China's Security Interests in the 21st Century

The collapse of communism in Europe, the quest for economic security and the war on terror have all affected China's view of security matters. This is intended as a comprehensive study of the new policy and security challenges that China may confront in the coming years. It includes chapters on Chinese concepts of security, the role of the United States, the Korean peninsula, Japan, Taiwan and China's quest for 'global power' status. The book covers all of China's current major security interests and concerns.

Dr Russell Ong is lecturer in Chinese Politics at the University of Manchester. He is also a research associate at the School of Oriental and African Studies (SOAS), University of London. His research interests lie in international security, international relations of Asia and Chinese foreign policy.

Routledge Security in Asia Series

China's Security Interests in the 21st Century

Russell Ong

Routledge
Taylor & Francis Group

LONDON AND NEW YORK

First published 2007
by Routledge
4 Park Square, Milton Park, Abingdon, Oxon OX14 4RN
605 Third Avenue, New York, NY 10017

Routledge is an imprint of the Taylor & Francis Group,
an informa business

© 2007 Russell Ong

Typeset in Times New Roman by
Newgen Imaging Systems (P) Ltd, Chennai, India

British Library Cataloguing in Publication Data
A catalogue record for this book is available
from the British Library

Library of Congress Cataloging in Publication Data
A catalog record for this book has been requested

ISBN13: 978-0-415-39215-0 (hbk)
ISBN13: 978-0-203-96222-0 (ebk)

To my parents

Contents

Acknowledgements

I would like to thank Eric Grove, Noel O'Sullivan, Christopher Coker, Stephen Chan and Rosemary Gosling for their assistance over the years. Special thanks must also be given to the computer support staff and library at the School of Oriental and African Studies, who have provided the necessary facilities to carry out my research.

Abbreviations

APEC	Asia-Pacific Economic Co-operation
ARF	ASEAN Regional Forum
BWC	Biological Weapons Convention
CCP	Chinese Communist Party
CentrasBat	Central Asian Battalion
CIS	Commonwealth of Independent States
CPSU	Communist Party of the Soviet Union
CSCAP	Council on Security Co-operation in the Asia-Pacific
CST	Collective Security Treaty
CTBT	Comprehensive Test Ban Treaty
CWC	Chemical Weapons Convention
DPP	Democratic Progressive Party
EEZ	Exclusive Economic Zones
EU	European Union
G-8	Group of Eight
GCC	China-Gulf Co-operation Council
GDP	Gross Domestic Product
GNP	Gross National Product
IAEA	International Atomic Energy Agency
IISS	International Institute for Strategic Studies
IMF	International Monetary Fund
IPR	Intellectual Property Rights
ISAF	International Security Assistance Force
KEDO	Korean Peninsula Energy Development Organization
KMT	Kuomintang
KWP	Korean Workers' Party
LWRs	Light Nuclear Reactors
MTCR	Missiles Technology Control Regime
NAFTA	North American Free Trade Area
NATO	North Atlantic Treaty Organisation
NDPO	National Defence Programme Outline
NIEO	New International Economic Order
NPC	National People's Congress
NPT	Non-Proliferation Treaty

NUC	National Unification Council
ODA	Official Development Assistance
P5	Permanent Five
PfP	Partnership for Peace
PFP	People's First Party
PLA	People's Liberation Army
PNTR	Permanent Normal Trade Relations
PRC	People's Republic of China
PSI	Proliferation Security Initiative
RMA	Revolution in Military Affairs
SCC	Security Consultative Committee
SCO	Shanghai Co-operation Organisation
SDF	Self Defence Forces
SEZ	Special Economic Zone
SPR	Strategic Petroleum Reserve
TMD	Theatre Missile Defence
TRA	Taiwan Relations Act
TSU	Taiwan Solidarity Union
ULO	Uighur Liberation Organisation
UN	United Nations
WMD	Weapons of Mass Destruction
WTO	World Trade Organisation
XPCC	Xinjiang Production and Construction Corps

Introduction

The aim of this book is to analyse China's security interests in the 21st century. The concept of security here is broadly conceived and this is congruent with the Chinese emphasis on comprehensiveness (*quan mian hua*). In particular, the aim is to better incorporate non-military elements of security – political security and economic security – in defining China's national interest. Geographically, this book focuses mainly on China's backyard of Northeast Asia, although Central Asia also receives attention. Apart from the traditional concerns, non-military issues such as human rights and the threat of peaceful evolution which are highly relevant to understanding China's security, will be explored. This introductory chapter is divided into three sections. The first surveys the current security environment in which Chinese policymakers assess national security interests. The second section of this chapter examines the coherence of China's security interests. The final section sets out the main arguments and structure of this book.

The context: the age of US unilateralism

This book focuses on China's security interests in the post-September 11 environment. To a certain degree, the terrorist attacks in the US in 2001 have affected the functioning of the international system and altered the foreign policy focus of major powers, including China. For the US, its concept of national security has been altered to reflect terrorism as the current biggest threat. Chinese scholars argued that under the George Bush administration, the US foreign policy focus has shifted from Bill Clinton's 'human rights and economics diplomacy' to national security and anti-terrorism.[1] This also implies that the US now has an excuse to assert itself in international politics in the name of countering terrorists or hostile states, as the wars against the Taliban and Saddam Hussein regimes, the pressure on Libya to abandon its nuclear ambitions, and plans to curb Iran's and North Korea's nuclear aspirations showed. More specifically, this adds to the argument that the world has become unipolar as the US pursues its war on terror and evinces a unilateralist tendency in international politics. Basically, this means China now needs to reassess the ramifications of such an assertive US stance. At the same time, China acknowledges that the key trend in international relations is globalisation (*quan qiu hua*). Accordingly, three entanglements will then need to be resolved: globalisation and sovereignty; power politics and sovereignty; and human rights and sovereignty.[2] The latter two entanglements centre primarily on the US, as the lone superpower is perceived as indulging in power politics and promoting human rights in order to undermine Chinese sovereignty.

For most parts of the Cold War era, China had manoeuvred between the two hostile superpowers, leaning from one side to another to enhance its national security in the strategic triangle. Today, the room for such manoeuvres has shrunk to a large extent as China often faces the US on its own. To counter US preponderance in international politics, China is now seeking to boost its ties with a former adversary, Russia. For instance, the border dispute with Russia, which had existed for over 300 years, was resolved in 2004 when both parties sealed an agreement.[3] This follows from the establishment of confidence-building measures with Russia as well as Kazakhstan, Kyrgyzstan and Tajikistan on their borders in 1996 and a troop-reductions accord with the aforementioned countries along those borders in 1997.[4] Those moves in the 1990s were taken by Beijing to bolster its military security on its northern and northwestern flanks, and they have finally come to fruition in relation to traditional rival Russia. They also relate to China's desire to develop its old economic base in the northeast and the interest of Russia's Far East region to tap into such developments. For instance, China and Russia are planning to build a highway running through the Heixiazi island in the Ussuri River, the scene of their 1969 war. The key point is that the threat from the north, posed by the former Soviet Union, no longer exists for China. In the military realm, China now aims to enhance its ties with Russia and the first-ever joint military exercise, 'Peace Mission 2005', was conducted in August 2005 in China's northeast region. Beyond the sphere of tactical collaboration, the exercise carries political connotations and epitomises China's objective of balancing against the lone superpower.[5] Overall, it is clear that US unilateralism in world politics, evinced in the war on terror, has pushed China to look more earnestly for allies who share reservations about America's assertive foreign policy.

It must be pointed out that China currently emphasises its economic ties with Russia as part of a wider strategic partnership aimed at countering US unilateralism as well as fuelling its modernisation programmes. Sino-Russian trade rose over 20 per cent to US\$21.23bn in 2004 and both sides have set a goal of US\$60–80bn in annual bilateral trade by 2010.[6] China is the fourth largest trading partner of Russia and Russia is China's eighth largest. In additional to military equipment, China's imports from Russia consist mainly of natural resources and raw materials. In return, China mainly sells Russia household commodities such as textiles, clothes, shoes and home electrical appliances, and these account for over 70 per cent of total exports. Basically, China wants from Russia military hardware to improve the capabilities of its armed forces and oil for its economic modernisation.

For Russia, stable relations with China could well be the single most important facilitator of economic development in the Russian Far East, as China is potentially its largest and most valuable market in Asia. Despite voiced discontent from the Russian population in the Far East towards the Chinese who have intruded into their areas, for Russia as a whole, its fragile economy can ill afford further reductions in Russo-Chinese trade. This fact can be used by China to enhance its economic security, for Siberia is rich in minerals and could be exploited jointly with Russia. Specifically, Russian energy resources are being sought by China for its economic modernisation goals. Given its projected energy requirements in the 21st century, China intends to diversify its supply in order to minimise over-reliance on any single source. Overall, Russia is important to China's quest for energy security, and Sino-Russian energy co-operation in oil and gas has considerable potential.

At the same time, China has to compete with states such as Japan for such as Russian resources. For instance, Russia recently approved a major oil pipeline to the Pacific Ocean that enables exports to Japan and the US, thus dropping the idea of a competitor route to China. At a geopolitical level, China still struggles to come to terms with strategic partner Russia's choice of Japan, especially given that Russia and Japan have yet to sign a peace treaty primarily due to territorial disputes in the southern Kurile islands/Northern Territories. In reality, competition including that for energy resources is endemic in international relations and China must learn how to cope with this by perhaps offering more attractive financial terms for the oil pipeline project.

Overall, Russia remains on good terms with China in Northeast Asia. In that region, China is still aligned with North Korea against the US and its Asian ally Japan. Although the ending of the Cold War has brought some modifications, such as the partial removal of the Soviet factor, the overall security structure in Northeast Asia did not undergo any fundamental changes, unlike in Europe. Today, the geostrategic and geoeconomic importance of Northeast Asia cannot be overstated, for this is a sub-region of Asia where four of the world's five recognised centres of powers – the US, Russia, China and Japan – meet and interact; where permutations of bilateral, trilateral and quadrilateral power games are played out on multiple chessboards with all their complexities and shifting configurations.[7] The US remains the sole superpower in the world and therefore in Northeast Asia as well. It has a strong influence over the region and plays an important role in shaping the strategic environment there. Chinese perceptions of the American strategy in Northeast Asia will be explored later.

The removal of East–West confrontation might portend instability in Northeast Asia; once the 'superpower overlay' has been lifted, it is possible that regional tensions might resurface.[8] Such tensions could include those between China and Japan, which had previously been suppressed to some extent by a shared common enemy in the form of the Soviet Union. Moreover, regional tensions might attract the intervention of additional extra-regional powers such as the European Union (EU) in the long run, something that China will be keen to avoid. The possible rise or resurgence of regional hegemons in Northeast Asia, namely Japan and Russia, is also a matter of concern for China; at the very least, an economically powerful Japan will pose new problems for China and any revival of Russian nationalism will also be regarded as a threat. At the same time, the ascendancy of

China itself causes concern for the smaller Asian states. All these scenarios make the region of Northeast Asia seem rather volatile, notwithstanding the ending of the Cold War.

Essentially, the 'democratic peace' thesis that democracies do not go to war would not apply in Northeast Asia as most of the countries there, including China, are not fully developed democracies.[9] Given their political culture, authoritarian regimes in Northeast Asia, would feel less inhibited than say, western European states, in using force to settle their disputes. At present, a host of territorial disputes still exist in Northeast Asia, and this has prevented the establishment of closer ties among states in the region. One example is the Southern Kurile islands/Northern Territories issue, which still remains an obstacle to better Russo-Japanese relations. More relevant to China is the contest with Japan over the sovereignty of Diaoyu islands/Senkaku islands.

Historically, China had fought several wars to maintain its security interests in Northeast Asia. Some campaigns were successful but others were not. China fought against Japan twice in the 1894–1895 and 1937–1945 wars. China intervened in the Korean conflict in 1950 when American military forces came too close to its northeastern border, within striking distance of its capital. In the aftermath of the Sino-Soviet split, China fought a small-scale border war against the Soviet Union along the Ussuri River in 1969. Although a direct military threat has been reduced today following the demise of the Soviet Union, it is true to say that China still faces some great powers in Northeast Asia, such as the US and Japan. Moreover, Northeast Asia constitutes part of the larger Asia-Pacific region, which is vital for China's comprehensive security. Beijing attaches great importance to stability in the Asia-Pacific region because this is a prerequisite for ensuring economic development. Essentially, China wants to use economic development as the basis to drive to truly global power status in the 21st century. The proposition here is that China is a regional power but it wants to become a global power.

Coherence of China's security interests

In analysing China's security interests, one needs to examine the degree of their coherence and internal consistency. This raises the question of how much a single factor exists in the formulation of such interests. In this book, China's security is generally taken to mean the Chinese Communist Party's (CCP); the reality is that the CCP has represented the security interests of the Chinese state since 1949, albeit largely through its monopoly of violence. It is not the purpose of this book to discuss Chinese domestic politics and how different factions in Chinese society, including dissidents, interpret security. At the same time, there is no doubt that security policymaking in China has become more decentralised, professionalised and pluralised post-1978.[10] Conceptually, one might argue that it is moving towards a 'bureaucratic politics' model.[11] The question is to what extent this affects thinking on national security totally. We can explore the nature of the Chinese political system to get some answers.

The Communist political system is in a transitional phase and one major weakness of such systems is the lack of an orderly process for the selection of new leaders. Various historical examples can be cited. For instance, after the death of Mao Zedong in 1976, there was a period of political struggle, with the purge of the radical 'Gang of Four' eventually resulting in the ascendancy of the late Deng Xiaoping. More recently, the power transition has been comparatively stable and less violent, as the assumption of CCP leadership by Jiang Zemin in 1992 and Hu Jintao in 2002 showed. At the same time, it must be noted that because there is no truly democratic process for the selection and removal of leaders, political selections still to a large extent take place through intra-party struggles behind the scenes. Key leaders often place their own cliques in key positions while counter-ing the manoeuvres of rival leaders and their followers. The classic case was the removal of the Yang clan from positions of power in the early 1990s.[12] For our pur-pose here, we need to bear in mind that such internal manoeuvres by various fac-tions within the CCP in the struggle for political supremacy may, to a certain extent, reduce the coherence in China's national security agenda.

In addition, the leadership succession issue in China raises questions on the likelihood of Beijing's security interests being dominated by internal concerns. For example, it is worth noting that during the Cultural Revolution, Mao Zedong paid more attention to internal affairs compared to foreign relations and external security concerns; in fact, the door to the outside was closed during most of that period. In the near future, it is possible that China's current leaders may be pre-occupied with internal struggles in the quest to achieve political supremacy in Zhongnanhai and therefore they might have less time and energy to present a clearer security agenda to the outside world. Furthermore, it is worth noting that competitive successors to the current leadership are bound to show no hesitation in exploiting nationalism in an era of ideological bankruptcy to strengthen their claims to the throne and weaken their opponents.

In particular, it is often noted that when dealing with strictly military security issues, one can see that there are often less major disagreements within the Chinese leadership. For example, on the Taiwan issue, Beijing's foreign policy has been unvarying in its basic orientation and goals, with a no-compromise adherence to the one-China principle. As the new generation of leaders generally lack the absolute authority of their predecessors, they will not be in a position to make compromises on issues of national sovereignty. They will be unable to move in new directions or reach compromises with foreign states as that will weaken their already limited power. Such potential developments need to be borne in mind when analysing China's security agenda.

At the same time, although the new nationalist elites might to some extent regard the Marxist–Leninist beliefs of their elders as outmoded, they are certain to share the same conviction that China should become a truly global power. That at least will remain an enduring feature of Chinese security thinking. However, when one moves across the range towards the non-military aspects of security, one is bound to discover much more diversity in Chinese thinking. For example, on issues relating to economic security, Chinese leaders have often been engaged in debates over how to reform the loss-making state-owned enterprises, with some advocating a move to the capitalist mode of pure private ownership while others stressing the importance of some remaining state control to avoid the pitfalls of liberalisation or over-integration with the international economy.

Apart from the question of whether the leadership will assert effective authority, arguments can also be made regarding the fact that a possible confluence of institutional and ideological crisis will radically transform or even-overrun the existing order. On the internal front, this may portend a protracted and inconclusive struggle for power that can encourage powerful local elites to demand greater autonomy from the central government. For example, the People's Liberation Army (PLA) might intervene in the affairs of political leadership. In general, causes that produce military interventions in politics, to a certain extent, lie in the structure of society, in particular in the absence or weakness of effective political institutions.[13] In actual fact, the best opportunity for the PLA to intervene might have been during the Cultural Revolution. This argument that political instability is a classic breeding ground for military intervention paints a scenario reminiscent of the final days of the Qing dynasty, which later gave way to warlordism in China. However, the view adopted here is that this is rather unlikely as China's political leaders, with Hu Jintao as the chairman of the Central Military Commission (CMC) since September 2004, retain control over the military and the military has shown no clear signs of breaking away from its political masters. As such, it is assumed that China will remain a unified state and there exists a fair degree of coherence in the formulation and articulation of China's security interests among the military elite and the civilian leaders.

Last, it is worth pointing out the impact of security threat perceptions on actual foreign policy behaviour. This applies not only to China but to every state in the international system. There are the larger questions of information processing, cost calculation and political decision making in Beijing. Perception is essentially a cognitive process; it may provide insights into a particular way of thinking but must still be subjected to different interpretations and debates. Therefore, certain key assumptions will frame China's security threat forecasts here. Domestic dissidence and regime factionalism will not jeopardise the CCP's control of the country, at least not totally. Otherwise, the traditional Chinese premise of 'internal unrest, external danger' (*neiluan waihuan*) will significantly heighten threat perceptions than the case actually is; attendant efforts to unite the country in an event of social fragmentation will surely magnify any existing external security threats.

Main arguments and structure

Overall, it is argued that certain basic premises of China's security interests have not been altered in any drastic manner. Moreover, relative stability of the political and economic priorities since 1978 encourages cautious projection for the present patterns of China's security interests and threat articulations. In sum, it is assumed that China will resemble some form of a unified state in the foreseeable future, and its security interests will show a certain extent of continuity with those in place at the time when this book was written. With these in mind, the central arguments of this book can now be set out.

China's security interests in the 21st century will to a large extent be affected by perceptions of the lone superpower. Specifically, Beijing is concerned about the implications of US unilateralism. Another key argument is that to achieve a thorough explanation of China's security interests, the political and economic dimensions must be more fully explored, in addition to traditional military concerns. In short, interaction of the military, political and economic aspects of China's national security must be more closely examined.

Theoretically, the call for a broader definition of security in international relations can be traced to the work of the Copenhagen School.[14] Such a definition of security will enable one to better understand China's policy towards countries such as the US, Japan, North Korea, South Korea and Taiwan. It will also enable one to understand China's security thinking in relation to issues such as peaceful evolution (*heping yanbian*), human rights and economic development.

The book will be structured as follows: Chapter 1 compares the Chinese concept of security with that used in the Anglo-Saxon study of International Relations. The key defining feature of China's security is comprehensiveness, that is, encompassing the military, political and economic.

Chapter 2 assesses the alleged Western strategy of peaceful evolution and how this still constitutes a key concern for Chinese leaders, despite the ending of the Cold War. US-led attempts to modify the regime in China through non-military means will be explored. More importantly, in the post-September 11 era, the strategy of peaceful evolution is also linked to the US notion of regime change.

Chapter 3 focuses on how China perceives the lone superpower, dealing with issue of US unilateralism in world politics. It will be shown that China calls for multipolarity in the international system primarily because it fears unipolarity.

Chapter 4 explores the Taiwan issue, and here the US involvement is critically examined.

Chapter 5 looks at China's security interests in relation to the challenge of Japan; it examines Beijing's concerns about the potential re-emergence of Japan as well as assesses the evolution of the US–Japanese alliance.

Chapter 6 deals with China's security interests in relation to North Korea and the emphasis here is on the enduring importance of this buffer state.

Chapter 7 looks at China's policy towards South Korea, examining the importance of economic security as well as how China views the US–South Korean nexus.

Chapter 8 focuses on Chinese interests in Central Asia, a region that is attracting the attention of other great powers such as Russia and the US. Beijing's search for political and economic security on its western flank will be delved into.

Chapter 9 examines China's search for ultimate security, that is, driving to truly global power status. This seems to constitute a threat in the eyes of its smaller neighbours and the West. The wider ramifications of China's ascendancy for the international system will be examined.

A final chapter restates the main arguments stemming from the various chapters. It is hoped that this book will encourage further research and debate on the evolution of China's security interests, which will have a major impact on international relations in the 21st century.

1 The Chinese concept of security

In this chapter, the focus will be on the theory of security. In particular, the aim here is to explore the Chinese concept of security in greater detail. This will be useful in illuminating the approach to be adopted in subsequent chapters. First, the debate on broadening the scope of the security concept in international relations, which coincides with the growing importance of economic issues in the post-Cold War era, will be explored. Second, the Chinese approach to security will be scrutinised, in comparison with non-Chinese ones. It will be stressed that the Chinese concept of comprehensive security is very much in line with the increasing widespread adoption of a broader definition of security in International Relations. We first turn to the concept of security.

The concept of security

Generally, what security means in the domestic and international contexts, and how the concept can be operationalised, is a much-disputed matter in academic circles. Essentially, security is a multidimensional concept; it is malleable and subject to different interpretations by both academics and policymakers at different times. What security means can be controversial and it remains an 'essentially contested' concept.[1] Despite the theoretical problems and controversies pertaining to the operational utility of the concept, few proponents would disagree that security is the core value of states. In the study of International Relations, the prominence of the security concept ranks alongside others such as power, balance of power, war and peace; in fact, one might even argue that security is more relevant than those other concepts and should perhaps replace them as the central focus of academic enquiry in this field.

It is possible to look at the concept of security from two perspectives: the first in terms of the 'level of analysis' and the second in terms of the different aspects of security.[2] The first, the 'level of analysis', is a well-documented problem in international relations theory and was first noted by David Singer.[3] This type of thinking basically posits looking at issues in international relations in terms of the three 'levels' of the individual, the state and the international system. International relations theorists such as Kenneth Waltz have applied this type of analysis to a study on the causes of war, looking at the three 'levels' of human nature, the state and the international system.[4]

Such an approach is useful in international relations but there are implications; theorists need to be competent in other fields in order to embark on such types of analysis. For instance, one would need a reasonable knowledge of psychology, which is essential for understanding human nature. Retraining in other skills will then be needed as analysts try to cope with other facets of a particular problem. Even if expertise in other disciplines has been acquired, there is a need to come to terms with the inter-linkages among various disciplines in such analyses. This means that the scope of a particular study might become too broad for most academics to handle comfortably and might at times even render the entire exercise too overwhelming. This constitutes a dilemma that academics working in the field of international relations and security studies have to contend with.

In security studies, it is possible to examine three 'levels' of security: individual security, state security or national security, and international security. This book deals primarily with the second level, specifically the Chinese state's security. In other words, it does not in general analyse security from the perspective of the Chinese citizen[5] or from the perspective of the international security system, unless in specific cases where they shed light on China's national security. At the same time, it is important to be aware of contradictions among individual, state and international security. What is viewed as secure from one level may be seen as insecure from another. For example, one can point to the classic contradiction between individual security (largely represented by the human rights issue) and state security, and in fact, arguments have been made that the individual should become a central referent in any attempt to discuss the concept of security.[6] For instance, Bill McSweeny posits that implicit in most studies of international and national security is the notion that the ultimate reference is people, and it is from the need to protect human values that the term security derives its meaning.[7]

It is not the intention here to delve into this type of debate, except to note that an individual's security interests may be threatened by the state that purports to represent his security interests. This type of contradiction appears in this book insofar as the ruling government in China perceives human rights as a national security threat and acts to crack down on dissidents. In general, state and individual security often do not coincide, especially in the case of totalitarian regimes. In the quest for national security, the Chinese state might actually threaten the individual security of its citizens. The human rights issue is most often linked with the Chinese government perceptions of the US pursuing a strategy of peaceful evolution (which will be explored fully in Chapter 2); this linkage demands more attention in studies on China's security interests.

Linkages and contradictions can also occur between the second and third levels of security, that is, the state and the international system. This is manifested in the form of the China threat theory (*Zhongguo weixie lun*). In the drive to maximise its own security, China is often perceived as posing a threat to regional or international security. In general, it is worth noting that China's search for security is reinforced by the anarchical nature of the international system. The conventional wisdom in international relations is that a state's security strategies do not exist in a vacuum; they are reactive to the external environment as much as they are proactive. Hence, it must be noted that the international security system does pose limitations to China's security strategies. At the regional level, the security system in Northeast Asia constitutes the milieu in which China assesses its security interests.

Having specified the Chinese state as the level of analysis in this book, it is worth pointing out that an approach focusing on this second level is not without its problems. There are numerous disputes over what is or what should be the second level. One might come up with alternative referent objects such as society.[8] The distinction between state and society is a familiar one in social sciences in general and domestic politics in particular; the two entities often pursue different objectives. Michael Mann's distinction between despotic and infrastructure power of the state is useful; the former refers to the ability of the state or the elites to act freely without regard to society while the latter refers to the ability of the state to penetrate society and organise social relations.[9] The Chinese totalitarian state – represented by the Chinese Communist Party (CCP) – retains much of this despotic power, and the Politburo is, on the whole, empowered to undertake a range of foreign policy tasks without routine institutionalised negotiations with nascent civil society groups. One can then envisage a continuum whereby at one end, states act completely in their own interests without regard to their domestic constituencies to another end whereby national security is primarily determined by domestic constituencies, at least in the abstract sense that the national interest embodies the collective interests of the domestic society. Through its monopoly of violence, it must be said that the CCP on the whole represents the security interests of the Chinese state.[10] This is especially true when one moves to the military realm, when society groups have little influence on national security thinking.

The non-military aspects of security

The question of what should be included in the study of security is not only an academic problem but also a practical one that policymakers have to contend with. In general, it is fair to say that the traditional concept of security employed in international relations has become increasingly anachronistic in the 21st century. Certain changes that occurred in global politics in recent times, such as the rising importance of economic issues, have hastened the need for academics and policymakers to come to terms with widening the concept of security. A clear illustration is the perceived need to use naval vessels to monitor the exclusive economic zones (EEZ) over which states have had legal authority since the early 1980s. Another example is the relationship between the burdensome foreign debt and environmental decay in some Third World regions. Yet another case is the threat of mass migration across national boundaries, which may in turn lead to conflicts between states.

Hence, security and the accumulation of military power are no longer seen as synonymous in the current era. Academics and policy analysts alike have already begun to take more of an interest in economic issues, thereby probing the frontiers of the security concept. For instance, as early as 1989, the London-based *International Institute for Strategic Studies* (IISS) published in its journal *Survival* a special issue on the non-military aspects of what it calls strategy, indicating a new way of examining security issues in the modern era.[11] On the theoretical front, the Copenhagen School has opened up the subject of security studies from its narrow traditions. This coincided with what an increasing number of specialists are calling for. For instance, economic, sociological and psychological dimensions of threats have been listed as important for security analysts in addition to military security.[12] Essentially, the interrelationships between these new dimensions and traditional military concerns call into question the distinction between strategic studies and security studies. Traditionally, the definition of strategic studies has been 'limited to issues of military operations'.[13] By contrast, security studies cover more ground; it embraces political and economic issues more systematically in explaining how states pursue their national interests as well as interact with one another. Today, there are very few analysts working in the field of security studies who still adhere to a narrow conception of security. The perspective adopted here is that explaining China's security agenda fully requires knowledge of certain non-military issues.

At the same time, it is worth noting that strategic studies and security studies are not mutually exclusive. While the non-military aspects of security might occupy more of a strategist's time than in the past, questions relating to the procurement, deployment, engagement and withdrawal of military capabilities still constitute an important approach to understanding national security. Also, it is worth noting that the inclusion of non-military issues, such as poverty and environmental decay, into the security agenda could destroy the 'intellectual coherence' of security studies.[14] Overall, it is fair to say that attempts to rethink security can be oblivious to the theoretical and political pitfalls that imperilled the enterprise in the first place. To some extent, one might argue that keeping the balance of power (implicitly military power) as the core variable in security studies might preserve 'intellectual coherence' because drastic changes within the discipline often brings costs to the practitioner. In sum, most academics now support the view that security should be conceived more widely, although the degree of commitment varies. The basic argument in this book is that national security encompasses more than just military interests, hence one must give emphasis to the political and economic dimensions.

China's comprehensive security

Having examined the general widening of the concept of security, we can now turn specifically to the Chinese case. The defining feature of China's security interests is comprehensiveness (*quan mian hua*). Essentially, this means that the security is defined not only in military terms but the political and economic dimensions are also regarded as key components. Therefore, Chinese strategic planners often use this more inclusive term 'comprehensive national strength' in discussing the country's long-term strategy. There is no shortage of discussions on the security concept in China. Five strands of thought can be discerned: peace and development constitute the core elements in security thinking; the concept of security encompasses non-state actors such as individuals; non-state related issues might slowly develop into high security concerns; there are linkages between the various aspects of security; and the most important referent object is still the state.[15] These elements are quite similar to those found in the Anglo-Saxon framework. For instance, Chinese analysts still note the enduring wisdom of Realism and see the nation-state as the dominant actor in international relations.[16]

Another representative manifestation of Chinese security formulation is found in the notion of a 'new security concept'; this concept was first proposed at the annual meeting of the ASEAN Regional Forum (ARF) in 1996, reiterated during a visit to Singapore in 1997 and more fully elaborated by former president Jiang Zemin at the United Nations Conference on Disarmament in 1999. The key characteristics of this concept are 'comprehensiveness, equality, mutual trust, mutual benefit and co-ordination'; the first indication of it being applied, according to the Chinese, is the major security agreement signed with Russia and other Central Asian states in 1997 and the announcement of a unilateral disarmament in the same year whereby China would further cut its border troops.[17] According to Beijing, the core purpose of the new security concept is 'to conduct dialogue, consultation, and negotiation on an equal footing', which then helps 'solve disputes and safeguard peace'; it is argued that 'only by developing a new security concept and establishing a fair and reasonable new international order can world peace and security be fundamentally guaranteed'.[18]

In reality, the new security concept is not really innovative. It is, in essence, a repackaged version of the Five Principles of Peaceful Coexistence that was first enunciated by Zhou Enlai at the Afro-Asian People's Solidarity Conference in Bandung, Indonesia, in 1955. Those Five Principles are mutual respect for territorial integrity and sovereignty, non-aggression, non-interference in each other's internal affairs, equality and mutual benefit and peaceful coexistence. One can discern that today, given the salience of economics, Chinese foreign policy thinking has gradually shifted from peaceful coexistence (*heping gongchu*) to peaceful development (*heping fazhen*).[19] Peaceful coexistence was advocated during certain periods in the Cold war era because China was relatively weak vis-à-vis the US-led capitalist bloc. On the whole, China did not wish to instigate a direct military confrontation with the West; it calculated that a period of peace would be useful as a breathing space to catch up with the West. The idea was to wait for the forces of socialism to become stronger so that China could then defeat and replace capitalism. Obviously, the blurring of capitalism and socialism in the 1980s in the reform era modified much of this strategic thinking. At a wider level, one can detect a slight shift away from a strictly zero-sum approach to international relations, which was apparent during the Cold War, to a more co-operative one today.

Furthermore, it is important to note the strong historical influence on security thinking in China. Drawing on its long civilisation, Chinese strategic thought can at times be linked to the Confucian emphases on peace as the best option (*yihe weigui*) and taking the middle path to avoid extremes (*zhongyong zidao*). At times, this implies that China has no desire to challenge another great power or another power bloc. In reality, one might argue that China still lacks the actual military muscle to challenge the status quo, so a good neighbourliness policy (*mulin*) seems to be the best option in the near term. China currently calls for peaceful development, with the aim of using economic growth to achieve parity with the Western nations. This in many ways vindicates the salience of economics in security policy formulation today. Economics is one of the three facets of Chinese security thinking that will be explored in this book, but we first turn to military and political security.

China's military security and political security

Military security is foremost in the minds of security planners, and it is the traditional concern in international relations and security studies. From a Chinese viewpoint, 'the military force shoulders the important mission of defending the state's territorial sovereignty and integrity, resisting foreign aggression and safeguarding state unification'.[20] Accordingly, it is necessary to develop a strong military to achieve this mission. This Chinese formulation is quite similar to the conventional concept of military security employed in Western strategic thought; the focus is on the interplay of military threats and mutual perceptions of military intentions. For China, direct military threats have on the whole diminished following the disintegration of the Soviet Union. More important today will be meeting new military challenges from a resurgent Japan and of course, the US. The latter's military prowess is currently unmatched in the world, and this raises acute concern for Chinese defence planners.

Beyond the traditional conception of military security, Chinese analysts contend that the armed forces of all countries should play a role in countering new security threats such as terrorism and that international co-operation is needed to resolve such threats; in fact, counter-terrorism, treatment of epidemic diseases, disaster preventions and fighting transnational crime have been identified as actions that countries need to undertake jointly.[21] Today, China supports existing counter-terrorism conventions and the related legal frameworks. For instance, it urges all states to ratify the conventions and reach consensus on the draft Comprehensive Convention on International Terrorism.[22] Furthermore, China has called on Southeast Asian states to strengthen co-operation to root out anti-terrorism and drug abuse in a regional seminar on non-traditional security co-operation.[23] Interestingly, China's perceived enemy, the US, also views terrorism and drug trafficking as major security threats, and this could inadvertently open up the possibility of Sino-US co-operative actions against such threats in areas like Central Asia.[24] In sum, it is important to note that China emphasises the need to strengthen its armed forces to meet military challenges from potential rival states but also sees a need to counter non-state enemies such as transnational terrorism. Here one can discern that even when discussing military security, the Chinese are aware that some non-state forces can be just as threatening as opposing great powers.

On political security, China emphasises that its political system must not be undermined and its sovereignty must not be encroached; it is adamant that 'no country shall meddle in the internal affairs of another country' and 'the superpowers should not be allowed to order other countries about, pursue power politics and impose their values on others'.[25] Political security essentially relates to the organisation and process of government and the ideology that gives the rulers of a particular country legitimacy. In China's case, the ruling communist ideology is severely under threat as Beijing becomes increasingly drawn to the capitalist orbit in the search for economic resources for its national development; one might even argue that there is little meaning to the term communism in China today as market reforms accelerate. Nonetheless, the potential collapse of communism in China is linked to the perceived Western strategy of peaceful evolution (*heping yanbian*), and this political security issue will be discussed in detail later. At a wider level, one might argue that China's political security, or more specifically the security of the current regime, is very much related to the wider contest between the communist and non-communist political systems.

From the Chinese formulations of military and political security, one can detect the impact of history. The coming of the West destroyed the Sino-centric regional security system, where China was at the centre and other states had to conduct their relations with Beijing in a deferential manner. Military defeats at the hands of the Western powers and Japan in the 19th century meant China lost its position at the top of the Asian hierarchy until the end of the Second World War. Therefore, the CCP that came to power in 1949 espoused anti-imperialist nationalism and based its legitimacy in part on an ability to defend the country from potential foreign invaders. Anti-imperialism has since become a central focus in the Chinese quest for security, with the result that there exists a certain obsession to eradicate any residues of imperialism. This becomes very clear when one examines China's whole-hearted embrace of the concept of sovereignty and the concomitant tenet of non-intervention in the domestic affairs of a given country.

Chinese leaders still emphasise the importance of nationalism – which encompasses anti-imperialism – as a means to come to terms with the 'century of humiliation' (*bainian guochi*) that lasted from the 1840s to the 1940s. This type of feeling is often shared by states that had been victims of European colonialism. In this light, one can understand why China supported liberation struggles in the Third World, such as in white-racist Rhodesia and Mozambique, against the colonial powers during the Cold War. Moreover, China wanted to be seen as the champion of the Third World, as it sought independence from the two superpowers. In particular, mobilisation against both the US and the Soviet Union were incessantly promoted during the 1960s and 1970s; an all-out struggle against the imperialists was deemed as important for China's own national security. Although one can say that the concept of imperialism employed by Chinese leaders has different targets at different times – it was largely the US in the 1950s and then the Soviet Union in the late 1960s and 1970s – the point is that this highlights China's firm belief that its security must never be undermined by foreign powers again.

Hence, China's anti-imperialist stance has an impact on its conception of political and military security today. This is in some ways related to its negative experience of alliances in the international system. Historically, China had no permanent friends or enemies because it was at the top of the Asian hierarchy. It was largely isolated from other great powers in the West before the Opium Wars. At the height of Western imperialism in the 19th century, China often sought to play one foreign power off against another. For example, as a means to safeguard China's political and military security, China had relied on France, Germany and Russia to dislodge the Japanese from South Manchuria after Beijing was defeated in the 1894–1895 Sino-Japanese War. To some extent, such policies were successful, at least in the short run, but they proved to be ineffective over the longer term. During the First World War, China fought on the side of the victorious Allies but Qingdao in Shandong Province was transferred from defeated Germany to Japan instead of reverting to Chinese sovereignty.[26] This was, of course, a setback to China's security interests and it sparked off the 1919 May Fourth Movement, with anti-imperialist nationalism reaching new heights. Eventually, Japan relented to international pressure and its military forces evacuated from Shandong in 1922. Later on in the early 1950s, a shared communist ideology with the Soviet Union presented China with an opportunity for a marriage of convenience. Although this was the first deliberately chosen alliance in Chinese history, it eventually collapsed over a host of issues, such as ideology, national interests, historical rivalry, foreign policy divergence, culminating in the Soviet Union becoming a key military threat on the northern border.

In short, China never had positive experiences when it formed alliances to enhance its security interests. This means that self-reliance appears to be a more realistic option, which in turn leads to the current emphasis on using economic development to achieve truly global power in the 21st century. It also explains why China continues to emphasise an independent foreign policy, refusing to align itself to any other power in a formal way. To sum up, as far as enhancing military and political security is concerned, China draws upon historical lessons – the two main ones being Western imperialism and Japanese aggression. We now turn to economic security.

China's economic security

From the earlier survey of the security concept, it has become clear that one needs to explore the economic dimension of China's security more thoroughly. Chinese worldviews have already incorporated Marxism and Realism, which as materialist theories give prominence to the role of economics in both inter-national relations and security thinking.[27] Compared to Western strategists, it is fair to say that Chinese experts tend to give more weight to development issues on the national security agenda. This is primarily because China is still a developing country, and it wants to catch up with the world's industrialised powers, and because development is deemed as critical for achieving truly global power status.

Essentially, economic security includes the promotion of growth, access to global markets and guaranteed supply of natural resources. It is increasingly important, not only to China, but to every state in the international capitalist system. Economic issues are sometimes taking precedence over political ones, and it can be argued that, in general, the dichotomy of 'high politics' (military) and 'low politics' (economics) in international relations has gradually blurred and proved to be a false one. Energy security is a case in point and it occupies substantial attention of Chinese security planners today. This is primarily because China became a net importer of oil in 1993, following three decades of energy self-sufficiency. It is soon to become the world's second largest consumer of oil after the US. According to the National Development and Reform Commission, it is estimated that China's oil consumption will rise by 5.4–7.0 per cent in 2006; China's two major oil producers, Sinopec and PetroChina, are going all out to meet huge industrial demands but the country would still need a refining capacity of 17 million tons to meet those demands.[28] Currently, China has to rely on imports, with some 60 per cent coming from the Middle East. It will therefore be affected by global oil price volatility and supply disruption; a related point is that developing countries tend to suffer more from oil price volatility than developed ones.

For China's energy security, a secure passage of oil from the Middle East via the Straits of Malacca is vital. China currently does not have the naval capability to patrol the major oil shipping routes, unlike the US. This is a weakness that can be exploited by the US; Washington does possess the means to stem the flow of imported oil to China if necessary.[29] To alleviate such fears, China has actually considered building a strategic petroleum reserve (SPR) in order to cope with situations of supply disruption.[30] Another option is to rely more on overland transportation, with pipelines emanating from Central Asia and Russia being important in this regard. In Central Asia, China has already embarked on a strategy to build pipelines connecting to the region as this could be safer than sea transport because the US is in a relatively weaker position on land. The search for oil also sees China furthering its diplomatic advances in the key region of the Middle East, where new mechanisms such as the China–Arab Co-operation Forum and China–Gulf Co-operation Council (GCC) Framework Agreement have been established to enhance energy security. Beyond the Middle East, China is keen to invest in the oil sectors of countries such as Sudan, Azerbaijan, Indonesia, Kazakhstan, Peru and Venezuela. In sum, economic considerations such as secure energy supplies are prominent on China's security agenda today.

In discussing economic security, one must explore China's integration with the international economic system, which is not without its problems. Financial crises are endemic in the global capitalist system and states cannot remain totally immune from them, the Great Depression in the 1930s being a case in point. Overall, in an age of globalisation, China can reap the benefits of international trade but it will also be subjected to global financial risks and crises; these risks and crises do threaten national security directly. The 1997 Asian financial crisis was regarded as a 'historical event' similar to the collapse of the Soviet Union, with the Chinese expressing concern that the International Monetary Fund's (IMF) loans to

South Korea, Thailand, Philippines and Indonesia included 'stringent' conditions imposed on these countries to 'obey' IMF guidelines to change, reform and open up their markets.[31] This clearly expresses China's fear that economic crises might lead to its sovereignty and security interests being compromised. As mentioned earlier, the principle of anti-imperialism is not only embedded in China's search for security in both political and military aspects, it is also evident in the economic one. The communist leadership in Beijing continues to see itself as being engaged in a continuing struggle to free China and defend it against economic imperialism in all forms, from the exploitation of China by the old colonial powers before 1949 to the dominance of the Western powers in the international economic system today.

The 1997 Asian financial crisis contains some lessons for China; specifically, it makes China realise that co-operation is needed in managing the international economy. Beijing argues that it helped to stabilise the regional economy by not devaluing the renminbi while implicitly recognising the importance of US leadership in preventing the Asian financial crisis from spreading. Such crises are likely to occur again and China must learn to cope with those types of economic threats more adequately. If China suffers badly from a major financial crisis, it might not be able to benefit from international assistance, partly due to the sheer size of its economy but more importantly, due to the linkage of foreign financial assistance to political considerations such as human rights. Moreover, the fact that growth rates in the developed world have stagnated since the early 1990s and trade imbalances could create protectionist sentiments in the form of emerging trade blocs in Europe and North America. A combination of recession and protection in world trade can paralyse Chinese export growth while domestic demands for employment and expectations of higher living standards continue to rise, and China's leaders might find it increasingly difficult to satisfy the demands of the masses.

Essentially, there is a price to pay for joining the international economy: a lot of issues that were originally internal political and economic problems might become internationalised. This presents a stern test for China's strategic planners. For instance, joining the World Trade Organisation (WTO) has led to disruptive short-term effects on the Chinese economy; China has to make concessions on a number of vulnerable domestic sectors and these sacrifices might have ramifications on the country's stability. Moreover, some Chinese leaders do not wish to see large parts of the state sector being denationalised and falling into the hands of foreign capitalists because all this might eventually affect the CCP's stranglehold on power in domestic politics.

In this sense, protection and furtherance of China's economic interests is crucial for domestic legitimacy. The CCP has now been compelled by the erosion of Communist ideology to shift its legitimacy to the economic sphere, with the corollary that the communist leaders must turn to modernising the economy and keeping the masses materially satisfied. The connection between the economic and political aspects of China's security has never been closer since 1949. The current regime needs to use economic development to re-establish popular legitimacy. With rising standards of living, people might become more tolerant of the leadership of CCP in return for growing prosperity and a relatively quiet life free from Maoist-style political campaigns. These types of political security issues are often linked to international factors and will be further explored in Chapter 2, as they are important ones not often fully explored in security studies on China.

Overall, it is evident that the Western industrialised powers have pressurised China to conform to global economic norms in an age of increasing integration. For instance, although China's average tariff dropped to 9.9 per cent in 2005 from 15.6 per cent in 2000, and almost all pledged cuts have been made by end-2005, this is deemed as inadequate in the eyes of the West.[32] Basically, the Western trading nations want China to fulfil its pledge to complete the transition to a full market economy and, in particular, reform certain trading practices that currently failed to fully meet WTO membership rules. These would include adhering to global principles relating to intellectual property rights (IPR). Another example is the debate on whether a free float of the renminbi or a widening of the peg's band would be better. Although the market already has built in considerable investor speculation, betting on a move sooner rather than later, the US continues to prod Beijing to switch to flexible exchange rates; from the US's perspective, the Chinese currency's dollar peg artificially lowers the cost of Chinese exports – making them more competitive while increasing the cost of imported goods in China. Obviously, the key principle is that competition is endemic in the global capitalist system. China often points out that economic competition should proceed in accordance with international rules and regulations, noting that friction sand differences are normal but they should be resolved through dialogue on equal footing, consultation and talks. The truth is that the US is a major economic competitor to China, and this is a prime concern to Chinese strategists.

Interdependence

Apart from competition, China must learn to come to terms with interdependence in the international economic system. In a bilateral context, interdependence refers to the mutual dependence that develops in any of China's economic relationships and how this dependence imposes constraints on its international behaviour.[33] The degree of dependence between China and another state can often be unequal and this is sometimes referred to as asymmetrical interdependence.[34] If one country is heavily dependent on the other, threats to curtail economic relations can give the less dependent country political leverage. Specifically, China is careful to avoid that scenario whereby economic powers such as the US might use this type of leverage against Beijing. Hence, the Chinese argue that 'state-to-state economic relations should be established on the basis of equality, co-operation, and common development', emphasising that 'no country should be allowed to apply economic sanctions to retaliate against the other, still less use economic sanctions to obtain political gains'.[35] At the same time, it appears that the developed countries as a whole have up to now been unable to act collectively to convert China's dependence on the world economy into political influence.

For example, economic sanctions imposed after the 1989 Tiananmen Incident did affect China for a while but Beijing was not seriously afflicted by them. This is partly because the sheer size of the Chinese consumer market is too important for the West to ignore; human rights do come into consideration but they might not constitute the sole guiding principle for Western foreign policymakers.

Another key point to note when discussing China's economic security is that this is inseparable from that of the Asia-Pacific. China benefits from a stable and economically vibrant Asia-Pacific and vice versa. In many ways, the region has already entered a new era where economic factors have become major principles underlying the decisions of states there. Today, rising multilateralism and economic interdependence mean Asian states have to redefine their roles as sole interlocutors for domestic and foreign economic relations as well as political ones. Furthermore, the development of economic co-operation – rooted in the tremendous growth of intra-Asian trade and investment dating from the mid-1980s when one country after another adopted liberalisation packages – has led to notions that cross-border economic flows linking sub-regions of states rather than those states' political centres are more relevant. For example, how states such as China adjust their political and security relations – as well as their economic development strategies – to this new trend of 'economics from below' may yield insights on how the interplay of competition and co-operation will shape the Asia-Pacific region's dynamics in the 21st century. The subsequent chapters will examine China's economic security in relation to countries such as Taiwan, South Korea and Japan.

At this stage, it is fair to say that China may find informal co-operation with its Asian neighbours particularly attractive for its economic security objectives, especially at a time when the official mechanisms for collaboration such as the Asia-Pacific Economic Co-operation (APEC) and the WTO appears in general too slow in achieving any concrete consensus on a regional or global framework for trade and investment. In fact, informal economic interactions might be particularly suited to the Asian context where there is a strong predilection for incremental rather than bold systemic change. For instance, much of the untapped potential in China's peripheries and hinterlands can be efficiently realised by capitalising on complementarities across its political borders. One example is linking up its northeastern region with Russia. This represents one way for China to further enhance its economic interests. Overall, informal economic co-operation with Asian neighbours also allows China to proceed along its own path of development, just like Mao Zedong had 'Sinified' the political ideology of Marxism to suit China's needs, without being subjected to stringent international standards and principles. More importantly, it permits China to achieve its goals without needing to agree with others states on any overarching regional economic goals that might curtail Beijing's independence foreign policy.

Conclusion

China seeks comprehensive security – military, political and economic – and this type of thinking has coincided with broadening of the security concept in

International Relations over the years. The aim here is to highlight that, for China, the ability to achieve national security is no longer wholly centred on military capabilities. One must study the political and military aspects of China's security more thoroughly. Political security is highly relevant to an authoritarian state like China, where the organisation, ideology and process of the CCP is being challenged from within and without. Economic security is given emphasis because of China's status as a developing country, its reliance on imported oil and its increasing integration with the global economy.

For China, the ramifications of being a part of the global economy are daunting. Although China was not affected in a major way by the Asian economic crisis of 1997, the lesson is that huge costs will be incurred if trade and other international economic interactions are disrupted in future. These costs arise because of growing interdependence with the wider world. On the whole, one detects a certain Chinese ambivalence in becoming more enmeshed with the international capitalist economy. On one hand, there are benefits from the classical market model of open trade, competition and private ownership that can be reaped, and the diffusion of economic decision making that entry to WTO requires can spur growth. China is able to benefit from access to foreign capital and technology and can undertake specialisation to take advantage of new export opportunities. On the other hand, amongst other negative effects, deeper economic integration with the world economy affects the structure of the domestic economy as Chinese firms are subjected to competition from imported goods. More worrying is how further participation in the global economy might entail an erosion of sovereignty. We now turn to explore China's comprehensive security – encompassing the military, political and economic dimensions – in relation to other states and the key issues.

2 The threat of peaceful evolution

This chapter explores the enduring impact of the Western strategy of peaceful evolution (*heping yanbian*) on China's political security. This non-military strategy is given an added significance in an era of the lone superpower, when American military might can provide the buttress. It can also be linked with the US notion of regime change, which often entails military intervention to bring about a desired political transformation in a particular state. Specifically, the strategy of peaceful evolution still constitutes a serious threat to China because Beijing needs to continue opening up to the West for the sake of economic modernisation. We begin with a closer examination of the concept of peaceful evolution.

The concept of peaceful evolution

First, China perceives that the strategy of peaceful evolution was adopted by Western nations towards socialist countries at the onset of the Cold War. The origins were traced to a statement made by John Foster Dulles in the 1950s during the Korean War; this strategy of the 'international monopoly bourgeoisie' formally came into existence when the former US Secretary of State explicitly proposed 'the use of peaceful means' to 'accelerate the evolution of government policies within the Sino-Soviet bloc' and to 'shorten the expected life span of communism'.[1] It became an acute concern in the 1950s given that the Communist regime had just come to power in China after decades of internal strife and war against foreign invaders.

Essentially, the strategy of peaceful evolution seeks to undermine the values of socialism through the political, economic, cultural penetration of Communist states. This penetration, especially in the later era, often derives from Western economic assistance and commerce. In this vein, the provision of such assistance is regarded as a bait to induce socialist countries such as China to abandon Marxism–Leninism. The aim of the West is the gradual undermining of the Chinese communist state system through increasing interactions with the outside world, in particular with the most advanced industrial capitalist nations. In general, peaceful evolution means transforming the Chinese political system by encouraging the introduction of private ownership, free-markets, human rights and liberal democracy, all of which would eventually lead to the erosion of

Marxism–Leninism as an official ideology in China as well as the end of the Chinese Communist Party's (CCP) political monopoly.

In the post-Cold War era, Chinese scholars have noted that the 'imperialist nations, backed by the threat of a mighty military machine', use 'non-military means, including the international mass media, to convert the socio-economic system, culture and thought in socialist nations to capitalism' with the ultimate aim of incorporating these socialist nations into 'the capitalist orbit'.[2] With demise of the Communist bloc in Eastern Europe, it appears that Western capitalist nations, led by the US, are now in a better position to subvert the Beijing regime through the strategy of peaceful evolution. One former Chinese leader, Deng Xiaoping, had even described this as the West 'waging World War Three', noting that this is a war 'without the smoke of gunpowder'.[3]

The key point is that peaceful evolution comes across primarily as a political security threat to China's leaders rather than a military one. Here the aim of the West is to undermine the organisation and process of government in China as well as the ideology that gives the rulers of that country legitimacy. The authoritarian political structure in China is being questioned today, with calls for liberalisation within the country as well as from the outside world. Moreover, as Beijing becomes increasingly drawn to the capitalist orbit in the search for resources for its economic development, contacts with bourgeoisie ideas and values will increase. This would in the long run undermine the ruling ideology – Communist or authoritarian. To a certain degree, one can even argue that China's political security is very much related to the ongoing struggle between the communist and capitalist political systems.

At the same time, the coherence of the concept of peaceful evolution needs to be explored. Used by the Chinese, the concept tends to be 'vague and all embracing; its meaning ranges from dark conspiracies involving the alleged plotters of the counter revolutionary rebellion (the official term for the 1989 Tiananmen event) to the broad spectrum of cultural, social and economic exchanges with the outside world'.[4] It is important to note that this vagueness has often allowed Chinese leaders to denounce security threats to their regime as manifestations of the negative aspects of bourgeois liberalisation. Notwithstanding the doubts on the coherence of the concept of peaceful evolution, there is no mistaking that it is still taken very seriously by the Chinese leadership. Concerns over peaceful evolution are in part magnified by the demise of communist regimes in Eastern Europe and the Soviet Union from 1989 to 1991.

After all, the Soviet collapse was attributed to the West's efforts in issuing 'propaganda about the inferiority of socialism'; in particular, the US had high-lighted economic difficulties arising from 'the implementation of socialism by the Soviet leadership'.[5] A general conclusion for the CCP is that it needs to be responsive to societal demands in order to ensure its own legitimacy. Hence, attempts to restructure the Communist Party of the Soviet Union (CPSU) were considered by the Chinese as a bad example of inducing political change; Mikhail Gorbachev's resignation as the general secretary of the CPSU and dissolution of the CPSU was described as 'the greatest betrayal in the international history of communism'.[6] Specifically from 1989 to 1991, it was evident that Chinese leaders were extremely concerned about their grip on power as the ideological underpinnings of their own regime had come under threat. To a large extent, the underlying concern remains that the Leninist system in China will never be fully accepted by the Western powers.

Basically, once the Soviet Union is perceived to have succumbed to the strategy of peaceful evolution, China sees itself as the next key target. China has now become the sole significant socialist power, alongside countries such as North Korea, Cuba and Vietnam, in a world where capitalist nations are preponderant. One can argue that this leaves China in a precarious position, for the socialist ideology that has sustained the CCP since 1949 is on the verge of extinction in the international system. This ideology – notwithstanding doubts about its practical relevance – still to a large extent underpins the CCP's internal legitimacy and the CCP's security is still primarily equated with national security. Despite embracing economic reforms since 1978, Chinese leaders are not willing to abandon Communism totally as this forms the basis on which they had come to power and have remained in power. Moreover, it is clear that a Leninist strand persists in the Chinese political system, as articulated in the Four Cardinal Principles, whereby the overriding role of the CCP and its ideology are emphasised.[7]

Another important point is that the strategy of peaceful evolution does not target the Chinese state directly. To a certain extent, this represents a slight departure from the traditional state-to-state type of analysis in international relations. The strategy of peaceful evolution works best through the dissemination of bourgeois ideas and way of life to the Chinese masses via educational, cultural and intellectual exchanges. Basically, the purveyors of this strategy hope that having absorbed some liberal values, via mass media such as the Internet, the Chinese masses would press for further political liberalisation or call for an end to the political monopoly of the CCP.

Therefore, Western media are seen as a threat to socialist ideology at various levels in non-capitalist countries such as China. For example, Western radio, television, newspapers and magazines are seen as capable of influencing social psychology, social opinion and social thinking as well as propagating capitalist ideologies and theories in China. The Voice of America, the British Broadcasting Corporation and other Western media are alleged to have contributed to the 'corruption' of the Chinese people with 'bourgeois spiritual pollution'; this reflects China's fears of Western attempts to subvert the Chinese socialist system through 'media propaganda', by confusing the Chinese people's minds and weakening their 'ideological commitment to communism'.[8]

Basically, the strategy of peaceful evolution assumes that opening up to the West will gradually imbue the Chinese population with notions of civil liberties, political pluralism and the like. Today, being the lone superpower that espouses a different set of political values, the US represents this threat most clearly in the eyes of Chinese leaders. Moreover, with the use of military force becoming less cost-effective in international relations, it appears to China that peaceful evolution might be a more viable foreign policy instrument that the West could use against Beijing. According to the reasoning of the peaceful evolution strategy, Western powers such as the US should then step up its efforts to spread bourgeois ideas in China through educational, cultural and intellectual exchanges. Given that China engages in strategic competition with the US in the international system over a range of issues, the strategy of peaceful evolution does constitute a key weapon for the Americans. Added to this is that some Western academics and analysts advocate a strategy of containment to keep a rising China in check.[9] To a large extent, the drive to truly global power status, which is paramount in the security thinking of Chinese leaders, both past and present, could be stalled or ended by the strategy of peaceful evolution.

Avenues of peaceful evolution

Among the various forms that the strategy of peaceful evolution might take, the West's advocacy of human rights and liberal democracy is perceived to be particularly dangerous, as far as Beijing's political security is concerned. After all, the lone superpower intends to spread liberal democracy to the rest of the world, as it believes this is the basis for a stable international order in the long run.[10] Today, US politicians regularly assert that the development of a free market economy, brought about by greater international trade and investment, creates the foundations for democracy and individual freedom in totalitarian states such as China. Moreover, the US insists that other great powers share common interests and values with itself, noting that China 'will in time find that social and political freedom is the only source of national greatness'.[11] It has also been asserted that 'American values are universal', with the corollary that other states should recognise that American interests and global interests are indivisible.[12] Naturally, China resents such assertions and often makes the point that its political values are different from those of the West.

As a post-revolutionary society, the US is often seen as exporting its democratic ideas and institutions abroad, with China now being a prime target after the demise of the Soviet Union. There is a perceived attempt by the US 'to remake China in its own image', this time by exporting a secular philosophy rather than by spreading religious teachings as it had done during the age of imperialism.[13] In fact, it has been argued that America's agenda is to change China, as evident in the century-long American 'missionary complex' underlying policy towards Beijing, and this agenda indicates a strong 'American paternalism towards China' that has been present since at least the 1920s.[14] It is this type of paternalism that irks China's leaders because they wish to enforce an authoritarian political system on their subjects. This is even more evident when the concept of sovereignty enters the equation, as China adheres to this legal concept vehemently, primarily due to the impact of the 'century of humiliation'.

At a wider level, there is definitely a clash of Chinese and US political values, and this is important in explaining the strategy of peaceful evolution. For instance, China has a different interpretation of democracy from the US. China does not reject democracy per se but argues that democracy is always relative and specific hence it must conform to and be compatible with the national conditions of a particular country; essentially, Beijing will undertake political reforms only in accordance with the goal to develop a 'socialist democracy suited to its national conditions'.[15] On the whole, Chinese leaders are often confounded by the American commitment to pluralism in domestic politics. To them, the coexistence of various channels of political participation in the US is often interpreted as a sign of the disintegration of the state control rather than an expression of the competitive dynamics of the domestic system. Compared to Western countries, the notion of liberal governance, which provides a space for societal autonomy, is generally less accepted by China.[16] For centuries, China has taken the stance that the state should be privileged over society, and America's frequent efforts to stress the latter's legitimacy are seen as unnecessary and often deemed as political interference.

Fundamentally, it must be pointed out that the US political model runs against the traditional Chinese desire for social order, which has throughout centuries been mostly achieved by the institution of an authoritarian system interspersed with Confucian principles. Essentially, the Confucian system places an emphasis on hierarchy and order in social as well as political life. For a developing nation like China, order is arguably more important as it attempts to cope with the ramifications of first-pace economic growth such as uneven development. In this vein, Chinese scholars argue that Confucianism has helped 'countries and regions in East Asia modernise at a much quicker pace' and 'steer clear of defects that the West encountered in achieving modernisation', suggesting that it might replace the modern and contemporary Western culture in the 21st century.[17] To a certain extent, the Western notion of competitive domestic politics with its relative lack of coherence in social and political agendas is regarded as undesirable for a country that wants to modernise rapidly. This proposition is also linked to the notion of 'Asian values', with various Asian leaders arguing that such values are more suitable for their countries' developmental needs.[18] The key point is that peaceful evolution strategy calls for political liberalisation in China, and this is often regarded as an impediment to development by Beijing's leaders.

Human rights

The peaceful evolution strategy also highlights a key area where Chinese and American political values collide – human rights. Since the ending of the Cold War, this issue has become more prominent in international relations. For instance, during the Sino-American strategic alignment to counter the Soviet threat in the 1970s and the 1980s, moral issues such as human rights generally received less attention in Beijing and Washington. The Sino-US strategic alignment meant that on the whole, China did not face severe criticisms on its human rights record, compared to other communist states in the Soviet bloc. Moreover, many of the Third World countries that Washington had close relations with were right-wing dictatorships, and human rights issues were largely not raised by mutual tacit agreements.

In the 21st century, China finds that most of the countries that it wants to deal with are democracies, and human rights issues are mostly on the agenda, albeit to varying degrees of importance. Furthermore, non-governmental organisations have also become an important international lobby, obliging various Western governments to take up the issue of human rights with China more forcefully. For example, enjoying greater access to US Congress and the media, non-governmental groups such as Asia Watch and Amnesty International have succeeded in placing political repression, imprisonment for political activities, torture and prison labour exports on the agenda of Sino-American relations at various points in time.

Given that China regards human rights issues as a matter of national sovereignty, it is hardly surprising that such issues are perceived as constituting a political security threat as well as a key obstacle for better relations with the US. Specifically, causes and consequences of the Tiananmen Incident have been given further prominence as a result. The US was held partially responsible for fomenting the demonstrations and contributing to their sustenance; at that time, the Chinese point out that 'leading political figures of the US monopoly capitalist class' trained 'some so-called fighters for democracy' and gave them economic aid so that they can 'play an important role for the US government's strategy of peaceful evolution'.[19] The late Deng Xiaoping himself had identified the Chinese 'counterrevolutionaries' as 'agents of Western subversion'; it was reported that at that time, Chinese students in Tiananmen Square quoted American revolutionaries.[20] At a time when the survival of Communism in other parts of the world was at stake, the Western call for political liberalisation in China to accompany the country's economic opening up since 1979 was therefore seen as a plot to undermine China's political security. In short, the threat of peaceful evolution was undoubtedly magnified in the period from 1989 to 1991.

During that period, China saw an urgent need to guard against the Western strategy of peaceful evolution. To avoid being further isolated in the international community, it sought to cultivate the hard-line East European states with high-level visits, which produced joint statements warning the need to combat peaceful evolution. The few governments that supported China included hardline communist states such as North Korea, Romania, East Germany and Bulgaria but most of these states later disintegrated.[21] It is evident that the Tiananmen Incident emphasised the Chinese leaders' concern for its political security or more specifically regime security and how dangerous the peaceful evolution can be. This concern has prompted Beijing to seek allies, primarily in the Third World, in its ideological contest with the capitalist democracies till this day.

In general, it can be argued that human rights issues do represent a threat to regime security and an avenue for peaceful evolution, for they represent an attack on the CCP's legitimacy and monopoly of political power. What is more debatable is whether the human rights threat pertains to the entire Chinese or just the CCP. As stated in the Introduction, the assumption here is that regime security is equated with national security as there does not yet exist a meaningful distinction between state and party in China. To the Chinese leaders, political security must come first: state sovereignty is the basis for the realisation of human rights, and to preclude human rights as a state's internal affair is contrary to international law.[22] Specifically, China sees US pursuing hegemony when its advocates the spread of human rights. Specifically, Beijing questions Washington's status as the 'global judge of human rights'.[23] It is worth noting that the US has adopted a tougher stance against China compared to other Western nations on the human rights issue. The US is at times at variance with its allies over human rights policy, as the case of the European Union (EU) arms embargo demonstrates; some European countries were more willing to lift the ban that was imposed in the aftermath of the 1989 event.

From a wider perspective, peaceful evolution is still relevant today to Chinese security thinkers because China and the US have different social systems, values, levels of development and historical traditions. Hence, it is inevitable that both countries will adopt different approaches to human rights, a key component of the peaceful evolution strategy. Basically, China views human rights as a 'Western package' that has been thrust upon itself as well as a means for the West to intervene in its internal affairs in the name of international standards. This resonates with the notion that China was forced to open up to the West during the 19th century and it had to absorb certain European norms and values. When viewed from China's recent experience as a victim of Western and Japan imperialism, it is hardly surprising that Beijing is adamant that no foreign power should intervene in its affairs again, let alone undermine CCP rule, be it in the name of human rights or any other pretext.

Conceptually, China counters the Western criticism of its human rights record by distinguishing between civil and political rights, and 'positive rights' (economic, social and cultural rights) and then prioritising the latter over the former. Whereas civil and political rights require governments to refrain from taking actions that violate them, 'positive rights' require government to make provisions for citizens; China is definitely more comfortable doing the latter. Moreover, it is generally acknowledged by Western human rights experts that 'positive rights' are less subject to theoretical controversy. Overall, the Chinese argue that human rights encompass not only include civil and political rights but also economic, cultural and social rights; this broader view of human rights is, in general, extremely suitable for authoritarian states that are experiencing high growth rates because it serves as a way to emphasise a particular regime's achievement in terms of raising living standards while de-emphasising its defects such as a lack of political liberties. Overall, the West's advocacy of values such as human rights – as part of the strategy of peaceful evolution – is seen as a direct challenge to the CCP's security as it calls into question the regime's legitimacy. We can now turn to how China's increasing integration with the world economy helps the West induce peaceful evolution in China.

Integration with the world economy

Given its perceived destructive potential to China's political security, why the Western strategy of peaceful evolution continues making inroads into China warrants further analysis. Fundamentally, the answer lies in the interaction between the political and economic dimensions of China's security. Economic security relates to a state having access to key mineral resources as well as to global financial institutions, which are to a large extent dominated by the Western industrialised states. China has opened up to the outside world since 1978, hoping to tap the world economy for its rapid modernisation goals.[24] It realises that market reforms are essential for bringing socialism's potential into play, especially after studying the problems of central planning in the former Soviet bloc. Today, China needs foreign loans, technology and expertise as well as access to markets in the industrialised states. It is inescapable that in the process of trade, increasing contacts with the West will serve as a conduit for foreign influences such as liberal values. In opening up to the wider world, the Chinese masses as well as the younger generation of CCP leaders will absorb some of those values. Calls for modifications to the political structure will then increase, putting the political security of the current regime at some degree of risk. Overall, the argument that economic growth and the concomitant of a middle class will spur political liberalisation has already been vindicated to some extent in Asian countries such as Taiwan and South Korea.[25] Such an outcome is what the CCP wants to avoid because it wants to hold on to its political monopoly in China.

The challenge for Chinese leaders is how to keep the populace free from Western bourgeois influence while absorbing the desirable impacts of Westernisation. This is in some ways reminiscent of the dilemma facing the reformers in the late-Qing dynasty. The proponents of the Self-Strengthening Movement wanted to adopt Western science and technology to boost China's military and economic capabilities but they also aimed to prevent the substitution of their Confucian values by foreign ideas and thought (*zhongxue weiti xixue weiyong*).[26] Such a strategy did not work – the Qing dynasty failed to bolster its position, arguably because it was overly fearful of uncontrolled foreign influence. Basically, the CCP today will not allow an uncritical acceptance of foreign values; there is an insistence that all foreign imports must be tailored to suit Chinese conditions. It has been noted that for Beijing, the onus is to achieve a 'Chinese' modernisation, not simply a 'transplant of the Atlantic culture'.[27]

At the same time, it is plausible that since the decline of Communism world-wide, the historical meaning of peaceful evolution has changed slightly. In that sense, one might argue that peaceful evolution is now more a case of the authoritarian political system in China being changed rather than Communist values being undermined. In any case, the CCP needs to find new substantive validating credentials in economic performance in order to appease the masses whom it retains power over, as it can no longer rely on the egalitarian justification of Communism. Market-oriented economic reforms and opening up to the West have undeniably played a large part in China becoming one of the few Communist countries to have succeeded in raising living standards. Generating economic growth can keep the masses materially contented for the time being; it seems the most prudent way to reduce demands for drastic changes in China's political system, thereby bolstering the political security of the CCP in the process.

This type of argument is further vindicated when one looks at Samuel Huntington's distinction between 'procedural legitimacy' and 'performance legitimacy'.[28] The former relates to the procedural aspects of competitive politics such as the recognition of minority rights, the freedoms of expression, contested elections and third party mediation while the latter focuses on the actual policy outcomes. Historically, regime authority in China has rarely been based on 'procedural legitimacy', but more dependent on 'performance legitimacy', in areas such as material well-being. Since 1978, it is clear that political legitimacy in China has gradually shifted from the ideological to the material, leading to the situation whereby promotion of economic growth and raising standards of living have become more important as a criterion for judging the Communist regime. In other words, for China's leaders today, their legitimacy as rulers is tied to the reforms they initiated. Unfortunately for them, to pursue these reforms entails opening up to the outside world, which in turn means being subjected to the Western strategy of peaceful evolution.

At a wider level, China's policymakers must learn to cope with the ramifications of economic interdependence, in particular the impact on national sovereignty, in the 21st century. It is clear that, today, autonomy carries the risk of costly isolation for China in all aspects – diplomatic, economic and technological. For example, it is generally acknowledged that during Mao Zedong's reign, autarkic policies such as those pursued during the Great Leap Forward had on the whole set the country backwards economically.[29] Today, withdrawing from the international economic system and pursuing an autarkic path of development is no longer a realistic option for China. Self-reliance still remains an important principle but it arguably takes second place to using foreign trade, technology, loans, grants and investments to achieve modernisation goals, which enhances economic security over the long term. Furthermore, in order to facilitate economic exchanges with the developed world, China will need to continue remodifying its internal institutions in order to become more attractive to foreign governments and investors. This is another form of peaceful evolution: the impact of trading with the West shifting from the economic realm to the political one, that is, from merely changing China's trading practices to having some influence on its political structure.

Linkage to regime change

The strategy of peaceful evolution can also overlap with the current US notion of regime change in the era of war on terror. Both approaches are similar in that they seek to alter the regime in a particular country, often according to the wishes of the progenitor. However, there are also important differences, the main one being that the strategy of peaceful evolution is non-military in nature while regime change often entails military intervention; the defeat of the Taliban regime in Afghanistan and the Saddam Hussein regime in Iraq are cases in point. Another difference is that the strategy of peaceful evolution is often identified with a wider capitalist bloc, no doubt spearheaded by the US, while regime change seems, at least in the present time, the sole preoccupation of the lone superpower. Furthermore, regime change is often associated with activities carried over a shorter time span, as military actions tend to be, while peaceful evolution constitutes a long-term approach to defeat enemy regimes.

In general, the policy of regime change entails the removal of a government hostile to the US or is considered illegitimate by the US and its replacement with a new one, mostly in accordance to the ideologies, values and interests of the lone superpower. Interestingly, the concept of regime change can to a certain extent be compared with dynastic changes (*gaichao huandai*) that had occurred in Chinese history. In those circumstances, it was deemed that the ruler's right to govern was removed by the divine powers when he was no longer capable of performing his task. The key point is that in a unipolar world, it seems that the US has emerged as the final arbiter of which regime has failed to remain accountable to its masses as well as conform to the norms and standards of the international community; the corollary is that such a regime would then have to be removed, by force if necessary. This type of inference will no doubt magnify the security concerns of China's leaders in an era where US military leadership is virtually unassailable.

Closely related to the US notion of regime change is the concept of the rogue state. For the US, implicit in the concept of the rogue state is that such a country will never moderate its behaviour. Given that the leaders of rogue states are demonised as evil dictators, regime change is assumed to be the only permanent way forward.[30] This is particularly worrying for China, who is one of the most ardent defendants of the Westphalian concept of sovereignty and non-intervention in the domestic affairs of a given country. From the US perspective, if more rogue states can be turned into democratic countries, then there will be less safe havens for terrorists, and the world would become a safer place.[31] To some extent, China recognises that putting this policy into practice will enhance international security but it still expresses concerns that the US can take the chance to impose political change in other states unilaterally. This type of change is also the aim of the peaceful evolution strategy.

Essentially, the US advocacy of regime change started in Iraq when George Bush's predecessor Bill Clinton signed into law the Iraq Liberation Act. The Act stated that 'it should be the policy of the US to support efforts to remove the regime headed by Saddam Hussein from power in Iraq and to promote the emergence of a democratic government to replace that regime.'[32] The goal has been largely achieved although the challenges of nation-building remain.[33] Another target for regime change could be China's ally North Korea (see Chapter 6). In Chinese eyes, although the Cold War has ended and ideology might seem less relevant in international politics, the US does to some extent treat non-democratic states as ideological enemies. In this sense, ideology – defined as 'an interrelated set of convictions or assumptions that reduces the complexities of a particular slice of reality to easily comprehensible terms and suggests appropriate ways of dealing with that reality' – retains its importance in the making of US foreign policy.[34] At a wider level, in the formulation of national security objectives, it is worth noting that ideology can impose a straitjacket on top foreign policymakers and indeed fundamentally shape their worldviews.[35] Today, the US regularly asserts that spreading liberal democracy to all corners of the world, through regime change policies if necessary, will enhance international security.

At the same time, there are hopes that regime change policies might not be sustainable in the long run. George Bush has domestic critics who believe that such policies have destroyed US's image in the world.[36] The case of insurgents in Iraq battling the occupying US forces is a case in point; regime change happened there as a result of military intervention and it might not guarantee a replacement of the whole administrative apparatus, existing bureaucracy and other regime remnants. China points out that the military occupation in Iraq has not achieved the desired outcome for stability, with the type of democracy espoused by the US having 'no market value' and 'failing to win the hearts and minds of the Arab people'.[37]

Interestingly, the lessons of Iraq could make the US rethink its strategy in future. Military options may not be totally effective or they may need to be supported by non-military means – exemplified by the strategy of peaceful evolution – in defeating undemocratic regimes, Communist or non-Communist. This implication is highly relevant for Chinese security thinkers as they ponder over a recent case of regime change. Although comparisons with the Iraqi and Taliban cases are limited, and despite subsequent assurances from George Bush that his administration is not actively pursuing regime change policies, Chinese leaders remain concerned over US inclinations to replace the political structure in certain countries. The key point is that non-democratic states such as China have the most to worry about the concept of regime change.

One key task for China is to gain more allies in the international community in order to counter the US tendency towards regime change policies. In this regard, China has actively sought the support of other great powers. For instance, it joined Russia and India to call for the democratisation of international relations, aiming to build a world order based on the norms of international law, equality, mutual respect, co-operation and multilateralism, with the United Nations (UN) playing a core role.[38] With France and Germany sharing concerns about US unilateralism, Europe as a whole could be another useful ally in checking US predominance and preventing the application of more regime change policies although Russia seems be the most important partner for this task right now. Overall, it is clear that the US's regime change policies and its unilateralism in world politics have pushed China to look more earnestly for allies who share reservations about America's assertive foreign policy. China also seeks to garner international opinion against the US practice of regime change in countering the wider, longer-term strategy of peaceful evolution.

From China's perspective, peaceful evolution is arguably less threatening in the short term because its military security is not directly threatened. However, in the long run, peaceful evolution is just as serious a threat to national security or more specifically regime security. For the CCP, the biggest fear today is that the US might become more outright in attempts to induce democratic change in China itself, thereby undermining its political monopoly. For instance, the US could step up the export of democratic ideas to the Chinese masses or offer more encouragement to Chinese dissidents than before. From China's perspective, the US notion of regime change serves as a reminder that the threat of peaceful evolution still exists; any linkages between the two concepts can only emphasise the enduring relevance of the latter.

Conclusion

Since the Cold War began and notwithstanding its ending, China still perceives itself as facing political security threats when it analyses the objectives of the West's strategy of peaceful evolution. Among the various ways to promote this strategy, spreading human rights and liberal democracy through economic engagement is probably the most threatening. To be more precise, Beijing views one of the goals of US foreign policy as seeking to subvert the few remaining communist states in the world through a process of peaceful evolution. This threat to China's political security has become even more pronounced because, as the major remaining communist power, Beijing sees itself as providing the symbolic ideological bedrock in an international system that has almost abandoned communism. The notion of regime change practised by the US in Afghanistan and Iraq, whereby military force was employed, magnifies China's security concerns as it overlaps with the concept of peaceful evolution.

At the same time, China's leaders know that they have to continue opening up their country to the outside world in order to stimulate economic growth. Further integration with the international trading system is needed as autarky is not a realistic option. In the process of economic liberalisation, Beijing will increasingly be confronted with an influx of democratic ideas, which are largely incompatible with the authoritarian rule of the CCP. From the CCP's perspective, the spread of Western values such as human rights to China are largely seen as unsuitable and threatening to regime security. The contradiction between the political and economic aspects of national security, or more specifically regime security, is most evident when one analyses the Chinese dilemma of economic opening-up to the wider world.

Essentially, the CCP must determine how to maintain close economic ties with the West while not allowing its authoritarian political system to be subverted through peaceful evolutionary pressures. The key question is how long they can continue to do so in an era where closer integration with the global capitalist system has on the whole induced varying degrees of political change – or peaceful evolution – in most other countries.

3   US global supremacy

In addition to the perceived American-led strategy of peaceful evolution discussed in Chapter 2, China is apprehensive of US supremacy in international politics. The objective of this chapter is to explore how the US dominance in the international arena might represent challenges to China's security – military, political and economic. Here, we need to examine how China perceives the US war on terror: the US appears justified in its merciless pursuit of terrorists because it was a victim of terrorism on September 11, but it also seems that the US has now used the global war on terror as a pretext to seek hegemony.

US war on terror

In order to understand China's security interests fully, one must delve into how China sees the US war on terror. First, the US rationale for the war on terror and ensuing efforts to further enhance homeland security comes from the September 11 attacks. Those attacks changed America's perception of its own security, and terrorism is now deemed as the biggest threat to national security. Specifically, George Bush has issued a doctrine: 'Either you are with us, or you are with the terrorists.'[1] This doctrine has implications for China, especially on the question whether total support should be offered to the US in the fight against terrorists. The war on terror is also linked to the US mission to defeat rogue states, as such states often provide military, financial and moral support for transnational terrorist networks. The definition of a rogue state varies but is generally understood to mean states that develop weapons of mass destruction (WMD), defy international norms and support terrorism.[2] Inevitably, these states have become more obvious military targets for the US after the September 11 attacks.

It is fair to say that the war against terrorists and rogue states has been fairly successful to date; the US won two battles – in Afghanistan and Iraq – and used diplomacy to force Libya to give up its nuclear aspirations.[3] The hunt for Al-Qaeda in Central Asia and indeed worldwide is ongoing. The prowess of the US military machine, as demonstrated through those missions, elicits concerns for China. Linked with the lone superpower's unilateralist tendencies, this portends unstoppable US dominance in the international system that China has to cope with. A specific concern for China is that the US might further violate the sovereignty of other states and intervene in their domestic affairs.

Moreover, in Chinese eyes, the war on terror is related to the US categorisation of states into three groups.[4] The first comprises allies and friendly states that the US can rely on. The second comprises countries that are neither allies nor outright enemies, with the future development of such countries being somewhat uncertain. The third group is made up of rogue states, including those in the 'axis of evil'.[5] These are the targets of US regime change, as noted in Chapter 2. China has been listed in the second group. This implies that the Bush administration does have concerns on how China fits in with the framework of the war on terror; China could emerge as a key ally in this war or it could scupper the US's efforts.

One aspect of the war on terror that China sees as particularly dangerous is the US strategy of pre-emption (*xianfa zhiren*), which entails using force to respond to an imminent threat.[6] This concept of pre-emption is perhaps the most controversial of all US military doctrines simply because its entails encroaching on the sovereignty of other states in the name of self-defence. The US argues that the existing legal right of pre-emption rests on the existence of such a threat – 'most often a visible mobilisation of armies, navies and air forces preparing to attack' – but it also advocates broadening the concept of imminent threat to better reflect the capabilities and objectives of today's adversaries because rogue states and terrorists do not seek to attack the US with conventional means.[7] Hence, the US argues that it needs to adapt its military strategies to fight these new adversaries. Terrorists groups like Al-Qaeda are 'irregular' threats because they employ 'unconventional' methods to counter the 'traditional' advantages of stronger opponents; these groups also pose 'catastrophic' challenges because they seek to acquire and use weapons of mass destruction.[8] Today, the US aims to forestall or prevent hostile acts by rogue states, terrorists-linked states and terrorists groups by, amongst other means, attacking them first before they have the chance to strike or use their weapons of mass destruction. China watched the US succeed in forestalling the threat posed by Saddam Hussein but more notably, it criticised Washington's occupation of Iraq, notwithstanding a joint undertaking to denounce terrorism and terrorist-linked states. With hostile nuclear aspirants Iran and North Korea possibly being the next targets for the US pre-emption strategy, China does have concerns about America using overwhelming military might to hit other sovereign states before being attacked.

To some degree, one might argue that the US stretched the concept of pre-emption well beyond its normal usage and actually declared a policy of preventive war.[9] Certainly, Washington recognises that 'under the most dangerous or compelling circumstances, prevention might require the use of force to disable or destroy weapons of mass destruction in the possession of terrorists or others or to strike targets (e.g. terrorists) that directly threaten the US or US friends or other interests'.[10] At a wider level, the US concept of pre-emption calls into question the basis for a just war and how a war should be fought in the current international system.[11] Added to this concern on how the US might employ force in future is the fact that China lags behind the US in terms of military power.

China had already expressed concerns about US military supremacy in the early 1990s when America scored an easy victory over Iraq in the 1990–1991 Gulf War. Moreover, Washington's success in mobilising a broad international coalition during the War suggested that Beijing simply could not afford to oppose the US – at least not directly – in the global arena without risking international isolation or marginalisation. International pressure was the key to China's public pledge to cease arms transfers to Iraq and China's positive vote on the first United Nations (UN) Security Council resolution calling for Iraq's withdrawal from Kuwait. Subsequently, in the 1999 Kosovo war, Chinese anxieties were further fuelled when the US and its allies in the North Atlantic Treaty Organisation (NATO) coalition defeated Serbia, displaying a degree of Western military sophistication beyond that was evinced during the Gulf War.[12] The current war on terror further validates the sheer might of the American military machine, albeit against lesser adversaries.

On the issue of nuclear security, China also has concerns about US superiority, and this explains why Beijing calls on all nuclear-weapon states to reduce the role of nuclear weapons in their national security policies, to honour their commitment not to target its nuclear weapons against another country and not to develop easy-to-use low-yield nuclear weapons.[13] In particular, China urges countries with the biggest nuclear arsenals such as the US to bear 'special responsibility' for nuclear disarmament and to take the lead in drastically reducing their arsenals. Of particular relevance to China are plans by the US to develop a theatre missile defence (TMD) system in East Asia. In its advocacy of nuclear disarmament, the conventional Chinese argument is that such systems undermine strategic stability and therefore should not be developed. The truth is that China lags far behind the US in terms of nuclear ability hence it is calling for a reduction in the role of nuclear weapons in international politics.

There is also a Chinese perception that the US leads military actions in the name of humanitarian intervention and peacekeeping in order to create an international order under its control. Under such a scenario, NATO will assume a 'global mission' and other US allies will be junior partners in this American quest for 'security dominance'.[14] Furthermore, some Chinese analysts see the geographical extension of NATO beyond Central Europe, with military force being used for an 'out of area crisis response', as foreshadowing a dangerous escalation in Western military alliances and US attempts to dominate the world.[15] For instance, whereas the US saw humanitarian motivations for organising a NATO-led coalition force to intervene in Kosovo, the Chinese leadership discerned a dangerous precedent that could later be used to oppose Beijing's designs on Taiwan and control of dissident ethnic areas such as Tibet. Knowing that, as permanent members of the UN Security Council, both Russia and China could, and probably would, veto military interventions in Kosovo, the Clinton administration was shrewd in working through NATO in 1999. This gave the Beijing leadership yet another grievance: the other members of NATO had conspired with the US, and this could compromise China's security interests over the longer term. Basically, China does not view US military preponderance as the only condition to preserve global security and has in fact called for the abrogation of all alliances such as NATO, arguing that they are often not the best means for maintaining peace.[16] With the overall concern over US assertiveness, it is clear that China is unwilling to give unqualified endorsement to American-led military interventions in any part of the world.

US hegemony

To the Chinese, the events of September 11 did provide the rationale for the US to wage an all-out war on terror, but what worries them more is that this war gives the US a good opportunity to further pursue hegemony. In general, Chinese analysts still largely adhere to a Realist approach to international relations whereby great power competition is deemed as central and inevitable; they see the US now taking steps to prevent another powerful foe, like the Soviet Union had once been, from challenging American hegemony.[17] This concern first manifested itself very clearly in the early 1990s after the demise of the Soviet Union; China had to face the US on its own in the absence of a strategic triangle. Today, the war on terror provides the US with further impetus to reinforce this 'new world order', whereby American military might will preserve international security through, among other things, defeating terrorists. Overall, the re-election of George Bush in November 2004 seems to portend the pursuit of an even more assertive US foreign policy in Chinese eyes.

Overall, the war on terror has provided the US with the chance to assert its preponderance in Asia as well as in the international system. The ongoing hunt for terrorists has enabled the US to enhance its presence in Central Asia, a key geopolitical region. Specifically, the war led to the US establishing bases in Central Asia – a region which was inaccessible during the Cold War as it had formed part of the Soviet Union. In other parts of Asia, the war on terror provided the US with the rationale to return its troops to the Philippines, where bases had been abandoned in the early 1990s. To a certain extent, the deployment of American forces in Central Asia and East Asia is perceived by China as the first stage of an encirclement process directed at itself.[18] In reality, one might argue that the US's national security strategy derives from a 'distinctly American internationalism' that reflects the union of its values and national interests; Washington will not only defend itself but also help make the world – including Asia – a safer place to live in.[19] Although China might agree with the need to rid the world of terrorists, it still often sees America's unilateral foreign policies as a smokescreen for pursuing hegemony.

It is important to note that usage of the hegemony concept as a key element in the Chinese theory of international relations is in many ways linked to the history of modern China and the country's experience of Western imperialism. Before the arrival of the Western powers, China played the role of a regional hegemon when it imposed its will on smaller neighbouring Asian states via the tributary system. Tracing the roots of the Chinese concept of hegemony further reveals that this concept actually dates back to ancient times. The character *ba*, the term from which *baquan zhuyi* (hegemony) is derived, can be found in Chinese political thought and has appeared in a variety of records beginning from the Warring States period.[20] In short, hegemony is not alien to the Chinese because they have actually pursued it and imposed it upon others when they had the chance to do so. The arrival of the Western powers in the 19th century led to China losing its hegemonic role in Asia – in fact, China's own security was actually undermined by those powers and Japan. Henceforth, China became suspicious of the hegemonist tendencies of other great powers, be it the US or the Soviet Union during the Cold War or just the US today.

It is also worth noting that Realist and Marxist strands in Chinese strategic thought have converged in the interpretation of hegemony. Chinese Realists might worry about a hegemon's ability to impose its will on others while Chinese Marxists interpret American efforts to expand the community of market democracies as a new form of hegemony. Both the Realist and Marxist perspectives give grounds for concerns that the US will use its power to seek hegemony and possibly eliminate the remaining socialist countries, including China. Opposing any form of US hegemony in the current era is therefore regarded as an important principle, and it is vital in preserving China's national security.

In opposing US hegemony, China advocates a multipolar world structure where America should ideally be just one of several poles of powers. This is primarily because China is fearful of a unipolar world where the US is dominant and can shape the global order to its disadvantage. The preference for multipolarity also lies in China's experiences in the international system following the collapse of the Sino-centric world order. In the age of imperialism, China had often manoeuvred between various imperial powers by playing one aggressor off against another with some degree of success.[21] After the Second World War, China viewed the US in the context of an international system that was largely defined by a bipolar world of East–West conflict, with Beijing's military and political security considerably entwined to this structure. China leaned towards the Soviet Union in the 1950s but later had to count on the moral and ideological support of Third World countries, especially Marxist ones, to meet the threat posed by two superpowers. In the 1970s, when parallel concerns about Soviet global power became evident, China tilted to the US. The point is that in a non-unipolar world, Beijing has more room to manoeuvre. That is not really the case today although certain European states and Russia might offer some sort of counterbalance to the US.

To China, the US global strategy is to completely replace the East–West bipolar system with an American-led unipolar structure in the 21st century. Accordingly, a key problem is how to stop the single superpower from aligning closely with the advanced industrialised democratic states in western Europe and Japan. One tactic is to exploit the differences between the US and its closest allies. For instance, Washington continues to pressurise its western European allies not to lift the arms embargo that was imposed after the 1989 Tiananmen event, even warning that lifting the embargo could have a negative impact on bilateral defence co-operation. From the US perspective, the embargo should be maintained for three reasons: serious human rights abuses persist in China, ending the embargo would have a negative impact on Asian regional and cross-strait stability, and no mechanisms are currently in place to prevent China from transferring technology and lethal weaponry to other, less stable regions of the world or to use it for internal repression. Compared to the Europeans, the US is definitely more forceful in demanding that China improve its human rights record. Hence, it is in Chinese interest to highlight the importance of bilateral ties, especially economic ones, with Europe in the hope of winning more diplomatic support there. This task is more pressing given that the US can affect China's military security, albeit marginally, by insisting that its European allies do not sell China specific types of weapons.

Tacit co-operation with the US

Notwithstanding the negative perceptions of the US war on terror, the war also gives China a chance to highlight its role as a responsible great power through a common undertaking to denounce and combat terrorism, at least in the short term. To the September 11 events, the China response was to describe terrorism as a 'common scourge' for the international community.[22] In general, China supports the US in the war on terror to show the international community that it can shoulder the responsibilities that comes with being a great power. This was evident in the first of the US's efforts, the war against the Taliban regime in Afghanistan in 2001. In the aftermath of the September 11 attacks, the US was determined to eliminate this radical Islamic regime, which had provided bases for Al-Qaeda. On this occasion, aware of strident global opinion against terrorism immediately after the tragic events in New York and Washington, China shrewdly distanced itself from the Taliban regime.[23]

China's role in fighting the Taliban regime was, however, rather limited and restrained. It shared some intelligence with the US as well as provided long-standing ally Pakistan with some economic aid and reassurances for Islamabad's support for Washington. The significance is that China did not actively seek to oppose US-led efforts on this occasion. At a wider level, Beijing knows that this tacit backing will serve useful as a bargaining chip in encounters with Washington over a host of important issues such as Taiwan, human rights and trade concessions later on. By not vetoing a proposed anti-terrorism action in the United Nations (UN), China hoped to see reduced US arm sales to Taiwan; basically, it earned some goodwill by backing the UN Resolution 1373 endorsing the use of force by an 18-nation International Security Assistance Force (ISAF) against the Taliban regime. However, this does not mask the fact that China was more worried about growing US unilateralist tendencies; therefore, it stressed the need to fight the terrorists through a proper international framework.

On its part, Washington recognised the value of having a strategic dialogue with China. While China was limited and restrained in its support for the global struggle against terrorism, it is significant that Beijing did not actively seek to oppose US actions or US-led efforts. In comparison to other powers such as US, Russia, Israel and India, China never perceived the Taliban as a great threat. Nonetheless, the Islamic regime's demise actually serves China's interests because potential spill-over effects into China's western regions were removed. As the US-led war on terror continues, China has been urged to play a bigger role by other members of the international community.[24] It is widely acknowledged that China has significant resources that can be used in this war but it remains to be seen whether Beijing wants to contribute more. The answer will probably become clearer after China has done a thorough cost–benefit analysis in relation to the war on terror.

Basically, China wants to centre its international anti-terrorist co-operation on the UN rather than the US.[25] It backs the adoption of anti-terrorist resolutions by the UN and has joined 10 of the 13 international anti-terrorism treaties, signing two of those treaties.[26] China currently participates in the UN anti-terrorist legislative process and pushes for the establishment of an international anti-terrorist legal system. China also ratified the International Convention for the Suppression of the Financing of Terrorism that aimed to check terror funding; the Convention comprises 28 provisions and urges all signatory countries to prevent and fight against 'terrorism financing crimes' through legislative, judicial and financial supervision measures.[27] Regionally, anti-terrorist efforts with organisations such as the Shanghai Co-operation Organisation (SCO) were increased. In bilateral co-operation, it is worth noting that China has stepped up exchanges with the law-enforcement departments of relevant Central and Southeast Asian countries and even concluded some anti-terrorism agreements with those countries.

At a wider level, more active participation in global anti-terrorism efforts would steer China towards the path of multilateral engagement in security issues, contrasting with the US's unilateral ethos. At the same time, it must be noted that China has traditionally never been keen on multilateral security dialogues, preferring to resolve specific problems on a bilateral basis instead. However, waging a successful war on terror today normally requires co-operation among the major powers; this gives China a chance to move cautiously towards some form of security arrangements with other countries in order to defeat terrorists. Apart from boosting the confidence of China in its role as a leading global actor, enhanced co-operation with other states also serves as a means to prevent any multilateral security regimes from exclusively targeting China. Moreover, joining regional efforts in the war on terror gives China a chance to assuage the concerns of smaller Asian states as well as the international community about its growing military strength.

Hence, it is in China's interest to further anti-terrorist co-operation with other states as this serves to demonstrate one of the positive aspects of Beijing's increasing clout in international relations. In the formulation of military security, China stresses that a country's military forces should have a wider role, including cracking down on terrorism. Like the US, China realises that terrorism poses a serious threat to international security. China needs a stable global economic environment to carry out its modernisation goals and terrorism can disrupt this. To a certain degree, the war on terror plays right into the hands of China because through combating terrorism, China can demonstrate its role as a responsible great power. Working more closely with other states to eliminate terrorism also serves to assure the world of its co-operative credentials and by extension, peaceful rise, which will be explored in detail in Chapter 2.

US dominance in the international economic system

Apart from military and political security, the US poses a challenge to China's economic security. It is fair to argue that military prowess helps the lone superpower maintain its dominance in the international economic system. Like Britain in the past, the US relies upon its politico-military dominance to ensure that the world markets are adequately accessible for the flow of its capital and products.[28] Today, globalisation of the world economy has further highlighted the need for US economic leadership. More importantly, China knows that as the leading Western trading nation, the US is the key to a more general acceptance of China into more international economic organisations. China is a member of the World Trade Organisation (WTO) but not yet in the less formal but important international grouping, the Group of Eight (G-8), which consists of the US, Canada, Japan, UK, Germany, France, Italy and Russia. International institutions such as the G-8 will almost certainly require China to satisfy various membership criteria for American support, overt or tacit.

A specific problem is that China needs ready access to US-dominated international economic institutions, such as the World Bank and IMF, for affordable loans to facilitate modernisation. US dominance in the international economics gives it the ability to link economic issues to political ones such as democratisation and human rights in its dealings with other states. Hence, China often criticises US laws that instruct American representatives in intergovernmental lending organisations, such as the World Bank, to oppose loans to countries that are guilty of human rights abuses. China needs affordable credit in order to facilitate its modernisation, and it knows that the US can hinder its search for funds. Overall, China resents the US linking economic issues to political ones such as human rights because Beijing wants to use the international capitalist system without being curtailed by Western liberal demands. To a certain extent, the human rights issue can then be regarded as a weapon used by foreign governments to impede the economic progress of China.[29]

The 1989 Tiananmen event is an important case to examine here. In the aftermath of that event, the US led a group of Western countries and Japan in imposing sanctions on China. Among other measures, Washington cancelled all high-level exchanges with China, cut off arms transfers and military-related sales, suspended financial credits and economic assistance and conditioned their restoration on substantial evidence of Chinese progress towards political reform. Fortunately for China, as a direct consequence of its co-operation in the 1991 Gulf War, economic sanctions imposed by the industrialised nations were rescinded and a major obstacle to China's desire to pursue economic development removed. Interestingly, in return for China's tacit co-operation in the Gulf War, the US eventually worked to end the moratorium on further World Bank loans to

China that were put in place after the Tiananmen Incident. One can detect a linkage in both events in the Gulf War and in Tiananmen Square; at a theoretical level, it means that the nexus between political and economic aspects of security needs to be more thoroughly worked out. Beijing now realises it has to learn how to deal with such types of complicated interconnections in international relations if it wants to cope successfully with the sole remaining superpower. The major short-term challenge facing China's foreign policymakers is how to accommodate American power without totally submitting to it while maximising Beijing's economic security. As China develops economically, it will be able to exercise greater leverage in international investment, finance and trade. For instance, the buying up of significant portion of US debt means that if Chinese investors redeem their bonds, the American financial system may malfunction.[30] One might argue that the balance of power in trade will slowly shift towards China as time goes by.

Essentially, China's current policy is to rely on bilateral trade arrangements while seeking to participate in a global market system through membership in organisations such as the WTO. This represents a realistic way for Beijing to enhance its economic security. Taking a wider historical perspective, it is worth noting that China had adopted a more confrontational approach to global capitalism during the Cold War. During the 1970s, it was generally recognised that China's delegates to the UN strongly supported the Third World calls for New International Economic Order (NIEO), backing the view that the industrialised and richer countries should provide more aid and better terms of trade and finance to the poorer ones. By the 1980s, Beijing has shifted its policy from challenging the US-dominated international economic system to seeking to become part of it. Deng Xiaoping's polices since 1978 mean that, instead of rejecting or seeking to reform international economic institutions such as the World Bank, International Monetary Fund (IMF) or WTO, China should join these organisations to extract whatever resources from them to satisfy its own development needs. Furthermore, China realises that it is more cost-effective to absorb foreign investment to hasten its modernisation rather than try to pursue an autarkic development programme, as was the case during Mao Zedong's reign.

Critically, increasing trading links with the US-dominated global capitalist economy can give rise to new problems for China. For example, China is bound to be more vulnerable to economic sanctions as its economy becomes increasingly interdependent with the US economy and the world economy in general. Essentially, the notion of economic security is fundamentally a tricky one. At present, one can discern that China will tolerate interdependence with America for the sake of its own economic goals. China is interested in international trade but only as a means to build up its economic power. In short, in an era of economic interdependence, growth is seen not as an end in itself but as a necessary means for China to achieve truly global power status in the long run.

Today, China has become a leading exporting nation but it still needs outside assistance to modernise, particularly in the areas of technology and management skills, and to overcome the overall shortage of capital for investment. In the 10th Five-Year Plan period (2001–2005), China actually used a total of about US$383bn of foreign funds, 34 per cent more than in the 9th Five-Year Plan period. The total includes US$286bn of direct overseas investment, US$38bn of funds raised by Chinese enterprises listing abroad and US$46bn of overseas credit.[31] On the whole, China has so far been rather successful in using foreign actors to serve its own needs. World Bank and Japanese government assistance to build China's infrastructure are examples. The use of international capital markets, sale of shares abroad and other sources of international finance will increase as a means to China's overall economic security. For the foreseeable future, China will continue to seek concessionary loans from financial institutions dominated by the West, in particular the US. It will also continue seeking Western venture capital and technology transfers. Another economic input sought by China is oil. Here China competes with the US, and foreign policies of both countries in regions such as Central Asia are driven by the quest for this vital resource. In general, China is perceived by the US in a negative light when it comes to energy competition; it is seen as attempting to 'lock up' vital energy supplies through a policy of 'mercantilism borrowed from a discredited era'.[32] Western energy analysts have noted that Chinese immense demand for energy has a major impact in driving global oil prices up and might eventually destabilise the entire market. Furthermore, Beijing's involvement in the global oil sector is often determined by arbitrary and non-market based administrative decision making and this worries Western oil experts. In any case, the first meeting of the US–China Energy Policy Dialogue and the establishment of the Department of Energy in Beijing by the US in June 2005 demonstrate the importance of energy issues to both states. Energy issues will constitute a significant factor in future Sino-US relations while having a major impact on China's economic security.

In bilateral terms, it must be pointed out that the US remains important to China's economic security. After all, the economic rise of China can to some extent be attributed to the US economy's openness to Chinese exports. Since the late 1980s, the US has been the largest market for Chinese exports. Natural complementarities exist between the world's foremost economic power and the world's largest developing economy. China wants access to the vast American market, advanced technology, financial investment and capital. Since 1978, economic reforms have transformed China from a typical state socialist economy with minimal foreign trade to a mixed economy in which foreign trade is growing in importance, and trade relations between China and the US have developed swiftly. At the same time, frictions exist between these two trading partners. By the late 1980s, the growth of China's exports to the US, which had followed the earlier path taken by Japan, South Korea and Taiwan, began to elicit accusations of unfair trading practices similar to those that Americans regularly voice against its other Asian trading partners. The Chinese export surge has now turned a positive American trade balance with China into a growing trade deficit.

Today, China's huge trade surplus with the US has led to charges that this resulted from unfair Chinese trade practices, such as bureaucratic practices, closed markets, dumping, evasion of quotas, violation of copyrights and currency manipulation, notwithstanding China's entry into the WTO in 2001. For instance, the US Congress' US–China Economic and Security Review on bilateral trade from 1989 to 2003 concluded that the US trade deficit with China during that period caused the displacement of production and some 1.5 million job losses in the US, with such losses doubling since China's entry into the WTO.[33] Another example would be the expiration of the quota-system governing global textiles trade at the end of 2004, which led to a surge of imports of Chinese clothing into America and the US textiles manufacturers urging Washington to take the necessary counter measures. In its 2005 scorecard on China's WTO commitments, the US–China Business Council concluded that despite certain progress, Chinese trade policies still violate WTO rules.[34]

On its part, China sees the US becoming more aggressive in its current trade policy, as Western countries in general are seeking to reinvigorate their economies. Washington is seen as interested in opening up the Asian markets further and increasing the vitality of its Asia policy. After all, the US had facilitated the East Asia economic boom during the Cold War era through its role as security guarantor, particularly for its allies Japan, South Korea and Taiwan. Today, the relative decline of the US economy vis-à-vis the Asian economy implies that Americans may take an increasingly hardline position on trade issues with China. For example, domestic budget deficits have limited the US's ability to give Beijing economic assistance or even to help finance American firms exporting to China. More importantly, a US that suffers from an international balance of payments deficit will be less willing to tolerate an increase in Chinese imports, barriers to American exports and the growing Chinese trade surplus.

At the same time, the US can ill afford to use economic sanctions against China today as most of its companies have invested in the China and because the US could actually lose more. This is similar to the situation in the 1990s: the annual debate in the US on whether to confer Permanent Normal Trade Relations (PNTR) status upon China occurred throughout that period but this arguably did not have a major impact on China's continuing economic rise. Arguably, America had realised that the delinking human rights to trade – under the rubric of engagement – was a better way to deal with a key trading partner that has a huge consumer market. As for China's leaders, they are aware that other countries need Beijing as a trading partner. For instance, although countries generally remain displeased with much of the Chinese government's domestic and international behaviour, companies throughout the Asia-Pacific region are rushing to trade with China and invest in China. Part of the reason why states do not restrict their investors is the fear of losing out in profiting from China's economic growth. Given that foreign companies benefit from doing business with China, the incentive is for more investment.

Moreover, the fact that one government refuses to do business with China does not stop other countries from grabbing their share of the huge Chinese market. This, of course, serves China's long term economic security objectives. China's leaders are aware that foreign investors prefer investing in countries that offer political stability because their main objective is to get a good return on their investment. In addition, China offers cheap labour and a large consumer market for Western goods. Ironically, it is thus the trade and investment of Western capitalist countries that constitutes one of the main reasons why China is expected to achieve high growth, inevitably enhancing Beijing's economic security in the process.

Conclusion

America's war on terror and its concomitant unilateralist tendencies in international politics have presented new foreign policy challenges for China. On one hand, the war has given China a chance to highlight its role as a responsible great power through a common undertaking to combat terrorism. On the other hand, from China's perspective, the US uses the war on terror as a pretext to strengthen its global hegemony in the post-Cold War era; this concern about hegemony has historical roots. Today, China is sceptical of the Bush administration's foreign policy, which it perceives as attempting to dominate the whole world with overwhelming military force. The events of September 11 do give the US a good opportunity to expand globally, into previously inaccessible areas such as Central Asia. More importantly, it seems that the US has emerged stronger than before and is now able to use this as the rationale of fighting terrorists to purse its strategic objectives in various places in the world.

At present, China has no alternative but to come to terms with a unipolar international system where the US is now the lone superpower and try to make the most of this situation. The fact that US military and political leadership is unassailable raises new concerns for China's security planners. From their perspective, there will arguably be fewer occasions when the US needs China's co-operation on strategic and regional issues once the war on terror is over. Washington might then adopt a more hardline policy towards Beijing, thereby threatening China's political and military security more directly than the case is now. In this sense, one can see why China is apprehensive about a US-inspired new world order, which is likely to be underpinned by an American-led coalition of Western industrialised states and Japan in the long run.

In the economic sphere, arguably one of the areas more amenable to Sino-US co-operation, relations between the two great powers have nonetheless strained. As a global economic power and the dominant player in the international trading system, the US is bound to have an impact on China's economic interests. Despite China's entry to the WTO and in principle full acceptance into the international trading system, a host of trade disputes with the US exists and will need to be carefully managed or resolved. From the Chinese perspective, the objective is to extract whatever resources it can from the US-dominated global capitalist system, at least until it moves higher up the international economic hierarchy. On the whole, because the US dominates the military, political and economic arenas of international relations, how the US pursues its foreign policy goals will have a major impact on China's security threat perceptions.

4   The Taiwan issue

This chapter looks at China's security in relation to the Taiwan issue. From the Chinese perspective, Taiwan does not represent a direct military threat but it poses a political challenge insofar as it is seen as seeking independence (*taidu*). More importantly, US involvement in the Taiwan issue constitutes an obstacle to China reincorporating Taiwan under its rule; for Beijing, the US commitment to Taiwan has indirectly encouraged the Taiwan independence movement. With the US acting unilaterally in international politics today, questions on whether Washington can now be more accommodating to Taiwan's interests will arise. Moreover, it can be argued that the US will offer Taiwan more moral support as part of its objective to export liberal democracy to the rest of the world. We first turn to China's military security and the US's commitment to Taiwan.

Military security and US commitment to Taiwan

Overall, American dominance in world affairs has an impact on the Taiwan issue, and this is a key concern for China. From the Chinese perspective, the US acts unilaterally in international politics today and is likely to become more accommodating to Taiwan's national security interests. This is especially true if the war on terror comes to an end; a common aim between China and the US to defeat terrorists would then disappear. Added to this is the strategic value of Taiwan in the US's East Asian strategy. This strategy stems from the Cold War, and the US still has an important role in guaranteeing the military survival of Taiwan today. By itself, Taiwan does not pose a direct military threat to China. However, with the involvement of the US, this threat is unduly magnified.

To be precise, American involvement in Taiwan dates back to the 1930s and was prominent in the 1945–1949 Chinese Civil War; the Chinese communists were prevented from gaining control over Taiwan then due in part to American aid to Taiwan. The outbreak of the Korean War in 1950 served as the catalyst for American enhanced support to Taiwan under the Kuomintang (KMT), and this backing was later further extended when the US sustained Taiwan's existence by the 1954 Mutual Security Pact, placing 'China's Taiwan province under US protection'.[1] The Pact was abrogated following Sino-American rapprochement in 1972 and since then, the US has not directly challenged the one-China policy.

However, the US stated at that time that it has an interest in a peaceful settlement of the Taiwan question by the Chinese themselves. With this prospect in mind, the US affirmed the ultimate objective of the withdrawal of all forces and military installations from Taiwan under the terms of normalising relations with China in 1979; essentially, there would be a progressive reduction of US forces and military installations on Taiwan as the tension in the area diminishes.[2]

Undoubtedly, the abandonment or sacrifice of Taiwan by the US was a security gain for China. However, the 1954 US–Taiwan Mutual Security Pact was replaced by the 1979 Taiwan Relations Act (TRA) that was passed into law by the US Congress. The Act assured a continuing American interest in Taiwan's security and it includes a US commitment to sell 'defensive arms' to Taiwan. From the Chinese perspective, any strengthening of Taiwan's military capabilities is regarded as a potential concern and can be viewed as an indirect challenge to its military security. In general, China regards US arms sales to Taiwan as one of the most sensitive area of Sino-American relations today; it consistently argues that such sales contravened the 1972 Sino-American agreement limiting arms transfers to Taiwan. A key Chinese argument is that US arm sales to Taiwan amount to an interference in China's internal affairs that obstructs and undermines the cause of China's peaceful reunification. This is of course premised on the assumption that Taiwan is part of China. From a wider perspective, one's likely explanation could be that defence contracts are shrinking in the Western countries and wealthy Taiwan represents a major potential market for Western defence industries. Overall, Beijing reiterates that the three communiqués of 1972, 1979 and 1982 should form the proper basis of Sino-American relations and be applied to the Taiwan issue as well.

The preceding historical analysis points to the fact that for China's leaders, the issue of Taiwan has been high on their security agenda since 1949. China still regards Taiwan as a renegade province and more importantly, it has never renounced the use of force to reincorporate Taiwan under its rule. This might seem somewhat unrealistic in a world where the efficacy in using military means to achieve foreign policy goals in international relations has gradually diminished, especially if the conflict is likely to involve another great power. To date, Beijing has flexed its military muscle to achieve political gains although this did not quite produce a totally desirable outcome. Shortly after Taiwanese President Lee Teng-hui's unofficial visit to the US in June 1995 and in the run-up to the first direct Taiwanese presidential elections in March 1996, the Chinese People's Liberation Army (PLA) launched a series of missiles at targets in the East China Sea. The first set of missiles fired in mid-to-late 1995 was intended to send a strong signal to Lee's government that it must not advocate Taiwan independence. The second set of missiles fired in early 1996 was aimed at intimidating the Taiwanese electorate so that they would not vote for Lee in the presidential elections.

Overall, the military manoeuvres in 1995–1996 were used to vindicate China's determination to deter any perceived independence tendencies in Taiwan. Although Beijing asserted that the exercises were routine, there were indications that China was really worried over the result of the 1996 presidential elections, or more specifically, that the voting result might ensue a more daring policy on Taiwan independence. China's military security also appeared to be at stake, at least indirectly, at that time when the US sent its aircraft carriers to the Taiwan Strait in a bid to counter Beijing's bullying tactics; this US commitment is extremely important from Taiwan's perspective. It is worth noting that such incidents have often acted as catalysts for actual conflicts. The 1995–1996 episode has been labelled as the Third Taiwan Straits Crisis; it can be compared to the previous two crises in the 1950s, when China bombarded the KMT-held islands of Jinmen and Mazu off the Fujian coast. Back then, the US reacted similarly with a dispatch of its navy to the Taiwan Strait in an attempt to deter further adventurism from Beijing. In all those three crises, the US was a key player: its support for Taiwan, be it for Chiang Kai-shek or Lee Teng-hui, was a concern for China. From another perspective, one can argue the Taiwan Strait Crises enable China to gauge the degree of US military commitment to Taiwan.

Another important area of inquiry is China's likely response if Taiwan formally declares independence, with or without implicit foreign encouragement. Specifically, the more hardline elements in China are unlikely to tolerate such a declaration; the People's Liberation Army (PLA) has stated that it will not 'sit idle' over the 'Taiwan independence' threat and has, in all aspects, indicated its preparedness and willingness to reunify China and complete what it regards as the 'the final phase of the Chinese Civil War'.[3] From Beijing's perspective, passing the Anti-Secessionist Law in the National People's Congress (NPC) in March 2005 provides the legal basis for using military means in achieving reunification with Taiwan, both internally and externally.[4] On its part, Taiwan countered the Chinese move by soliciting support from its allies, who sent a joint a letter to the United Nations (UN); its argument is that Anti-Secession Law violates the UN Charter, which opposes the use of force or the threats to use force to resolve inter-state disputes. However, those allies of Taiwan are small and weak states that have little weight in world affairs.[5] What really matters is that the great powers, the US in particular, have in general stuck to the one-China policy. Hence one detects a certain US strategic ambiguity in relation to the Taiwan issue; it wants to prop up and sustain Taiwan but is at the same time concerned about escalating tensions with China over the Taiwan.

On the whole, one might argue that active Chinese military pressure on the Taiwan independence movement today, as distinct from threats, does not appear to be a very promising option for China. Analysts have argued that prospects for seizing Taiwan through amphibious assaults are poor but noted that the Chinese submarine threat to Taiwan is possibly the most serious.[6] More importantly, a Chinese use of force against Taiwan is likely to cause a major international crisis, and American military intervention may follow. Most critical of all, such an unstable political environment will have catastrophic consequences for China's economic modernisation drive, thereby hindering Beijing's drive to truly global power status in the 21st century. Moreover, it must be noted that the Taiwan Strait is important for China's supply of energy; China relies on oil imports and wants to ensure the safety of delivery of supplies from the Persian Gulf via the Straits of Malacca to its eastern coast. In the event of a conflict in the Taiwan Strait, the US could use its naval superiority to disrupt China's oil supplies.

From a wider perspective, the Taiwan issue is intricately linked and entwined to China's perception of the US. From the Chinese perspective, the Taiwan issue is used by the US to partly justify its ongoing military presence in Asia; the issue also creates the basis for US intervention in the Taiwan Straits, if and when needed, as well as arm sales to Taipei.[7] This is of grave concern to China, given the lone superpower's unassailable military leadership. One detects a linkage to the earlier era whereby Chinese defence planners pointed out that America wants to take Taiwan as an 'unsinkable aircraft carrier' against China.[8] The current proposed US$15bn arms procurement package from the West, which is supported by Taiwanese president Chen Shui-bian, is indicative of such Chinese concerns.[9] Although approval for this package has stalled in the parliament, the US affirmed that any Taiwanese legislature decision will not alter its obligation to aid Taiwan in defending against a Chinese attack.[10] This obligation is linked in many ways to the notion of a China threat (to be explored fully in Chapter 9); the US would then use Taiwan to check China's ascendancy.[11]

From Taiwan's perspective, it is in the national interest to play up the China threat theory to garner more support from the US and its allies. Hence, stressing the ambitious modernisation of the Chinese military and the implications for a more assertive Chinese foreign policy in Asia is useful. For instance, Chen Shui-bian suggests that China's medium and long range missiles and intercontinental missiles target not only Taiwan but also Japan and the US. The Taiwanese government also noted that the modernisation of the China's submarine fleet is not just aimed at blockading Taiwan but rather at expanding influence into the Pacific Ocean; this is an attempt to warn other countries about China's quest for a blue-water navy, which will in turn help Beijing in its power projection. In this sense, Taiwan is in the 'first island chain' with regard to China's gateway to the Pacific; controlling this 'chain' will give China the platform to counter the naval superiority of Japan and the US in the longer term.[12] Obviously, such reasoning has implications for defence planners in the US as they entertain the prospect of growing Chinese naval strength.

Apart from the US, it is worth noting that Taiwanese president Chen Shui-bian has actively sought allies who share similar concerns about China's growing military strength. For instance, he advocates that both Japan and Taiwan should further upgrade their substantive relationship into a quasi-military alliance, arguing that China's military expansion is something that no country in the Asia-Pacific desires because Beijing poses a threat to the region.[13] Moreover, there were attempts made to get international organisations directly involved in cross-strait affairs with suggestions of UN-level inspections of the cross-strait security situation whereby staff and inspectors dispatched by the UN will make regular reports on security in the Taiwan Strait. Essentially, from Taipei's perspective, the expansion of China's military muscle is aimed at achieving beyond its stated purpose of deterring Taiwanese independence.[14] On the whole, one can discern an endeavour by Taiwan to internationalise the cross-strait issue. This surely raises China's security concerns because in general, China still prefers a bilateral approach to security issues, eschewing any advanced forms of multilateralism. Nowhere is this preference more obvious than in the Taiwan issue, which China regards as its own internal affairs.

Political security and Taiwan independence

Although China's military security is not directly challenged by Taiwan, its political security can be undermined by Taiwan insofar as it seeks independence. In this respect, continuing arms supplies from the West, in particular the US, can provide the basis for further bolder political actions by Taipei, apart from enhancing the military capabilities of Taiwan. It would be useful to examine the ascendancy of the Taiwan independence movement briefly here. Chronologically, the movement roughly coincided with the end of the Cold War; it partly resulted from the democratisation of Taiwan's domestic politics, associated with a new generation of political leaders such as former president Lee Teng-hui and the current president Chen Shui-bian. For example, in Taiwan's Legislative Yuan elections in December 1989, independence for the first time became an issue. Another milestone was the October 1991, when the Democratic Progressive Party (DPP) came to prominence in Taiwanese politics and adopted a resolution calling for an independent Republic of Taiwan, running counter to China's goal of reunification. The legalisation of the advocacy of Taiwan independence and the subsequent ascension of the DPP has since been interpreted by Beijing as a political security threat.

Before the DPP came to power in Taiwan, KMT leader Lee Teng-hui's use of 'flexible diplomacy' and 'dollar diplomacy' to gain diplomatic status for Taiwan in the international system was particularly dangerous in Chinese eyes. Notwithstanding its ambiguity, the Taiwanese independence movement represented by Lee during his reign was regarded as a problem for China's security policymakers. Lee Teng-hui's overtures to Washington in the mid-1990s – epitomised by his unofficial visit to his alma mater, Cornell University, with US permission in 1995 – were worrying. Beijing on the whole perceived that the US had implicitly encouraged this move. Lee's visit to America was seen as an 'inevitable move on the US strategic chessboard'; it was part of the US strategy to cope with a rising China in the post-Cold War era.[15] In short, even a private visit by the Taiwanese president to America was perceived by the Chinese as an acute security concern: Lee's visit appeared to signify a certain degree of acceptance and recognition of Taiwan by the US, and Beijing was worried that the rest of the world may eventually follow suit.

When Lee Teng-hui contested in the first-ever direct presidential elections in 1996, Beijing resorted to verbal attacks on him as well as a military show of force. The Third Missile Crisis vindicated China's goals of undermining the Taiwan independence movement and achieving reunification with Taiwan, although it was evident that a better understanding with the US on this issue is required. In the end, China reaffirmed its stance in the aftermath of the Crisis, stressing that 'changing the way Taiwan leaders is chosen and the results of this change cannot alter the fact that Taiwan is part of Chinese territory'.[16] This reaction is naturally expected, but more importantly, it evinces Beijing's concern that a new political leadership in Taiwan might further threaten its political security interests. Subsequently, in July 1999, Lee was accused by China of distorting cross-straits relations as 'state-to-state relations, or least special state-to-state relations' and more generally, encouraging the 'fallacy of Taiwan independence' and lobbying for 'dual recognition' or 'two Chinas' in the international arena.[17] China's predictable response was to continue linking the one-China principle to safeguarding its sovereignty and territorial integrity, and restating that principle's basis, both de facto and de jure, is unshakeable.

The end of Lee Teng-hui's reign in 2000 did not give Beijing any breathing space: the DPP became the ruling party in Taiwan that year. Given its emphasis on an independent identity and denunciation of China's missile build-up, the DPP's foreign policy has been watched just as, if not more, carefully by Beijing's leaders. The latest challenge came when DPP leader and Taiwan president Chen Shui-bian announced that the National Unification Council (NUC) and the National Unification Guidelines – which symbolises Taipei's own concept of reunification as opposed to independence – have 'ceased to function' and 'ceased to apply' respectively. Interestingly, Chen's decision was also backed by the Taiwan Solidarity Union (TSU) – the most ardent advocate of Taiwan independence today – which actually called upon the US to back Chen's case.[18] China reacted by criticising Chen's move as an attempt to deceive Taiwan public and international opinion, arguing that Chen wants to pursue de jure independence, which is linked to his constitutional reform plans.[19] At the same time, one can question the magnitude of this issue as the US is likely to demand that Chen abide by his promise to maintain the status quo; essentially, Washington advocates no unilateral change in this status quo by either Taipei or China due to the fear of escalating tensions.[20] Hence, for the time being, it appears that Washington can play a role in checking any further radicalisation of Taipei's foreign policy but the reliability of this pressure will continue to be carefully scrutinised by Beijing.

Moreover, one might argue that the DPP has in general softened its stance on the independence issue since it became the dominant party in government in 2000. From a historical perspective, the closer the DPP came to assuming political power in Taiwan, the greater the difficulty the internal consensus became on how to achieve Taiwanese independence. For example, within the DDP today, there are those who argue that Taiwan is already a de facto independent sovereign country and it is far more practical to protect Taiwan's current independent status than to advocate the establishment of a de jure independent republic. Although the commitment to promoting Taiwan independence is enshrined in the DPP platform, it is plausible that this principle only serves as a symbol of the party's basic stance nowadays. Hence, one might argue that the concept of Taiwan independence itself is ambiguous; it can mean different things to different politicians at different times. Nonetheless, China is unlikely to relent on its incessant pressure on Taiwan as the theoretical ambiguity of Taiwan independence is equally likely to be manipulated by hardliners in Washington or the more radical elements within Taiwanese politics.

In theory, the biggest threat to China's political security today comes from the secessionist TSU, which has Lee-Teng-hui as its spiritual leader. This party has stressed to the Taiwanese public that it is the only one sticking to its promise of producing a new constitution and not changing its insistence on national independence and autonomy. Claiming that it is the only party that can resist Chinese pressure, it comes no surprise that the TSU portrays the rise of China as the biggest threat to regional security.[21] More worrying for the Chinese leaders is that Chen Shui-bian acknowledges that the DPP and TSU are 'ideological allies and action partners' and both parties have the shared goals of strengthening Taiwan's national identity.[22] Essentially, the closer that a political consensus can be achieved in Taiwan regarding foreign policy towards China – although that also has to include main opposition party KMT – the more threatening the Taiwan independence movement becomes in Beijing's eyes.

Since the passing of the Anti-Secessionist Law in March 2005, Beijing has shown its preference to deal with the opposition in Taiwan in an effort to marginalise the role of the Chen Shui-bian administration. The Chinese Communist Party's (CCP) attention and 'united front' work – again with longstanding rival KMT – are now aimed at isolating the pro-independence forces in Taiwan. This is done by courting the opposition leaders such as Ma Ying-jeou of the KMT as well as James Soong of the People's First Party (PFP).[23] Although the KMT and PFP politicians received much attention from China, it is safe to say that they could not accomplish much as outstanding functional issues would require agreement from the Chen administration. This is the real limitation to China's strategy, as long as the DPP remains in power in Taiwan.

Externally, in order to consolidate its political security, China seeks to deny Taiwan any legitimacy in the international arena. In international relations, recognition of a state or government has been commonly regarded as crucial for the entity's legitimacy and status. Given that the concept of external sovereignty entails that independent states should be treated as equals in the international arena, Taiwan must therefore be prevented from achieving the status of an independent state in Chinese eyes. To a certain extent, China has achieved this goal of strengthening its political security on the international front, vis-à-vis Taiwan. Since 1972, Taiwan's diplomatic status in the world has declined. In practical terms, Taiwan was marginalised in world politics and reduced to the status of a pariah state until the end of the 1980s, when the country's move to democracy generated some rethinking by the wider world.

In order to deny Taiwan statehood, China constantly reminds the international community that most countries have recognised Beijing since 1972, after the US had switched recognition from China to Taiwan. In addition, China justifies its status vis-à-vis Taiwan by citing formal international agreements such as the Cairo Declaration and the Potsdam Proclamation made by the major powers during the Second World War, which stated that Taiwan should be 'restored to China' following the Japanese withdrawal.[24] Therefore, Beijing is totally against giving Taiwan 'any international living space', such as representations in international organisations; essentially, it argues that Taipei must never be allowed to join the UN.[25] In this regard, China has criticised Taiwan for engaging in 'dollar diplomacy' in an attempt to buy votes in the UN; for instance, Taiwan offers aid to poorer countries in exchange for their support vis-à-vis China.[26] As one of the economic success stories in East Asia, Taiwan does employ aid as one of its foreign policy instruments. However, the efficacy of such a policy is questionable, given that the huge consumer market and investment opportunities that China offers are arguably more attractive to other states in the long run. Countries choosing between China and Taiwan for diplomatic recognition will thus be more likely to opt for the former. In many cases, China actually forces these countries to a make a clear-cut decision, leaving no room for diplomatic ambiguity.

Adhering to the strict notion of sovereignty, China is only willing to accept ties with Taiwan on an unofficial basis, such as in the form of the Ku-Wang talks that facilitate the quasi-official framework for further cross-strait exchanges. Ultimately, China wants to see the return of Taiwan under its rule, just as the British colony of Hong Kong did in July 1997, and the Portuguese enclave of Macao did in December 1999. This is in line with the rationale of the 'one country, two systems' approach that China advocates; the notion is that Taiwan will eventually, as a special administration region of China, be able to preserve its own social and economic system, maintain a more democratic form of government than the rest of the China, receive a degree of autonomy in internal affairs and even have the right to maintain its own armed forces. In this vein, China rejects any comparison between the reunification with Taiwan and German or Korean reunification, arguing that both the two Germanys and the two Koreas had existed or are still existing as independent and sovereign states. In Chinese eyes, Taiwan has never existed as an independent and sovereign state.

Countering Taiwan's democratisation

Essentially, one might argue Taiwan can gain more support from the West in an age when the US intends to export liberal democracy worldwide. Moreover, Taiwan's democratic credentials can be employed as an instrument of foreign policy against China. Today, Taipei makes claims to legitimacy in the world community by stressing its identification with global trends towards democratisation and capitalism. The island republic has moved away from its KMT-dominated authoritarian political system, with the US playing an influential role in Taiwan's democratisation process. For example, the US Congress conducted hearings on the KMT's human rights abuses in Taiwan and the continuance of martial law on the island republic in the 1980s. The Taiwanese president at that time, Chiang Ching-kuo, eventually lifted martial law in July 1987 and removed the ban on forming new political parties in Taiwan.[27]

Clearly, democratisation constitutes another basis that can be used by the Taiwan independence advocates to further their cause, a danger that has to be stopped as far as China's political security is concerned. Today, Taiwan is governed by the rule of law while China is not; the contrast becomes even sharper when one compares the 1989 Tiananmen event and Taiwan's democratic transformation during that time as well as today. China is bound to be concerned that the international community might gradually accept Taiwan as an independent state, in an age when the lone superpower aims to export liberal democracy to the rest of the world. After all, Taiwan is not only one of the few thriving democracies in East Asia but more critically, an important component of the US's East Asian strategy. If the US hardens its commitment to Taiwan on ideological grounds, that will be seen as unfavourable to Beijing's objective of reincorporating Taiwan under its rule. Such a scenario will magnify the political security concerns of China's leaders.

On its part, Taiwan realises that China will continue to undergo peaceful evolution because of the spill-over effects of political liberalisation in the island republic; it is right to emphasise that what 'communist China fears most is the democratisation of Taiwan'.[28] The current Taipei government has explicitly stated that democracy will 'defeat' China's authoritarian regime.[29] This type of political legitimacy issue affects the political security of the CCP, as Chapter 2 on peaceful evolution has argued. A democratic Taiwan is likely to gain more recognition in the international arena and simultaneously highlight the need to induce change in China's illiberal political system. Obviously, the onus is on China to counter the democratic credentials of Taiwan. China had already pushed forward the concept of 'one country, two systems' in 1979 to placate fears that Taiwanese will lose their autonomy in the event of a Chinese takeover. China has also strengthened its legal work on the Taiwan issue. Domestically, the Legislations Bureau of the State Council's Taiwan Affairs Office was set up in August 2005 to implement the basic strategy of 'running Taiwan according to the law' and successfully handling Taiwan-related work.[30] The main duties of the Legislations Bureau include drawing up Taiwan-related laws and policies, co-ordinating with relevant departments in the drafting of such laws and studying the laws currently practiced in Taiwan as well as related trends in cross-strait affairs. The efficacy of such undertakings remains to be clearly seen.

Another Chinese strategy to counter Taiwan's democratic credential is to emphasis the authoritarian nature of the KMT regime on Taiwan, albeit before the 1980s. The target audience not only includes the international community but also the Taiwanese masses. For instance, China has reminded the Taiwanese people of the KMT's actions just after the Chinese Civil War. When the KMT first arrived from the mainland and imposed its rule on island of Taiwan, its troops launched a brutal crackdown on native Taiwanese protesters who demanded political reforms to root out autocracy and corruption in the KMT government. China often portrays the 28 February 1947 incident as the expression of the Taiwanese people's democratic political movement, criticising the KMT for its violent suppression.[31] Taking a longer perspective, Beijing is keen to remind the Taiwanese people that the CCP had come to power in 1949 as an advocate of egalitarianism – in the Marxist sense – over the elitist dictatorship of the KMT. It is also clear that

China still seeks to exploit any remaining suspicions between the native Taiwanese and the mainlanders who came to Taiwan in the 1940s. In discrediting the authority of the KMT, the CCP hopes to claim some sort of legitimacy over the Taiwanese masses. However, such tactics have lost much of their utility because Taiwan is no longer the authoritarian regime that it once was.

Hence, China needs to better present itself as a tolerant and benign government to the Taiwanese masses today. China must win the hearts and minds of the Taiwanese masses if it hopes to take over the country peacefully. History shows that the KMT regime of the 1930s and 1940s had failed to win over the masses, compared with the CCP at that time. The importance of political security is evident; CCP wants to enhance its legitimacy and this policy is also being applied to Chinese across the Taiwan Strait as well. For example, when China conducted military exercises in the waters close to Taiwan during run-up to the 1996 presidential elections, it stated that the Taiwanese people need not worry because the actual targets were 'independence-seekers, with support from some international forces bent on splitting China'.[32] One can also argue that China's leaders will increasingly turn to nationalism in an attempt to outmanoeuvre their counterparts in democratic Taiwan. Basically, nationalism is a sentiment shared by Chinese on both sides of the Taiwan Strait. Given the Japanese occupation of Taiwan from 1895 to 1945, an anti-imperialist form of nationalism is particularly useful in discrediting the proponents of Taiwan independence, some of whom praise Japanese rule and use this as the theoretical basis for advocating independence. These proponents, who are often associated with the DPP, argue that the Qing empire had betrayed the Taiwanese when it ceded Taiwan to the victorious Japanese after the 1894–1895 Sino-Japanese War; such historical arguments lend justification to Taiwan's existence as a separate entity since 1895. However, China denies the notion of Taiwan as a separate state by adopting a nationalist agenda instead. Beijing constantly reminds the Chinese and Taiwanese masses of the need to avenge China's century of humiliation – by Japan – in relation to the case of Taiwan.[33]

Economic security

The notion of economic security also looms large in China's strategies towards Taiwan. As argued in the previous chapters, the top priorities of China's leaders include sustaining the country's economic growth and raising living standards. In order to do so, China needs resources and capital. To a certain extent, capital-rich Taiwan can play an important role in this regard, hence China sees the three direct links of postal, trade and transport services between both sides as a sound approach to improving bilateral relations.[34] In 2004, Chinese statistics showed that bilateral trade rose 34 per cent to reach some $78bn while Taiwanese ones recorded a 33 per cent hike to $61.6bn.[35] The fact that political differences have failed to impede the acceleration of economic ties warrants further analysis.

In general, China's stance is that political differences between the two sides should not affect or interfere with economic co-operation. Hence, China has been quite receptive to Taiwan's economic policies since the 1990s, which encouraged greater contact, trade and commerce between both sides. To be precise, Taiwan has played a critical role not only as Beijing's trading partner but also as a source of investment capital, technology and management skills. The investment and business talent flowing into China from Taiwan have inadvertently made a major contribution to Beijing's economic development goals. This contribution is most evident in southern Chinese provinces, the close economic bond between the province of Fujian and Taiwan being a prime example. In contrast to the cautious stance adopted by the politicians, it must be said that Taiwanese businessmen have shown a remarkable readiness to invest in China in their bids to make profits in China's huge market. They are in general very keen to tap the Chinese markets because factors such as geographical proximity as well as the affinity of cultural and linguistic ties bring advantages of doing business in China. Overall, China supports cross-strait personnel contacts as well as economic and cultural exchanges as long as they endanger the goal of reunification with Taiwan.

With the aim of enhancing economic security in mind, China is generally more accommodating towards Taiwan's participation in regional economic organisations such as the Asian Development Bank and the Asia-Pacific Economic Co-operation (APEC). Basically, China does not wish to jeopardise its role in these economic organisations by adopting overly hardline policies against Taipei's membership because such policies might lead to unnecessary disputes between China and its other trading partners. In general, regional economic organisations are useful for fuelling Beijing's own modernisation drive, hence China has tolerated to a certain extent Taiwanese participation in them. Nevertheless, Beijing still insists that Taiwanese participation represents only 'ad-hoc arrangements and cannot constitute a "model" applicable to other inter-governmental organisations or international gatherings'.[36] In short, China insists that political recognition of Taiwan by the regional or international economic community must never be allowed.

Further economic integration with Taiwan also gives China leverage in their political rivalry. From Taiwan's perspective, its investment and trade are highly concentrated in China, and China has become a major engine for its economic growth since 1992; this over-dependence on one country might harm its economic security.[37] Overall, the Taiwan government stresses the virtues of a cautious approach to investing in China, arguing that Taiwanese businessmen should always put overall national interests above their corporate interests; in addition, there are concerns that certain high-tech products or advanced technologies might reach Chinese hands, and the Taipei government sees the need to create laws to regulate such exports.[38] Taiwan also sees China as an economic threat in the longer term; it often points to China's exploitation of cheap labour and frequent violation of international environment and labour standards means. The reality is that China has not fully subscribed to international trading norms, despite accession to the World Trade Organisation (WTO). Furthermore, the political leaders in Taipei are right in fearing that if market forces were given free rein, Taiwan might develop a deep economic dependence on China and Beijing could then exploit this for political purposes. For example, Beijing could impose economic sanctions on Taiwan, or perhaps detain Taiwanese business people in China as hostages, in an effort to force Taipei to make political concessions or even compel Taipei to submit to reunification under Beijing's terms and conditions. More importantly, it is plausible that economic power will be a major determinant in the outcome of cross strait rivalry. In this rivalry, China's sheer size could prove to be the deciding factor in the long run, and resource-poor Taiwan will eventually lose out.

One might argue that in the long run, China sees reunification with Taiwan, which would include the appropriation of Taiwan's resources, as part of the solution to sustain Beijing's economic growth. A merger with the Taiwanese economy will add size, boosting China's economic security in the process. A key point that needs to be grasped is that economic integration with Taiwan cannot be achieved by the use of force; this basically provides another incentive for Beijing to achieve reunification with Taiwan in a peaceful manner. China also realises that disturbance of the international system, especially if close to home and whereby US intervention takes place, will seriously undermine the long-term development goals upon which China's global power future lies. Proponents of economic interdependence will argue that cross border trade and investment can mitigate the political hostility across the Taiwan Strait; the interdependence in discussion can also include that between China and the US, a key player in the Taiwan issue. In reality, it is primarily due to China's quest for a peaceful regional environment – in order to carry out economic modernisation – rather than interdependence in its own right that rules out a military incorporation of Taiwan under Chinese rule.

Conclusion

In sum, China does not see Taiwan as a direct military threat, unless one factors the US directly into the equation. It is worth noting that on the Taiwan issue, the international community generally views China as the potential aggressor, not Taiwan or the US. In analysing the Taiwan issue, one key element is the continuing US military commitment to Taiwan; this acts as deterrence against any Chinese attempts to achieve reunification by force. To the Chinese, American involvement in Taiwan, which began with support for Chiang Kai-shek's Nationalist Party in the 1930s, is often regarded as the latest episode of foreign interference in its domestic affairs; many of them still regard Taiwan as the final phase of the Chinese Civil War. Added to this is the fact that Taiwan is today a thriving democracy, in contrast to the illiberal regime in Beijing, and liberals in the West might therefore increase their support for Taipei. Till this day, it must be noted that the Taiwan–US linkage remains an important determinant of China's foreign policies in general and those pertaining bilaterally to Taiwan and the US in particular.

In the quest to enhance its political security, China is determined to eliminate the Taiwan independence challenge because this represents an obstacle to achieving reunification. In this process, China has associated the US directly or indirectly with the issue of Taiwan independence as well as linked this issue to Chinese nationalism on both sides of the Taiwan Strait. Beijing's basic strategy is to isolate Taiwan in the international arena and discredit successive governments in Taipei; those manoeuvres have been conducted with the objective of bolstering China's political security while undermining Taiwan's. At the same time, by its threat to use force to reunify Taiwan, it is safe to say that Beijing has inevitably limited Taipei's foreign policy options. This limitation is more conclusive when one takes into account the fact that the US does not endorse the Taiwan independence movement outright as it generally favours a status quo in the Taiwan Strait.

In terms of economic security, Taiwan looms large in China's quest for national development and modernisation. Taiwan is a thriving economy and its resources and capital can help China further its economic rise. Indeed, one can argue that China sees reunification with Taiwan, which would include the appropriation of Taiwan's resources, as part of the solution to sustain its fast-paced economic growth. From the Chinese perspective, this reunification should be achieved through peaceful means. Basically, China seeks economic modernisation and accordingly needs a stable regional environment for this to be carried out. Analysing Beijing's security through the prism of economics therefore leads one to conclude that China is unlikely to resort to the use of force against Taiwan, unless there are drastic changes to the cross-strait situation.

5   The challenge of Japan

This chapter examines the role of Japan in relation to China's security interests. The first section looks at how Japan can actually enhance China's security interests, particularly in the economic sphere although frictions between both sides must also be analysed. The next section assesses Japan as a potential political and military security threat to China, at a time when Japan itself shows signs of re-emerging as a great power. This is then examined in relation to Japan's ties with the US. On the whole, it will be argued that Japan is seen as constituting a stiff challenge to China's security interests.

Japan's economic contributions

One of the main objectives of this book is to emphasise China's quest for economic security, a subject much neglected in most security literature on Sino-Japanese relations. As far as China's economic security is concerned, Japan is generally seen in a positive light. Essentially, Japan has played a role in China's modernisation drive. For a thorough analysis of China's economic security, the interplay with history is important, and therefore it needs to be discussed. Initially, China attempted to seek compensation from Japan for its wartime actions in relation to resumption of diplomatic ties. However, informal Japanese pledges of positive economic co-operation during the process of normalising bilateral relations meant that China subsequently abandoned its claims for war indemnities. This abandonment has since given China grounds to believe that it should get the best treatment from Japan, in terms of economic benefits, compared to other countries in Asia. In this vein, China has repeatedly reminded Japan as well as the wider world about the Second World War events such as the Nanjing Massacre, where Japanese military invaders had conducted atrocities against Chinese civilians. In truth, perhaps one might argue that other Asian countries, notably the two Koreas, suffered just as much as China under Japanese rule. In fact, Japanese occupation of the two Koreas took place over a longer time span than that of China. It was also total in geographical terms in the two Koreas, compared with partial control of China during the Second World War.

Nonetheless, China has adopted a basic strategy of using the 'the debt of history'; to its advantage.[1] To a large extent, history has served as a tool for China to solicit more economic aid, trading benefits and technology transfers from Japan since 1972. After all, China's modernisation requires as much help as it can get in order to achieve growth in the shortest possible time; Japan's economic, technological and financial help is indispensable in many ways. By building up its economic base, with Japanese help, China will then eventually be able to achieve truly global power status. This is at the heart of China's security interests.

In examining Japanese contributions to China's economic security, bilateral trade is an important element, and this began in the early 1950s. China initially responded to former Japanese Prime Minister Shigeru Yoshida's interest in resuming economic ties in 1952 in a cautious manner; the Yoshida doctrine basically emphasised the importance of economics as the principal means for conducting foreign relations.[2] Nonetheless, Japan's place in the opposing capitalist bloc did not help the cause of enhancing trade links. This situation lasted until 1972, when the normalisation of relations between Japan and China gave an impetus to economic ties. Since then, bilateral trade grew rapidly, topping some $169bn in 2004 from $2bn in 1972.[3] Japan is currently China's second largest trading partner, behind the US.

In general, Japan is a rich market for Chinese products, and China's exports to Japan are essential in accumulating foreign reserves. Japan produces and exports many consumer and capital goods such as machinery that China needs. Proximity adds another positive element for increasing bilateral trade as transport costs are reduced. This reinforces the notion discussed earlier that cross-border economic ties might to some extent outpace political ones as the 21st century progresses. From Japan's perspective, China has replaced the US as its top trading partner since 2004.[4] Also, China has risen to become an important product assembly site for Japanese exports. As Japanese companies develop new subsidiaries in China and move existing subsidiaries in the rest of Asia to China, the market for Japanese components shift to China as well. From China's perspective, many of its exports to other markets are therefore indirectly dependent on the importance of Japan as a trading partner. In short, given that China and Japan are at different levels of development, mutually beneficial economic relations can form the basis of Sino-Japanese relations and more importantly bolster China's economic security.

Overall, Japanese trade policies also suit the official line of the Chinese Communist Party (CCP). The leaders in Beijing do not want market reforms in China to be followed by political changes, whereby people and other forms of organised interests might replace the dominant role of the party. To a certain extent, the CCP believes that the authoritarian political system based on its absolute leadership is the only way forward. This in some ways resembles the Japanese mode of development, where there is an emphasis on strong state control and intervention in the domestic economy; after all, Japan was the classic and original development state in Asia.[5] In fact, China can learn a great deal from some of Japan's experiences in achieving economic modernisation. It can study the mistakes made by Japan and aim to avoid the pitfalls of quick development, bolstering its economic security in the process.

It is also worth noting that China views Japan as a more reliable trading partner, especially in comparison to its most important trading partner, the US. This type of issue illustrates the interplay between the economic and political dimensions of security. For instance, Japan's promotion of freedom, democracy and human rights is more indirect and stands in contrast to the US's more forceful approach. As the foremost and oldest democracy in East Asia – South Korea and Taiwan are new arrivals by comparison – Tokyo does have a role in spreading liberal values in the region, but its approach tends to be low-key. In general, Japan does not link political issues such as human rights to trade. It has provided China with economic assistance without completely linking it to human rights policies since the Tiananmen Incident. Even during the 1989 incident, Japan's concerns about China's treatment of dissidents were less visible. Protests from Tokyo were strong but brief and carefully phrased, somewhat different in tone from those of Western governments. Basically, Japan sought the understanding of other Western governments on its special historical relationship with China in mid-1990 and soon thereafter announced the planned resumption of yen loans.[6] To the Chinese, such Japanese actions suggest that trading with Tokyo carries the advantage that political considerations such as human rights issues tend to be given less emphasis. The corollary is that Japan is less likely to make aid to China contingent on Beijing's human rights records.

To a certain extent, one might argue that Japan's policy of engagement towards China has shaped the China policies of the world's largest trading nation, the US. Indeed, subsequent improvements in Sino-Japanese relation after the Tiananmen sanctions were lifted, as well as improvements in relations between China and Western Europe, spurred the US to change its sanctions policy and improve relations with China in general. China knows that, as long as it does not appear to threaten Japan's security interests directly, Tokyo appears willing to support the current regime in Beijing no matter what the other Western countries' view of human rights might entail.

Japan's role as China's second largest trading partner is reinforced by its position as a major provider of foreign capital to the developing world. Large scale yen loans are indispensable to a number of developing countries, including China, for consolidating their investments in economic and social infrastructures. China is the largest recipient of Japan's Official Development Assistance (ODA) bilateral aid, taking US$1,158.16bn or 13.46 per cent of the total.[7] In general, Japanese government loans to China have been given high marks because of their low interest rates, long repayment periods, accurate choice of projects and good results. They have contributed to China's development, especially in the initial stages of reform and opening up. Perhaps the only major problem is the appreciation of the Japanese yen over time, which will increase China's debt repayment burden to some extent.

In general, Japan has welcomed and supported Beijing's modernisation programme and open-door policy since the early 1980s. In this regard, Japan's direct investment is essential to China's development, although this has been traditionally cautious compared to its trade relationship with China and its ODA programmes. It is no secret that China desires more Japanese direct investment, and Chinese scholars question why the Japanese have underestimated the potential of the vast Chinese consumer market, especially given that countries such as the US and those in Europe compete fiercely for entry.[8] More specifically, given that science and technology is vital to achieving economic development in a shorter time span, technology transfer from Japan is something that China urgently seeks. However, the percentage of Japan's technology exports to China accounts for only a small proportion of total Japanese direct investment throughout the rest of the world. Japan's refusal to transfer its more advanced technology, especially technology that could be used for military modernisation, is understandable given its concerns about a rising China threat.

In general, the answer to traditional cautious Japanese direct investment in China lies in the fact that China's reformers have problems managing the transition to a capitalist economy. Considerable constraints are still being placed on the conduct of free-market activities, and there is still uncertainty over the eventual success of China's economic reforms. All these have perhaps discouraged Japanese businesses from participating more in the Chinese economy. Specifically, the 2005 Japanese White Paper has singled out the problems linked to investing in China, which include income distribution between the booming coastal provinces and the interior, an overheated investment climate, the protection of intellectual property rights, possible energy shortages, anticipated increase in labour costs and soft reforms of state-owned enterprises; accordingly, the solution is to balance such risks by expanding Tokyo's interests in Southeast Asia.[9] From Tokyo's perspective, Japanese businesses should not put all its eggs in the Chinese basket.

At the same time, from an international perspective, China can adopt a strategy of trading its markets for capital and technology. China can use Japan as a balance to the US investment and would encourage a contest between Japan and the US for the Chinese consumer market. In essence, this is a strategic triangle that gives China more choices in trade relations. China can therefore engage Japan as a hedge against the US from becoming too dominant in the international trading system. The aim is to achieve a balance between its reliance on Japanese capital and technology, and its economic relations with other countries such as the US.

In sum, the negative aspects of Japan's past have, to some extent, enabled China exploit them to its own advantage, primarily in terms of enhancing Beijing's economic security. In the quest to achieve its economic security goals, China has often asserted that Japan should lend maximum assistance to Beijing in its ambitious modernisation programme, in the light of Japan's historical debt to China. However, this type of assertion is beginning to come a full circle. It is also possible to argue that as time progresses, a growing economic interdependence has emerged between China and Japan, and could, ironically, lead to China curtailing its criticism of Japan's past.

Japan's global economic clout

Above all, Japan is a global economic power, and hence it is well placed to contribute further to China's modernisation. Japan is one of the major players in international economic, financial and monetary institutions. Although Japan encounters continuing difficulties in playing a bigger political–military leadership role globally, Tokyo finds it easier to expand its role in international economic and financial organisations. In particular, Japan is a very big contributor to aid programmes in general and to the funding of the United Nations (UN) in particular. The key point is that Japan can help China further its economic security because Tokyo has a certain level of influence in several international economic organisations. China might therefore count on Tokyo's support to protect or further its interests in organisations such as the International Monetary Fund (IMF), the World Bank and the World Trade Organisation (WTO).

China's partial dependence on Japanese clout in international economic organisations is further reinforced by the relative position of the two countries in international banking organisations. China is the main recipient of loans from the Asian Development Bank, which Japan dominates. China is also one of the World Bank's biggest borrowers. While the US remains the dominant force in the World Bank and has on certain occasions tried to cut off cheap loans to China, Japan's presence is now, officially at least, on a par with America's. This means that at times, Japan might maintain a fairly high level of funding to China to safeguard its own economic interests, regardless of any contrary US policy towards China. In this sense, Japan does serve to balance overriding US dominance in international financial institutions

In general, Japan's influence in the international economic arena is further reinforced by global trends towards regional trading blocs, with countries becoming more interested in the economic activities of their particular regions rather than the world as a whole. In the light of these trends, China might see mutual dependence and co-operation with Japan as increasingly important if the world economy moves closer towards regional trade blocs such as North American Free Trade Area (NAFTA) and the European Union (EU). While some analysts may dispute the claims that regional trading blocs will become the most important form of economic activity in the years to come, there is no doubt that policymakers in every country, including those formulating economic security strategies in China, need to take these global trends into account. Both the Chinese and Japanese economies rely on the Asian economy, and this regional economy in turn needs co-operation between China and Japan. Basically, China and Japan share an interest in maintaining stability in the Asia-Pacific in order to promote growth for their respective economies.

Nonetheless, over the longer term, China and Japan are likely to engage in economic competition. From Japan's perspective, the growing economic importance of Asia followed a surge in private-sector investment into the region, provoked by the rising yen since the 1980s. This emerging Asianism was also sparked off by Japan's lessening economic dependence on the US and its growing ties with East Asia in general. The Chinese are particularly concerned that a series of economic policies, including the careful deployment of foreign direct investment and ODA, has given shape to a strategy that seeks to lay the basis for a soft region-wide integration of economies under Japanese leadership.[10] For instance, Japanese firms have been successful at creating production and distribution networks linking Asian economies and the consolidation of Japanese corporations in other East Asian economies. This type of Japanese dominance in East Asia is perceived by most Chinese leaders as an undesirable phenomenon because it reminds them of the East Asia Co-prosperity Sphere that the Japanese tried to impose on Asia during the Second World War. The last thing that Beijing wants is Japan imposing its economic dominance in Asia alongside possible military and political control. Although this type of scenario is unlikely in the foreseeable future, the Chinese leaders are nevertheless cautious to prevent such situations from happening. Historical events play a huge role in shaping Chinese security thinking, none more so than China's experience of the Second World War.

In this sense, when taking a long-term perspective, Beijing seems to have mixed feelings about Japanese investment in China and other parts of Asia. The Chinese leaders want technology and capital, but they are concerned about Japanese domination of the Chinese and other Asian economies. This must be understood in the light of China's own aim to become an economic powerhouse, possibly matching or even surpassing what Japan has already achieved. Essentially, China needs to prepare for stiffer economic competition with Japan in the longer term.

In addition, energy competition is endemic between China and Japan. Both these oil-poor and energy-hungry nations will contest for energy resources in Asia and perhaps beyond. For instance, one can analyse China's dispute with Japan over sovereignty of the Diaoyu/Senkaku Islands in terms of Beijing's search for economic resources. The Islands lie just 166 km northeast of Taiwan and are situated halfway between Taiwan and Japan's Okinawa. The real important issue is the legal jurisdiction over about 21,645 square kilometres of continental shelf that is believed to hold up to 100 billion barrels of oil. China is, after all, seeking to discover its own offshore oil to replace imports. This is also the case of the Japanese government granting exploring rights in East China Sea to Japanese companies in April 2005. Another case of economic rivalry relates to the oil pipeline from Siberia; the Russians announced in December 2004 that this will be built to Nakhoda on the Pacific, which is favoured by the Japanese, over a competitor route to China.

Japan as a politico-military threat

The economic rise of Japan also implies that the country would become a military power one day. Among many others, those paying attention include Chinese leaders when they formulate their security strategies. Specifically, the end of the Cold War has hastened the need to assess the Japanese challenge among China's policymakers, spurred on to some extent by signs of Japan's continuing alliance with the US. Historically, it was Japan's rise that undermined China's long dominance in East Asia. Japan emerged as a great power in East Asia after the 1868 Meiji Restoration. Its expansionist policies had directly affected China's security, and this has left an indelible mark on the minds of China's leaders. An imperialist power that contributed to China's 'century of humiliation', Japan first encroached on China's security in the 1894–1895 war. As the defeated nation, China had to accept the terms of the Treaty of Shimoneseki; the Qing dynasty had to cede Taiwan to Japan and agree to the independence of Korea, which had up till then been a key vassal state in the Chinese tributary system.

A further blow to Chinese security interests was dealt when Japan formally annexed Korea in 1910. In the First World War, both China and Japan joined the Allies and were victorious but Tokyo attempted to pressurise the warlord government in Beijing to accept the Twenty-One Demands, which amounted to a de facto concession of China's own sovereignty. Japan had endeavoured to encroach on China's security and sovereignty in every sense. The weak and disunited government in Beijing gave in partly to Japan's demands, and defeated Germany's colonies in China were transferred to Japan instead of reverting to Chinese sovereignty. It took mass protests in China, symbolised by the May Fourth Movement in 1919, as well as opposition from the other great powers for Japan to relent, eventually evacuating Shandong in 1922.

By the 1920s and 1930s, it became clear that the threat of Japan to China had become more direct. Tokyo took advantage of a disunited China during the warlordism era and moved into Manchuria, setting up the puppet state of Manchukuo in 1931. While Chinese leaders at that time clearly recognise the military threat posed by Japan, they were unable to present a stiff challenge; essentially, the Nationalists and the Communists were embroiled in the struggle against each other although they later formed an 'united front' to fight the Japanese. More importantly, the international community did not do much to help China; the League of Nations was ineffective in preventing the Japanese occupation of Manchuria. Japan finally launched a full-scale invasion into China in 1937 and managed to occupy parts of eastern China until the end of the Second World War.

The above historical events are vital to the analysis of Sino-Japanese relations, and their relevance can be found in all strands of Chinese strategic thinking. In fact, history constitutes an important influence on Chinese security policy towards Japan, as evident in the economic security discussed earlier. From China's perspective, Japan's threat to its military security is arguably the most serious one posed by any state in modern times. While China had been subjected to treaties of extraterritoriality by Western powers such as Britain in certain treaty ports during the 19th century, Japan has so far been the only power that actually invaded China proper in the modern era. Therefore, Japanese foreign policies from the 1868 Meiji Restoration to Second World War have resulted in a very important legacy in China.

With this historical evidence in mind, it is only natural that Chinese leaders continue to worry about Japan recovering to its position as a great power in Asia. Fortunately for them, after the Second World War, Japan was restrained from becoming a military power largely by its own pacifist constitution and the 1952 Mutual Security Treaty it signed with the US. That restraint prevailed during the Cold War era. Moreover, when China faced the hostility of the Soviet Union, Japan was pulled into its anti-Soviet orbit: the normalisation of relations between

China and Japan in 1972 was accomplished in an atmosphere of growing Chinese concerns of a hegemonic threat from the Soviet Union at that time.[11]

The ending of the Cold War has cast doubts on the long-term ambitions of Japan. Questions on whether Japan might adopt a 'normal' strategy to rebuild its economy and military and then bring these to bear in the international system had already been apparent even before the Cold War ended. Nowadays, it has been argued that Japan is deviating from its traditional notion of comprehensive security (*sogo anzen hosho*) – emphasising a cautious balance of military and non-military elements – to a harder-edged military stance that seems more 'normal' in international relations.[12] More importantly, China shares the Realist conception that historically, 'countries with great power economies have become great powers, whether or not reluctantly'.[13] Japan's stunning economic successes, combined with the ending of the Cold War, imply that Tokyo is bound to reassess its role in international affairs. As skilled exponents themselves in turning limited national power to maximum use, the Chinese leaders cannot imagine that Japan will abstain from translating its economic strength into at least political power in the international arena. We can discern a slight difference in the forms of security threat that Japan poses to China in the past and in the near future. In the earlier period, Japan was more of a military threat to China. Nowadays, with the efficacy of the use of force in international relations gradually declining, it appears that an economically strong Japan will emerge as a country with more political clout in the international arena and that could impinge on China's security interest. Japan's ODA policy exemplifies this strand of thinking.

At the same time, China insists on using Japan's past to check a possible reversion to militarism by Tokyo. In fact, China has also chosen this legacy as the starting point in its bilateral relationship with Japan. Constantly highlighting specific key incidents, such as the revision of Japanese history books on Tokyo's wartime atrocities in Asia and the anniversary commemorations of Japanese wartime aggression, serves as a way for China to exert pressure on Japan to denounce its past. Moreover, China is sensitive to the potential rise of right-wing politicians in Japan. For instance, during the anti-Japanese protests in April 2005 in several key Chinese cities, Beijing expresses concern over the Japanese Diet's ambiguous 'non-apology' resolution on Tokyo's record of aggression.[14] Visits by Japanese Prime Minister Junichiro Koizumi and right-wing politicians to the Yasukuni Shrine are viewed as evidence of rightist tendencies in Japanese politics. Such tendencies are seen as paralleling the rise of Japanese military leaders in the Tokyo government earlier this century, a process that ended with dire consequences for China's security.

Right-wing elements in Japanese politics, such as Tokyo governor Shintaro Ishihara, have long lamented Japan's loss of strategic independence but as the Cold War waned in the 1980s, there was more resonance among centrists for the call for Japan to become a normal, ordinary state.[15] That would entail shaking off the shackles imposed on the country following its Second World War defeat and taking on more responsibility for the country's own defence. This is not incompatible with the Realist emphasis on anarchy, where self-help is regarded as the foremost principle in international relations. Unfortunately, China, and other Asian countries as well, have shown little understanding let alone sympathy for these Japanese aspirations and have been quick to condemn their articulation as proof of a resurgence of militarism in Japan.[16]

On the whole, China is still wary about the possibility of Japan acquiring further military power. The Chinese often question the size of Japan's defence spending, which stands at about US$25bn, some 50 per cent more than China's.[17] Given that China's territory is 27 times the size of Japan, they argue that Japan's rhetoric about China's defence development is designed to divert public attention from its own heavy defence expenditure, thus paving the way for its rapid future build-up, which in turn serves the way for Japanese and the US ambitions in East Asia and even beyond. Yet despite its relatively high defence budget, it is likely that Japan's Self Defence Forces (SDF) cannot conduct a war without the direct support of the US. Accordingly, this reliance on the US should not feed the perception of Japan as a military threat in its own right. Nonetheless, Chinese analysts still analyse the changes in Japanese defence doctrine from 'exclusive defence' of the home island to enlarged 'surrounding areas'; they are worried about various Japanese developments such as the redeployment of forces from Hokkaido to western Japan just opposite China and the Korean peninsula, streamlining of the SDF, procurement of new forces projecting air and naval weapons platforms and increasing closer integration of intelligence, training and planning with the US forces.[18]

While China sees Japan as a threat, this perception is mutual. In the 2004 National Defence Programme Outline (NDPO) – covering the period from April 2005 to March 2009 – Japan names China, in addition to North Korea, as security concerns for the first time; this contrasts with the previous outline in 1995, which avoided referring to specific states by name.[19] Japanese foreign minister Taro Aso has noted that China is beginning to pose a considerable threat, citing the elusive nature of Beijing's military expenditures and its nuclear arsenals.[20] Not surprisingly, China has pointed out that it does not threaten Japan but rather it was Japan that had invaded China during the Second World War. In reality, China and Japan have the military potential to do damage on each other.

Overall, it must be said that Japan still needs the alliance with the US to enhance its diplomatic standing in Asia; in addition to its historical record of aggression in Asia, Japan's negative image is partly attributable to its peculiar geopolitical position. Japan is situated in Asia, but until recently it maintains only loose relations with its Asian neighbours, especially in political terms. It is thus unlikely that Tokyo can easily claim to represent Asia in international affairs in short span of time, a point that the Chinese will be keen to take advantage of. If Japan does attempt to form an Asian bloc without China, Beijing is bound to oppose such a move in the most vehement manner.

Japan's wider role

Although Japan may be unacceptable as a political leader in Asia, it must be pointed out that the burden of its imperialist past tends to weigh much less heavily at the global level. For example, responding to calls for greater international responsibilities, Tokyo had earlier tried to take a more proactive role in places such as Cambodia in the early 1990s. However, this triggered a largely negative response in China. In general, China remains sceptical and apprehensive about Japanese participation in these multilateral peacekeeping efforts because it fears the possibility of the Japanese military's growing role in the global arena. Furthermore, Japanese military involvement in global crises will help erode Japan's isolationism and induce Japan to become more involved in multilateral security policymaking, thereby increasing the country's influence in the international arena.

Beyond Asia, Japan's quest to become a permanent member of the UN Security Council elicits concerns for China. After all, the UN has long been a pillar of Japan's national security strategy, along with self-defence and its alliance with the US. Today the question of UN reform, triggered to a certain extent by disagreement about the invasion of Iraq, has given Tokyo a chance to push further for a seat in the Security Council. Much of this push is based on the fact that Japan contributes to some 20 per cent of the UN budget. Along with Brazil, Germany and India, Japan had unveiled a proposal to expand the Security Council by six permanent member and four non-permanent member seats.[21] These four countries, the G4, want to claim four of the six permanent member seats, with the other two going to African nations. The G4 states have also promised to support each other's bid for a permanent seat. Japan was also prepared to drop its demand for a veto for 15 years, notwithstanding the fact that it had previously complained that a permanent seat without a veto was not satisfactory.

Apparently, Japan felt that forming an alliance in the form of the G4 would garner additional support and perhaps fend off some its critics, although not China. The entire plan was derailed in 2005 when it encountered stuff opposition from just about every one, including the US. Japan has the support of the US in gaining a permanent membership in the Security Council – but without veto power. The lesson for Japan is that it needs work more closely with the US on this issue. A fundamental problem is that reforming the UN Security Council ranks rather low among US priorities. Nonetheless, there is still a degree of US backing for Japan, and some US officials have even called on China to reconsider opposing Japan's claim. Ultimately, the permanent five (P5) members of the Security Council have the final say over any changes, and it is very unlikely that China would agree to any proposal that gives Japan a permanent seat. The fundamental obstacle to UN Security Council membership – the deep and bitter antagonism between P5 members and G4 aspirants – should remain for some time, none more obvious than in the Sino-Japanese case. From the Chinese perspective, granting the seat to Japan will enhance Japan's standing in the world and accordingly give Tokyo a greater role in East Asia.

To ensure that Japan does not play a greater role in international affairs today, Beijing is adamant to emphasis Tokyo's historical record of territorial aggrandisement, often comparing this with Germany's Nazi past. From China's perspective, Japan must seriously examine itself over its wartime actions before it can gain the trust of Asia and the world. This is in spite of the fact that Japan is not surrounded by weak neighbours, as was the case in the 1930s. For instance, countries such as South Korea and Taiwan are militarily stronger than they were in the interwar years vis-à-vis Japan. More importantly, the US is much more directly involved in East Asian affairs unlike in the 1930s when it pursued an isolationist policy. Nevertheless, given the damaging effects that Japan's past actions had on China, Beijing still remains wary of Japan and urges its Asian neighbours to remain vigilant against Japan.

There is also a shift on the part of Japan towards a wider conception of national security, which had hitherto been limited to homeland defence. Japan now wants to engage actively to improve international security environment, driven to some extent by its support of the US war on terror. This conformity with the US global strategy portends a wider role for Japan in the international system. The Japanese conception of self-defence moved from domestic safety to global security although this should not constitute a major surprise to China. On the military front, both the US and Japan have now agreed to enhance co-operation in their armed forces to ensure effective responses to emergencies in the Asia-Pacific.

Essentially, the NDPO introduced major policy shifts, such as a more active role for the SDF in international peacekeeping activities. Legislative measures would be taken to refine the categorisation of such activities under SDF duties, implying that the government is ready to upgrade such overseas operations to a principal duty of the SDF. Specifically, in the age of war on terror, Japanese Prime Minister Junichiro Koizumi has introduced a seven-point programme to respond to the new international environment, coming up with new measures such as allowing the SDF to provide logistical support to the US military in the emergencies, strengthening security checks at key facilities in Japan, despatching Japanese troops to gather information, stepping up immigration controls, giving humanitarian and economic aid to affected states, assisting refugees fleeing areas that might be affected by US retaliation in the war on terror and working with other states to stabilise the international economic system.[22] Some of these measures were applied in the conflicts in Afghanistan and Iraq as well as in relation to the North Korean nuclear issue. In July 2004, Japan's House of Representatives passed a package of contingency bills that enabled the country to be more ready for war despite its pacifist constitution.[23] Koizumi seems to believe that a tighter relationship with the US is vital to Japanese national security interests and wants to push towards a global alliance with the US from a regional one in the era of the war on terror. To a certain extent, it must be said that the concerns of Japan were magnified by the threat posed by North Korea; after all, regional developments such as the 1993–1994 Korean nuclear crisis had already moved the Japanese public to accept a more expanded role for the SDF.

The US–Japanese alliance

Obviously, a key Chinese concern is the evolution of Japan's alliance with the US, which is linked to Japan's future as a global power. On one hand, the alliance can constrain Japan. The US can still influence Japan's foreign policy in a number of ways through the 1952 US–Japan Mutual Security Treaty. From the Chinese perspective, the emphasis of this Treaty has shifted from protecting Japan to controlling Japan, including prevention of any resurgent militancy in Japan, as time goes by. Therefore, American forces in the region are seen as pre-empting the need for Japan to become a formidable military power – an outcome desired by no nation in East Asia. Moreover, a continued US presence, even if reduced in size, reassures states in East Asia that Japan will not be drawn into a power vacuum. It is important to note that, in Chinese eyes, relying on the US–Japan Mutual Security Treaty to check Japan is only a short-term policy. China will not be willing to put its faith in the US keeping Japan in check as the alliance between Tokyo and Washington might be altered in the longer term.

At the same time, notwithstanding the utility of the US–Japan Mutual Security Treaty, Beijing is wary of possible American–Japanese collusion against its own security interests. This is, in some ways, reminiscent of a certain episode during the Cold War when the former Soviet Union and the US were perceived as being in collusion against Beijing while engaging in superpower rivalry simultaneously. More recently, China has criticised the joint opposition of the US and Japan to the lifting of the EU's weapons embargo on itself. Another example is the US not recognising sovereignty claims made by China on the Diaoyu Islands. China sees the loss of the Diaoyu Islands as a result of Japanese past aggression, for it was forced to cede the territory of Taiwan, which then included the Diaoyu Islands, to Japan under the terms of the 1895 Treaty of Shimoneseki. Japan placed the Diaoyu Islands under the trusteeship of the US during the signing of the 1951 San Francisco Treaty, and the US handed those islands back to Japan via the 1971 Okinawa Treaty.[24] It is quite clear that Beijing prefers to deal with Tokyo on a bilateral basis. Any other powers, especially the lone superpower, supporting Tokyo's foreign polices will constitute a further potential security threat to China. This stance is evident when China asks Japan not to expand or broaden the scope of the security treaty with the US on grounds that it might complicate the situation in East Asia. What China really fears is that the US and its junior partner, Japan, might join forces to contain itself.

Another key worry for China is the enhanced US–Japanese military collaboration. This is to a certain extent represented by the Theatre Missile Defence (TMD) system that the US is developing with Japan. China argues that the transfer of such US technology to Japan is a clear violation of the Non-Proliferation Treaty, which is crucial to the stability in East Asia. Under the Japan's new NDPO, a ban on arms sales will no longer apply in areas like anti-missile defence. Arguably, North Korea's possession of missiles that can reach Japan has persuaded some Japanese that their country should rely less on the US – and more on itself – for security. The Chinese People's Liberation Army's (PLA) crash programme to develop land-attack cruise missiles is also of some concern to Japan and the US, as no TMD system is effective against such missiles. However, Japan's new NDPO does not incorporate a controversial suggestion by certain forces in Japan that it should consider acquiring a pre-emptive strike capability against missile bases in an enemy country: that would have reminded China of the current US emphasis on pre-emption. Tied in with these is Japan's participation in the US-instigated Proliferation Security Initiative (PSI) aimed at stemming the flowing on weapons of mass destruction and support for further missile defence co-operation with the US. In general, US–Japanese military collaboration is viewed in a negative light by China.

Essentially, China aims to pre-empt any possibility of further US–Japan collusion and seeks to exploit any tensions between the two partners. It is a well-known fact that Americans resent Japan as an economic threat and unfair trader; Japan's leaders have also faced increasing domestic pressures to stand up to US on trade matters, given that the Soviet military threat has disappeared and the need for a strong alliance with Washington has diminished accordingly. Another issue is the cost sharing. Although both Japan and the US agreed to extend the current agreement on Japan's cost sharing covering US forces on Japanese soil for another two years in December 2005, this issue remains a debate between the two allies over the longer term.

At a wider level, it is helpful to compare the different perceptions of the US–Japanese alliance by the US and Japan, which can be exploited by China. In the past, there were fewer differences between the two allies because there was a clear-cut distinction between the protector and protected. Today, questions have been raised on how long the US can prop up an old alliance with Japan without the shared Cold War values and commonly perceived Soviet threat that created the alliance in the first instance. Specifically, there have been arguments in the US that Washington 'can no longer anticipate the degree of diplomatic compliance Tokyo exhibited during the Cold War'.[25] Today, whereas the American approach to the US–Japanese alliance is more global and highlights the importance of the use of force to achieve objectives, the Japanese stance focuses much more on the Asian region and stresses the non-military instruments of policy. The Bush administration wants to look to Japan to continue forging a leading role in regional and global affairs based on common interests, common values, and close defence and diplomatic cooperation; work with South Korea to maintain vigilance towards North Korea while preparing the alliance to make contributions to the broader stability of the region over the longer term.[26]

However, Japan has in principle rejected that the US–British 'special relationship' as a model for its alliance with the US, which was advocated in the Armitage report.[27] Specifically, this report called on Japan to expand its security responsibilities in Asia; perhaps the most controversial was the observation that Japan's decision not to exercise the right to collective defence was an obstacle to the functioning of this alliance. Although the Armitage report was cautious in stressing that the decision on the Japanese Constitution must be thoroughly considered by the Japanese peoples, some foreign policymakers in Tokyo could interpret this as an endorsement for a revision of the Constitution. The key is that constitutional revision or reinterpretation of it will allow for collective defence by Japan under the UN Charter. This is bound to raise concerns for China.

From the Chinese perspective, its security is then partially dependent on the transformation of the US–Japanese alliance. Although Washington might have a hands-off policy, surely it must be pleased that Japan now seems more willing to take on a bigger role to counter new security threats. The biannual Security Consultative Committee (SCC) meeting between the two allies in February 2005 locked in the impressive progress that has been made in the security dimension of the alliance over the past four years and committed Washington and Tokyo to continuing efforts to modernise their alliance. There was a break with the past with both governments agreeing that interdependence and the proliferation of weapons of mass destruction (WMD) erases old distinctions between national, regional and global security; a list of regional and global strategic concerns, including military modernisation efforts within the region, were articulated.[28] Although no country is specifically identified there, China was later encouraged to embrace more transparency in its military affairs. Previously, Japan had gone to great lengths to avoid naming China as a direct national security concern. The readiness to do so in the SCC statement signals a slight shift in Japanese thinking about China.

In relation to Taiwan, the SCC statement did not specifically call for co-operation between America and Japanese SDF in case of a military conflict in Taiwan Strait, but it does hint at the US intention to lay ground for such co-operation if tensions increased there. The Chinese have argued with the US and Japan not to include Taiwan under the scope of their military alliance, arguing that inclusion of the island would breach the terms of a bilateral framework. Earlier, the Guidelines for Japan–US Defence Co-operation 1997 had already enlarged the scope of their joint defence, and China was concerned that Japan's definition of the 'peripheral state of affairs' actually included the Taiwan Strait.[29]

However, it must also be stressed that on the issue of Taiwan, a Japanese colony from 1895 to 1945, Tokyo is still generally recognised as a supporter. Like the US, Tokyo broke off diplomatic relations with Taipei in 1972 in favour of Beijing and has yet to alter its one-China stance. For example, Japan's reactions to China conducting large-scale military exercises during the run-up to the Taiwanese presidential elections in March 1996 were muted, merely calling for self-restraint on the part of Beijing. This stands in contrast to the US's forceful response where the Seventh Fleet was put on high alert. In general, it must be said that Japan's policy towards Taiwan is still in line with China's attempt to isolate Taipei in the international community.

While China has in theory rejected bilateral alliances as outmoded relics from the Cold War, it seems that the US–Japanese alliance represents a unique arrangement. China has not really directly raised the US–Japanese alliance with Japan; there were no discussions between both parties on the implications of a US withdrawal, let alone the ending of the alliance. Indeed, it is unthinkable to conceive of a structure of regional order without the US–Japanese alliance. It is the absence of a regional security architecture that underscored the continuing relevance of the US role in Asia, supported by military deployments in Japan as well as South Korea. From the Chinese perspective, a viable option is remain ambiguous about the future of the Japan–US Mutual Security Treaty. If Japan is seen as the main danger, then a continuing American role is essential to prevent the Japanese from becoming too powerful. Beijing's security can be enhanced by manoeuvring between Washington and Tokyo, as it did between Washington and Moscow during the Cold War. If China does tolerate a strong American presence in East Asia at all, then it is with countering Japan in mind. As long as Japan is tied to the US security umbrella, then any potential Japanese assertiveness and militarism could be at least kept in check until China itself becomes stronger to meet the Japanese challenge. After all, one of China's underlying strategic goals is to delay Japan's advancement towards becoming a major military power.

Conclusion

On the whole, at present, Japan seems to enhance China's security interests more than it poses as a threat. In particular, Japan has an important role to play in relation to China's economic security. To build up its economy, China needs Japan's assistance. China gains from trading with Japan, especially in the form of obtaining yen loans. By using the 'debt of history' as the key argument, China has pressed for considerable Japanese contributions to its economic development. Furthermore, given that Japan is less likely to link economic aid to human rights issues, it is regarded as a more reliable trading partner by China. As far as China's economic security is concerned, Japan is on the whole a contributor.

In general, it must be said that the fluidity of the post-Cold War period encourages Japan, and China as well, to strengthen its military in order to meet any possible challenges and problems that might have hitherto been suppressed by the Cold War framework. From China's perspective, this phenomenon seems like the rise of Japan once again. On a wider scale, strategic rivalry between China and Japan for prominence in East Asia is a likely outcome in the 21st century. Ironically, even if Japan is not drawn into a power vacuum in East Asia that partially arose with the ending of the Cold War, Tokyo may be pushed into it by Beijing's drive to global power status. From China's perspective, a status quo Japan would be ideal. From Japan's perspective, its ultimate interest is to avoid either internal instability and chaos in China or to avoid fostering a China that is a strong military power threatening its neighbours. From the perspective of regional security, China and Japan will have to work out their relationship's formidable bilateral problems, just as France and Germany did years ago.

For now, any potential manifestation of an aggressive Japanese foreign policy has hitherto been kept in check by the US–Japan Mutual Security Treaty as well as Japan's pacifist constitution. Overall, the US can play a role in restraining the ascendancy of Japan into a regional hegemon as well as checking any potential expansion of Japanese military power. Hence, from China's perspective, the future development of the US–Japanese alliance is important. In the meantime, China seems satisfied with manoeuvring between Japan and the US in another strategic triangle, for this will give China time to develop its economy and build up its military power.

Above all, China's strong interest in Northeast Asian stability is currently reinforced by the US–Japanese alliance, which provides an indispensable basis for regional security at a time when there is a degree of uncertainty in the strategic landscape. Beijing's primary interest is to maintain a stable East Asia in order to sustain its economic growth, and Japan can contribute to this by continuing its presence in the US–Japan Mutual Security Treaty, in a manner that is acceptable to China. A stable environment in East Asia gives China the space to build up its economic base. This base constitutes the springboard for China to achieve truly global power status, after which Beijing will be able to cope with any future Japanese threats on its own.

6   The alliance with North Korea

This chapter explores the strategic interests of China in relation to North Korea in general and the North Korean nuclear issue in particular. It examines China's perceptions of North Korea in the 21st century. For China, North Korea is still needed as a friendly buffer state as well as a political ally. China's economic goals in relation to North Korea will also be explored; this relates in particular to how North Korea might disrupt the stable environment that China desires.

Military security

First and foremost, North Korea shares a border with China and is therefore regarded as vital to Beijing's military security. From Beijing's perspective, an adversary force controlling the Korean peninsula, especially the northern half, can use it as a launching pad to invade China itself. After occupying Korea in 1910, Japanese troops used the peninsula as a springboard for attacks into China proper in subsequent years. During the Korean War, American troops under the auspices of the United Nations (UN) advanced northwards to the Yalu River from southern parts of the peninsula, too close for China's comfort. China then responded militarily, by sending in volunteers troops to aid the North Korean regime of Kim Il-Sung, as it perceived its own national security was at stake.

North Korea's importance as a buffer state to China – at least in psychological terms today – is further reinforced by an historical relationship; China actually controlled parts of Korea before the founding of a unified Korean state in the 7th century.[1] Korea then became a key tributary state of China or a part of the Chinese world order. Control over Korea was often regarded as a natural order, with Chinese script and Confucianism, for example, being readily absorbed by the Koreans. When the Manchu dynasty weakened at the end of the 19th century, a rising power in East Asia, Japan, challenged Chinese suzerainty in Korea. In the 1894–1895 Sino-Japanese War, which was to a large extent about Korea and fought largely on Korean soil and maritime waters, Japan emerged victorious and China had to accede to the independence of Korea. Later, Japan's competition with Russia over Korea, as well as Manchuria, culminated in the Russo-Japanese war of 1904–1905; the Manchu dynasty was largely a helpless bystander as foreign powers fought for the control of a former vassal state.

Japan subsequently annexed Korea in 1910 and ruled the country until the end of the Second World War.

When China became strong again in 1949 after decades of disunity, it aimed to revive its interests in Korea but this was soon challenged by another great power, the US this time. During the Korean War that pitted the Communist North against the capitalist South, China backed the North Koreans, primarily because its own security was deemed to be at stake.[2] From the above historical analysis, it is evident that North Korea occupies a central place in China's conduct of international relations. This is still the case today despite changes brought about by the ending of the Cold War. For instance, the Sino-North Korea Friendship and Mutual Assistance Treaty of 1961 continues to be valid – at least technically.[3] China is today the principal donor to North Korea and continues to supply the reclusive state with energy and food.

In actual fact, China knows that the risks of allowing North Korea to develop nuclear weapons are huge, as there are implications for China's own security. For instance, if the US fails to fulfil its commitment to protect South Korea, then Seoul might seek nuclear weapons itself.[4] Japan might also acquire its own nuclear weapons in response to the nuclearisation of North Korea, and Taiwan might follow next. All these developments would deprive China of being the sole nuclear power in the region and accordingly reduce its concomitant clout in international politics. Such developments are also likely to trigger a nuclear arms race in Northeast Asia and make the regional environment more volatile. This is precisely what China does not want.

Political security

Perhaps less obvious but of no lesser importance is North Korea's role as China's ideological ally, and this relates to China's political security. Here one must explore the organisation and process of the Chinese regime, and the ideology that gives the rulers of that regime legitimacy; essentially, the Chinese Communist Party's (CCP) 'blood ties' with the Korean Workers' Party (KWP) must not be overlooked. Beginning with the anti-Japanese war in the 1930s and 1940s, those ties were subsequently strengthened by the Cold War rivalry that pitted Communist states against capitalist ones. Today, the Chinese still remind themselves of the Korean War and stress the importance of comradeship with their North Korean counterparts. In terms of ideology, it is only natural that China sustains its bond with North Korea, its last Communist ally. After all, the collapse of Communist regimes in the Soviet Union and the Eastern European states has implications for Communism as a political ideology. China and North Korea are currently among the few Communist regimes left in the world and Communism, in any variant or form, still constitutes the ruling ideology and more importantly, the basis on which those respective regimes came to power and had retained power for such a long time.

In the post-Cold War era, rather than strict emphasis on any form of Asian communism movement of the global proletariat, both China and North Korea place emphasis on fighting against foreign subversive influence and outside interference in their internal affairs through for example, the Western advocacy of human rights. Both sides also continue to stress the common need to preserve the ruling authoritarian parties' hold on power by defeating the US-led strategy of peaceful evolution. As discussed earlier, this strategy aims to undermine Communist regimes through non-military means, primarily via commerce, cultural exchanges and infiltration of foreign ideas, especially human rights and liberal democracy. The current situation is one where Beijing and Pyongyang both face a lone superpower keen on promoting liberal values worldwide, and this provides a common ideological enemy for the two East Asian Communist states.[5] Furthermore, given the impact of the century of humiliation, the Chinese have become the most ardent defendants of the Westphalian concept of sovereignty, and they criticise virtually any foreign intervention in a given state's domestic affairs. This is accorded greater prominence in the light of Chinese perception of US interference in Iraq and possibly later in North Korea. It is also worth noting that North Korea supports China in criticising the latest US National Security Strategy report, arguing that the report wrongly criticised Chinese foreign policy and the direction of China's development, as well as represented interference in China's domestic affairs.[6]

Essentially, one can detect an ideological bond between China and North Korea against the US. Ideological elements also exist in US foreign policy, including that towards North Korea. For instance, North Korea has been labelled as a rogue state by the US. Implicit in this concept is that rogue states will never moderate their behaviour; the leaders of such states are demonised as evil dictators, and regime change is often assumed to be the only permanent way forward. Having practised the policy of regime change in Iraq and perhaps contemplating a similar move in Iran, the US has definitely given the North Koreans cause for concern. For instance, for a certain period, the labelling of North Korea as an 'outpost of tyranny' by US Secretary of State Condoleezza Rice heightened this concern, justifying Pyongyang's belief that it is at risk from a nuclear attack by the US for its 'roguish' behaviour.[7] The US National Security Strategy has also identified North Korea as one of the seven 'despotic governments'.[8] What this means is that such a US posture tends to drive North Korea even closer to China as well as China to North Korea as both these East Asian totalitarian regimes perceive US export of liberal values negatively.

For the Chinese, one of the ways that US can induce change in rogue states, besides employing military force, is through the strategy of peaceful evolution. A key element in this strategy is to foster democracy in North Korea. Certainly, America has launched a human rights offensive on North Korea with the North Korean Human Rights Act of 2004. The Act encourages the US administration to focus on the well-being of ordinary North Koreans; it authorises humanitarian aid to refugees and provides nearly US$24 million a year to non-profit organisations to support human rights, democracy, rule of law and the development of a market economy in North Korea.[9] The Act also allows modest funding for refugee assistance efforts and directs the US to accept North Korean refugees if they choose not to go to South Korea. To North Korea, this Act is viewed as part of the US policy of seeking political change in enemy states such as itself. Despite subsequent assurances from Bush that the US is not seeking regime change in North Korea and is still committed to six-party dialogue, North Korean leaders remain concerned over US plans to modify their Stalinist regime.[10] Given that the Chinese regime resents the US export of human rights and liberal democracy, Washington's ideological stance towards Pyongyang is seen as hostile to Beijing by extension.

Economic security

From the standpoint of economic security, North Korea plays an important role in China's quest for a conducive regional environment because its hostility towards South Korea can undermine stability in Northeast Asia. It is therefore in Chinese interests to prevent any further radicalisation of North Korea's foreign policy. In terms of economic security, North Korea is situated close to Manchuria, a key industrial region of China. In the past, the natural resources of Manchuria had attracted the attention of imperial powers such as czarist Russia and Japan. To further expand their economic as well as military and political interests in Manchuria, Japan and Russia fought a war there in 1904–1905, when China was too weak to resist foreign intrusion. Another war on the peninsula today would mean that China would have to come to the aid of North Korea in some form, lest its inaction be regarded as a sign of Beijing's declining military standing in the world. In any case, conflicts on the Korean peninsula will be detrimental to China's quest for a stable regional environment, which is a necessity for its economic development in the race to catch up with the Western industrialised nations.

Today, China aims to promote regional economic co-operation, an example being the UN backed Tumen River Area Development Programme that envisaged converting a sparsely populated outpost into an international trading centre that could rival the world's busiest ports. The five members of the Programme – Russia, China, North Korea, Mongolia and South Korea – recently agreed to extend the 1995 agreement on joint development for another 10 years as well as expand the geographical coverage to the three Northeast provinces and Inner Mongolia Autonomous region of China, the entire territory of North Korea, the eastern provinces of Mongolia, the eastern port cities of South Korea and the Russian Far East.[11] This Greater Tumen Initiative aims to focus its main activities in the areas of transport, energy, investment, trade and tourism, which can only be beneficial to China's economic security. Furthermore, China is carrying out a 3-year project to lay some 1,400 km of railways in the northeastern provinces of Liaoning, Jilin and Heilongjiang to boost infrastructure and facilitate trade with North Korea. In particular, there is a Chinese plan to turn Dandong, the largest town on the border with North Korea, into the transport hub of Northeast Asia.

Undoubtedly, the economic well-being of North Korea is essential to China. Should the North Korean regime collapse, China will have to face an exodus of refugees. Even in the event of domestic instability in North Korea, China will have to respond in some manner. Hence, it is quite evident that Chinese interests require the gradual evolution of North Korea towards economic reform rather than sudden transformation or collapse. China definitely cannot condone the wholesale change of the Pyongyang regime as this would have implications for the security of the Beijing regime. Overall, the economic systems of Communist countries are intertwined with their political ideologies. Both the Korean and Chinese communist parties have come to power by adopting the same political ideology and will not be able to renounce Communism entirely. What China hopes is that North Korea will follow the path Beijing has taken in order to ensure the survival of the Communist regime in China. Pursuing economic growth and ensuring the continuing material well-being of the masses, as the reformers in China would argue, could be one way to stave off demands by the masses for political change. On its part, North Korea is impressed by China's development path, especially in the southern provinces of China.[12] There is potential for North Korea to follow China's path to economic reforms without accompanying political liberalisation although this will entail giving up some of the cherished principles of self-reliance.

In the quest to maintain stability in the northeastern region, China could also induce the opening of North Korea to the rest of the world. Overall, the need to prevent any radical actions by North Korea forms part of China's emphasis on peace and development (*heping yu fazhan*). This emphasis also ties in with China's desire to assure the world of its co-operative credentials and by extension, its peaceful ascendancy. On its part, Pyongyang has shown interest in attracting foreign investment and joining international financial institutions. In this regard, South Korea is generally willing to offer assistance. For instance, South Korea has continued to push for economic engagement with its northern neighbour, with the Kaesong Industrial Zone under construction in North Korea some 40 miles north of the demilitarised zone.[13] South Korea has also stated it is in principle willing to provide the north with massive economic assistance if North Korea abandons its nuclear ambitions. In fact, South Korea's Unification Ministry has already drawn up seven specific projects to help rebuild North Korea's economy in the event that Pyongyang agrees to give up its nuclear programme; these include providing energy assistance, modernising railways and ports, establishing joint farming complexes, and organising tours to the North's highest peak of Mount Paektu, afforestation projects, and joint utilisation of rivers across the border.[14] However, this plan will still be dependent on, at least, the US and South Korea dropping their severe restrictions on trading with North Korea and supporting Pyongyang's membership in international economic institutions such as the Asian Development Bank, the International Monetary Fund (IMF) and the World Bank.

Certainly, Beijing encourages such positive responses from the outside world, if only to ensure that it does not have to bail its North Korean ally out financially. To be precise, China's strategy in prompting North Korea to engage in economic reforms is not designed to bring about liberalisation of the North Korean political system but to promote stability in its buffer state; the strategy has been formulated with the prime objective of enhancing security on China's borders. It is China's self-interest that primarily drives its foreign policy towards North Korea and the related issues. Nonetheless, China can play a key role in opening North Korea to the rest of the world. Basically, China is likely to gain economically if North Korea opens up to the international capitalist system. Increased trade activities in the Yellow Sea region – China, the two Koreas and Japan – may be one way to bring this about. At present, it seems the economic and political climate is not ripe yet to formalise any form of Yellow Sea rim economic co-operation but in the longer term, some form of inter-governmental arrangement might create a strong enticement for Pyongyang to become involved. In such a situation, it would be plausible that China and North Korea initiate a bilateral economic agreement first before extending it to Japan and South Korea.

Great power role

North Korea's posture in international relations, in particular on the nuclear issue, has also given China a great power role. This issue has come under the international spotlight since the early 1990s and it captured the world's attention most recently when the Stalinist state admitted its nuclear capabilities in early 2005.[15] In essence, North Korea's nuclear intentions remain, despite the recent pledge to halt its development programmes in principle.[16] Those intentions are often interpreted as a threat not only to regional security but also international security. Recently, the isolationist country has consistently sought to stifle the six-party talks aimed at resolving the North Korean nuclear issue. Those talks involve regional players such as Japan and Russia, but the roles of the US and China are much more critical.

Overall, Tokyo's ability to pressurise Pyongyang is limited and comes primarily through economic aid, given the lack of progress in establishing formal bilateral ties. Essentially, North Korea still insists on reparations for Japan's occupation of Korea from 1910–1945 in return for normalising diplomatic relations.[17] Moreover, Japan's pacifist constitution forbids the projection of military power abroad, and this means it is unable to assume regional responsibilities one might ordinarily expect a country of such economic prowess to shoulder. As for Russia, a former ally of North Korea, it is less capable of influencing Pyongyang today compared with the Cold War era. Since losing its superpower status when the Soviet Union disintegrated, Russia has abrogated its 1961 alliance with North Korea, and its overall influence in Northeast Asia has waned. Today, Moscow joins other powers calling for Pyongyang to return to the negotiating table but its role is marginal rather than primary. For our analysis here, the key point is that North Korea's foreign policy suits China. Pyongyang's policy calls for normalising relations with the US and Japan first before normalising relations with South Korea. This means that China has an intermediary role to play between North Korea and the US, as well as North Korea and Japan. It gains further leverage in its political manoeuvres against those great powers because it now becomes the key player in persuading Pyongyang to normalise relations with Tokyo and Washington in the long run.

Notwithstanding the dangers a nuclear North Korea poses to China's interests, Pyongyang's nuclear threat has in many ways enhanced China's great power status. A brief historical analysis of the nuclear threat is useful here. North Korea joined the Non-Proliferation Treaty (NPT) in 1985 but had until 1992 refused to sign an International Atomic Energy Agency (IAEA) safeguards agreement as it was obliged to do by the treaty, arguing that it would not sign such agreements unless all US nuclear weapons are withdrawn from South Korea. The end of the Cold War brought a partial solution to the issue. In September 1991, US president George Bush Senior announced that all tactical nuclear weapons would be withdrawn from South Korea, paving the way for both Koreas to sign a joint declaration on the de-nuclearisation of the Korean peninsula.[18] However, North Korea continued with its aim of developing nuclear weapons, which ultimately resulted in the 1993–1994 nuclear crisis. At that time, Pyongyang rebuffed demands by IAEA for inspections and threatened to withdraw from the NPT. Subsequently, under the 1994 Agreed Framework, the US and its allies consented to provide Pyongyang with heavy fuel oil and two light nuclear reactors (LWRs) in return for freezing nuclear-related activities.[19] However, in the latter half of 2002, North Korea restarted its nuclear reactor at Yongbyon and refused to co-operate with UN inspectors, eventually withdrawing from the NPT in January 2003.

During the 1993–1994 nuclear crisis, China had already acted as some sort of liaison for the West while remaining as North Korea's friend and ally. This made China look like a responsible great power in the eyes of international organisations such as the IAEA and the international community in general. At a time when the security order in Northeast Asia was still very much in the process of being shaped, in particular with much depending on how the nuclear issue in North Korea developed, any positive input from China to resolving the nuclear impasse was vital. Today, once again, the onus is on China to persuade Pyongyang to re-engage in dialogue in the form of the six-party talks; more specifically, China's good offices are needed to persuade North Korea to halt its nuclear activities immediately. At the same time, it is common acknowledgement that there are limitations to how much Beijing can actually accomplish in reshaping Pyongyang's national security thinking and behaviour. North Korea's heightened economic dependence on China may constrain its foreign policy to some extent, but this does not necessarily make the reclusive state any more co-operative. It is equally true that North Korea's potentially destabilising behaviour can jeopardise China's interest in maintaining a peaceful environment for its economic modernisation goals and its relations with South Korea, Japan and the US.

From a wider perspective, the entire Korean peninsula is important to China's conduct of international relations, in addition to being a vital component in Beijing's comprehensive security. This was first evident during the Korean War, when China intervened and later enhanced its prestige as a great power by holding the US to a stalemate on the 38th parallel. More recently, China's influence on the Korean peninsula was enhanced with the normalisation of relations with South Korea in 1992 (see Chapter 7). On the surface, the normalisation seems to indicate a shift towards Seoul from Pyongyang but the reality is that Beijing has extended its influence to the southern half of the Korean peninsula in the post-Cold War era, a feat that was unachievable during the Cold War. Today, China is one of two great powers – the other being Russia – that has formal ties with both North Korea and South Korea. This gives China an opportunity to enhance its status in the international system. The underlying guiding principle is that China needs to compete with other powers, primarily the US, in an anarchical international system.

China and the US on North Korea

Given that the US and China are engaged in strategic competition, it is inevitable that they will have different perceptions of North Korea that stem from their national interests. For China, those interests include sustaining its Communist ally in military and political security terms. Furthermore, Beijing uses its leverage over Pyongyang, which no other state in the world currently possesses, to elevate its status in the international system. For the US, exporting liberal democracy is one of its foreign policy goals and North Korea is a target. More importantly, North Korea's nuclear intentions constitute a threat to US interests in Asia, and this challenge has to be dealt with appropriately. The US has assumed responsibility in preserving stability in Asia since the Second World War. This was achieved through a series of bilateral alliances that stemmed from the Cold War era, the most important one being the US–Japanese alliance. In that era, the main antagonist was the Soviet Union. Today, despite the dissipation of the Soviet threat, the US still needs to underwrite stability in Asia for various reasons. For instance, Washington needs to maintain the military security of its traditional Asian allies such as Japan and South Korea. For Seoul in particular, the US still provides a military commitment to deter the threat posed by North Korea. Moreover, the US wants to preserve the existing liberal trading environment in Asia, partly because it has economic interests there and partly because such an environment would foster further economic interdependence and promote peace.[20] The key point is that the US sees North Korea as a threat to its interests in Asia as well as its Asian allies.

Beyond Asia, North Korea is also seen as a threat to America's global interests. As the lone superpower and the self-proclaimed guarantor of global security, the US has taken on the challenge of dealing with North Korea's nuclear intentions. In essence, the root of this problem lies in the nuclear brinkmanship practised by Pyongyang, which can be traced back to the 1993–1994 crisis. From North Korea's perspective, a settlement on the nuclear issue is only possible if three conditions are met: the US recognises its sovereignty, gives assurance of non-aggression and does not hinder North Korea's economic development.[21] At a wider level, North Korea poses a challenge to US security interests with regard to issues such as weapons of mass destruction (WMD) and nuclear proliferation. Ostensibly, justification for the US-led campaign to topple Saddam Hussein in Iraq was achieved on the grounds that his regime might use WMD against other states. Having achieved the Iraqi objective, the US might turn its attention to North Korea.

Certainly, North Korea has not only exported Scud missiles to US enemies such as Iran and Syria but also to Egypt, Pakistan and Libya; its proliferation of missiles, missile parts and their technology has been regarded as one source of strategic instability in South Asia and the Middle East.[22] From North Korea's perspective, the sale of such weapons is necessary for increasing export earnings and in turn, alleviating its economic burden.[23] As Pyongyang and its clients are not members of the missile technology control regime (MTCR), which restricts the exports of missiles to limit the proliferation of WMD (nuclear, chemical and biological), the process of keeping North Korea in check becomes even harder. For instance, both the Pakistani Ghauri and Iranian Shabab missiles projects are based on the North Korean No Dong programme.[24] If North Korea can be convinced to stop its missile exports, the Iranian programme will slow down significantly.[25] Iran and North Korea belong to the 'axis of evil', and the US would want to prevent further missile development exchanges between those two states.

Essentially, there is a consensus in the US that Pyongyang must not be allowed to sell nuclear materials to other countries or terrorist organisations as the six-party talks continue; the impetus for this consensus was provided by the events of September 11 and the concomitant emphasis on homeland security. In addition, having demonstrated the willingness to put its pre-emptive national security doctrine into practice in Iraq, one might argue that Bush administration has not totally ruled out a similar policy towards North Korea.[26] The Bush administration's decision to freeze the assets of eight North Korean companies – viewed as WMD proliferators – and level sanctions against a Macao-based bank for aiding North Korea's black-market and counterfeiting operations has not helped cause of the six-party talks.[27] Washington argues that such measures were necessary for its own defence and independent of the diplomatic efforts that it is pursuing, but Pyongyang disagrees. Essentially, the US policy is not to give economic aid to North Korea until the country totally abandons its nuclear programme. There is also an insistence that North Korea must return to the negotiating table and disarm without preconditions.

Given that North Korea poses a threat to international security because of its nuclear intentions, how to deal with this threat is likely to constitute a key concern for Washington for the foreseeable future. In general, engagement strategies with recalcitrant states are only successful if there is some sense on the part of the advocator that the target state's intentions are amenable to change. Engagement will not be appropriate if the target's actions are aggressive or revisionist. Pursuing an engagement policy despite uncertainty surrounding the target's intentions, on the assumption that such intentions can be transformed, would therefore be costly and dangerous.[28] If this is the case, it might be better for the US to work more closely with other great powers or international institutions to resolve the North Korean issue rather than pursue the case wholly by itself.[29] As the case of combating terrorism illustrates, the US needs to work closely with other great powers to resolve such thorny international security issues. This is where China comes into the equation, and we can examine the prospects for great power management, that is, some form of co-operation between China and the US over the North Korean issue.

Overall, it must be said that the Bush administration, driven by domestic security concerns, have clashed with the view held by other powers such as China and Russia, which are prepared to offer North Korea more to a deal on the nuclear issue. At a wider level, the six-party talks are a test of whether the key participants can collectively deal with regional security concerns. Those talks might lead to a broader regional security forum at a later stage. To a certain degree, one can compare the US approach to the North Korean and Iranian nuclear issues. In the latter, the US acts much more in concert with other powers: Washington would support significant incentives that the European Union (EU) has offered to Iran in exchange for an EU promise to back tough measures proposed by the US if EU–Iran talks fail. The key point here is that in the North Korean case, China, which exerts the main influence on North Korea, is deemed more as a strategic competitor to the US. Hence the US is naturally more willing to compromise with the EU in the resolution of strategic issues such as the Iranian nuclear case.

Beyond the North Korean issue, it is important to note that Sino-US strategic competition exists in other key areas of international politics. US unilateralism and its dominance in international politics are resented by China, which desires a multipolar world where the US should just be one of several poles of power. In this sense, it is plausible to view North Korea as a key piece as China plays out its confrontation with the sole remaining superpower on the strategic chess-board; Beijing can use the North Korean card to establish a stronger bargaining position vis-à-vis Washington on a wide range of issues such as Taiwan, human rights, Northeast Asian security and trade. Confrontation over those issues would surely reduce the likelihood of China and the US co-ordinating tactics over the North Korean issue.

Nonetheless, China continues to be the key intermediary between the US and North Korea, and this is one of the roles that it plays in the six-party talks. In general, the international community has looked to China in helping to resolve the North Korean nuclear issue because the US has difficulties dealing with North Korea bilaterally. After all, it was Beijing that encouraged Pyongyang to adopt a more conciliatory stance towards Washington even before the end of the Cold War. For example, when the US eased its restriction on diplomatic contacts with North Korea in the 1980s, Beijing hosted a series of North Korea–US councillor-level meetings. Today, China continues to encourage North Korea to increase efforts in repatriating the remains of US servicemen who were unaccounted for at the end of the Korean War.

One can also identify a common interest in Beijing and Washington in stemming nuclear proliferation in East Asia. For China, a nuclear North Korea would not only undermine its own nuclear monopoly in East Asia but also give regional states such as Japan, South Korea and Taiwan further justification to develop their own nuclear weapons. In this sense, China has a vested interest in halting North Korea's nuclear ambitions. Compared to the US, it must be said that China's interests in preventing nuclear proliferation are still narrower and largely confined to East Asia, primarily because Beijing has yet to emerge as a truly global power.[30] Nevertheless, it must be noted that China also takes a keen interest in global nuclear proliferation issues, the Iranian impasses being a case in point.[31]

Moreover, Sino-US interests converge to a large extent on the Korean Peninsula as both countries are anxious to avoid another conflict there. China knows that North Korea's potentially destabilising behaviour can jeopardise its quest for a peaceful environment to carry out economic modernisation goals as well as complicate its relations with other Asian states. In this vein, preventing any further radicalisation of North Korea's foreign policy is a primary objective. Eyeing the dangers of instability on the Korean peninsula, China will not let the six-party talks fail totally. To Beijing, continued dialogue – no matter how ineffective – is better than an escalation of hostilities that might result in a military conflict on the peninsula. Persuading North Korea to stay on the negotiating table is crucial because another full scale war on the Korean peninsula will disrupt the regional environment, making it harder for China to carry out economic modernisation, which is essential for achieving truly global power status to rival the US in the long run. As for the US, it wants to preserve regional and international security by countering the nuclear threat posed by North Korea. More specifically, the US wants to stop North Korea from further developing its nuclear capabilities. This might be more effectively achieved through economic engagement rather than adopting a hardline policy towards a member of the 'axis of evil'. In sum, both China and the US do not have much to gain from an outbreak of full-scale conflict on the Korean peninsula.

It is clear that the North Korean policies of China and the US as well as how these two great powers manage their divergent worldviews and differences are important to resolving the North Korean nuclear issue comprehensively. Great power management can to a certain extent contribute to the sustenance of regional security and international security. The intransigence of North Korea might be a key stumbling obstacle to stability in East Asia, but if US and China can reach to some form of mutual understanding on their North Korean policies, Pyongyang's bargaining power will be reduced to a certain extent. Consequently, North Korea would not be able to use China to the fullest against the US. It would not be able to practise nuclear brinkmanship, which it has so far been very successful at; in the long run, Pyongyang might have no alternative but to rethink its nuclear aspirations.

At the same time, even if any understanding between China and the US is reached, it might be undermined by a weaker power – North Korea. In the near term, Pyongyang will continue to underscore the importance of concluding a separate peace treaty with the US rather than with South Korea, as it believes this will guarantee its political legitimacy and independence. Moreover, from North Korea's perspective, developing a nuclear weapons programme seems to be a cost-effective deterrent and strategic equaliser in its competition with South Korea. This nuclear weapons programme can be used to open negotiations with the US, representing the only way that North Korea can offset South Korea's diplomatic advances and also perhaps secure more economic assistance from the West. In short, great power management and a moderation in Pyongyang's foreign policy are both required for a complete resolution of the North Korean nuclear issue.

Conclusion

North Korea remains vital to China's security interests, despite various changes in bilateral relations and the strategic landscape in the 21st century. In terms of military security, North Korea remains indispensable as a buffer state – at least in psychological terms. Essentially, the loss of North Korea means China could face hostile military forces on its doorstep along the Yalu River. It is also worth stressing that both Beijing and Pyongyang share common military threats in the form of the US and Japan. In terms of China's political security, survival of the communist regime in North Korea is highly relevant because few communist states remain in the world today, and the US is seen as a hostile superpower pursuing the strategy of peaceful evolution to end Communist rule in China itself. This is further reinforced by the outright advocacy of liberal democracy by the US and its concomitant regime change policy. Essentially, the similarity of the Chinese and North Korean political systems means that the demise of one will have implications for the other. The future evolution of the North Korean regime also has implications for China's economic security. In its attempt to emerge as a global power in the 21st century, China needs a stable regional environment in order to realise its ambitious modernisation goals quickly. Hence, China would like to see a North Korea that does not engender conflict on the Korean peninsula because this will disrupt Beijing's wider regional environment.

Finally, China's influence over North Korea gives Beijing a means to enhance its regional power standing and fits in well with its aspirations for global power status. All the major powers – the US, Japan, Russia and China itself – have strategic interests on the Korean peninsula, and the nuclear issue has sharpened these interests and increased the importance of being involved at the centre. This issue, which affects not only regional security but also international security, illustrates that North Korea's co-operation on nuclear matters requires at least tacit Chinese participation. Being Pyongyang's key ally has given precisely China a huge role in this regard. Aware that the interests of Russia, Japan, and the US – as well as the wider world – are all at stake in avoiding a major war on the Korean peninsula, China can use its influence on North Korea to enhance its status in the region and at a global level. Therefore, North Korea remains vital to China's security interests in a divided Korean peninsula for the foreseeable future, notwithstanding some changes in the strategic landscape there since the Cold War ended.

7   The role of South Korea

This chapter explores China's security interests in relation to South Korea. First and foremost, South Korea is increasingly important for China's economic security. The emphasis here is on how much Seoul can contribute to China's ongoing modernisation programmes. Second, having a degree of influence on South Korea enables China to manoeuvre against the lone superpower. Specifically, this relates to the role of South Korea in countering the dominance of the US in the military and political arenas in the international system. Hence, we need to explore Chinese perceptions on the South Korea–US alliance, as this is arguably the US's most important strategic partnership in Asia after the Japanese one. Third, having influence on South Korea allows China to increase its presence on the Korean peninsula as a whole, with North Korea being the traditional client already. China can, for instance, have some inputs in the issue of Korean reunification. These three themes are analysed in turn.

Economic security

First, South Korea is increasingly important for China's economic security. Basically, the realm of economics had become too important for Beijing in relation to the Korean peninsula, and this explains why China established ties with South Korea in 1992. By extending its relations to the southern part of the Korean peninsula, China hopes to discover new opportunities and avenues to facilitate its ongoing economic modernisation programme. China is a developing country with an enormous supply of low cost labour and abundant resources. South Korea, despite the economic crisis it experienced in 1997–1998, is an industrialised nation with a booming economy and has many technology-intensive industries.[1] In many ways, China sees South Korea as the natural economic partner for achieving its development goals. In fact, South Korea is China's third largest trading partner and second biggest foreign capital source.[2] From South Korea's point of view, China has already supplanted the US as its chief trading partner.

A testament to the strong economic complementarities between Northeast China and South Korea is the rapid shift in South Korean investment from China's southern provinces to the Bohai Sea areas in recent years. In particular, South

Korea is well poised to transform China's Shandong Province, which lies across the Yellow Sea from the Korean Peninsula, as another export-launching pad because much of its investment and trade is concentrated nearby. South Korea began its investment in Shandong in 1988 and currently, 15 out of South Korea's top 20 businesses, such as Daewoo, Hyundai, Samsung and LG, have invested in the province. Its investment in Shandong surpassed that of Hong Kong for the first time in 2001, and South Korea has been the largest source of Shandong's foreign capital ever since. Today, South Korea's investment in Shandong is changing from labour-intensive industries to capital- and technology-intensive industries and covers fields such as finance, real estate and navigation. According to local Chinese government statistics, Shandong Province is expected to take up half of China's actual use of foreign capital from the South Korea by the end of 2005.[3] By November 2005, the actual use of South Korean capital-by Shandong had reached US$15.7bn, according to the latest data of the Shandong Provincial Department of Foreign Trade and Economic Cooperation; ahead of Hong Kong with US$14.2bn. Today, South Korea figures positively in China's internal policy shift towards emphasising development of the Bohai Seas in order to cope with uneven economic development. For China, this represents one way of reducing economic development disparities between the northern and southern provinces. More importantly, such policies clearly enhance China's overall economic security as well as political stability.

One can also contrast South Korea's contributions to China's development goals with the notion of North Korea being China's economic burden. In reality, since the Second World War, China's relations with North Korea has been characterised by a large lop-sided economic aid programme and barter trade for Pyongyang's benefit, with almost all economic transactions based on political considerations. The nexus of the political and economic aspects of security is important here. When it comes to economic interests, China is in this case prepared to put its military and political ties with North Korea at some degree of risk. For instance, it did keep North Korea informed of the normalisation process with South Korea but probably calculated that friendless North Korea had no choice but to accept this. Today, China's economic engagement with South Korea has often drawn criticisms from North Korea although in reality, there is not much an economically weak and isolated North Korea can do to stop this trend.

Notwithstanding the importance of South Korea to China's economic security, one must recognise that trade frictions might increase between China and South Korea over the longer term. For instance, South Korean manufacturers have complained that they are suffering losses in China due to rising labour costs in Qingdao, Shandong Province, and some are relocating to inland areas including Xian and Guangxi.[4] Overall, it is possible that South Korea fears being overwhelmed by the rapid growth of China's economy and might seek to lock in preferential trading arrangements with its security patron, the US, to maintain its qualitative edge in technology and export products. From the US perspective, striking bilateral trade agreements with Asian countries is also a way of countering China's aggressive economic diplomacy in the region and ensuring that US companies will have optimal access to important Asian markets. Hence, China's policymakers need to work out the triangular trading relationship between China, South Korea and the US when formulating its economic strategies.

Overall, China's effort to develop economic ties with South Korea is not only aimed at immediate trade benefits, but there is also the intention to allow China to diversify its economic partnerships and reduce its technological and economic dependence on a few foreign sources. Moreover, South Korea's economic structures and technology may be more suitable for China's modernisation programmes than Japan's and other Western countries' in terms of expense and technology transfer. By normalising relations with South Korea, China not only added a major trading partner but Seoul can, to a certain extent, help reduce Chinese dependence on trade and investment from other major trading partners, especially the US and Japan. For the Chinese leaders, this represents one way of coping with insecurity that is generated by economic interdependence.

Furthermore, South Korea has proved to be more reliable as a trading partner for China compared to the Western countries. Although Sino-Korean relations underwent a temporary setback following the Tiananmen Incident in 1989, Seoul was keen to improve bilateral relations as soon as possible. Although human rights issues form a component in South Korean foreign policy today, they are not the top priority.[5] It is worth stressing that until the 1980s, South Korea had been under authoritarian rule with its own Kwangju Incident in 1980 often being compared to China's Tiananmen Event.[6] In reality, South Korea's experience of democracy is relatively short. Moreover, a shared Confucian tradition with China – advocating status quo and social cohesion in general – implies that Seoul is not likely to embrace Western-style liberal democracy fully. In general, one might argue that South Korea is thus less likely to link bilateral trade issues to political ones such as human rights. This is regarded as a bonus in China's eyes as the aim is to achieve economic development quickly without being hampered by political considerations, as the case of Japan has to some extent indicated.

To a certain extent, South Korea also acts as a successful economic model for China. Basically, Beijing is interested in the way Seoul has combined the achievements of rapid economic growth with an authoritarian political system, at least up to the 1980s. The coincidence of South Korea's move to democracy with its recent economic difficulties may also have some resonance in Beijing, perhaps suggesting that a more pluralistic political system is not conducive to achieving or sustaining rapid economic success. Ideally, the leaders in China want to have the best of both worlds: they want to enhance economic security while maintaining the political security of the Chinese Communist Party (CCP).

At a wider level, improvements in the relations of Sino-South Korean economic co-operation reflect both a foundation of naturally endowed economic complementarities and a degree of political confidence between the political actors. In this regard, it is hardly surprising that booming Sino-South Korean economic transactions constitute the most advanced component of the Yellow Sea Economic Zone. This Zone – comprising China, South Korea, North Korea and Japan – has a population of 354 million, or 5.8 per cent of the world's population and its gross domestic product (GDP) is 3.5 per cent that of global GDP, exceeding the 1.8 per cent of the Association of Southeast Asian Nations (ASEAN) and the 3.1 per cent of Mercosur; it has a 7.2 per cent share of global trade, which has continued to rapidly expand in recent years with the economic growth in China.[7] The region is fast becoming a global production centre for products such as semi-conductors, telecommunications equipment and automobiles. The Yellow Sea Economic Zone is also much more promising that the UN-endorsed Tumen River Area Development Programme, which despite Chinese encouragement, has thus failed to ignite due to, amongst other things, lingering security tensions between the two Koreas.

In the search for economic security, China as well as South Korea and Japan will aim to promote regional economic co-operation.[8] Specifically, the China–South Korea component of the Yellow Sea co-operation has made the most headway in both economic and political terms, while relations with China and Japan are processing at a more gradual pace. One reason is the historical animosity between Japan and China. At the same time, the global trend towards the dominance of economics emphasises the shift from superpower confrontation to regional economic security. Viewed from a global perspective, Yellow Sea rim economic co-operation has much potential in Northeast Asia as China, South Korea and Japan can carve out a sphere of influence that is not only cost-effectively grounded but that also fosters better political and cultural ties.

Influence on South Korea

Another key Chinese strategic interest is to exert political influence on South Korea. This influence has been existent for centuries, apart from the 1910–1945 interregnum when Japan controlled Korea. During the Cold War, Korea was divided into two states and South Korea tilted towards the US. Hence, rapprochement between China and South Korea was slow before the Cold War ended; the first official contacts occurred in 1978 and did not increase until the 1980s. The fear of losing its ideological ally, Pyongyang, means that Beijing on the whole made diplomatic ties with Seoul contingent upon the implementation of formal links between North Korea and US as well as Japan. Essentially, the East–West conflict and the concomitant bipolar structure meant China could not proceed too quickly to normalise relations with South Korea, who is a key ally of the US in East Asia.

However, the end of the Cold War brought about transformations in the pattern of inter-Korean relationship as well as in the structure of great power relationships around the Korean Peninsula. Russia established formal diplomatic ties with South Korea, North Korea began talks with the US and Japan on normalising relations, and Japan adjusted its Korean policy to a more balanced one focusing on both Koreas instead of one tilting towards South Korea. From a strategic perspective, these changes in the geopolitical landscape mean that China had to revise its traditional Korean policy of focusing just on North Korea and try to extend its influence to the southern half of the Korean peninsula. In particular, the normalisation of ties between the Soviet Union and South Korea in September 1990 presented an attractive new opening and precedent.

Therefore, as a member of the Security Council, Beijing did not veto Seoul's application to join the United Nations (UN) in 1991. This was in spite of the fact that, for decades, South Korea's suggestion of simultaneous participation with North Korea in the UN had been vehemently opposed by Pyongyang, who regarded this as symbolising national division. China's decision not to veto South Korea's application to join the UN had in effect left North Korea with little alternative but to set aside its declared principles and apply for simultaneous UN membership in 1991. It also appeared that, at that time, Beijing was worried that supporting North Korea might jeopardise its relations with other permanent members of the Security Council, who were all backing South Korea's position. Basically, the consensus of other great powers on this issue to a certain extent pressurised China to lean towards South Korea rather than North Korea. The UN acceptance of South Korea was followed by the normalisation of Chinese–South Korean relations.

A key Chinese reason for re-establishing relations with South Korea in August 1992 was trade and investment, as discussed earlier. A complementary factor was the 'Northern Policy' that South Korea adopted in the late 1980s to improve diplomatic relations with China and the former Soviet Union. With regards to China, this South Korea policy had the twin objectives of strengthening bilateral economic ties and establishing political dialogue with China on North Korea. Although China reacted cautiously initially, the pragmatist policies adopted by Chinese reformers after 1978 played a part in gradually allowing Beijing to alter its traditional aversion to a two-Korea policy. Besides, from the Chinese perspective, recognising South Korea in 1992 also means that the last of Taiwan's diplomatic ties to any state in Northeast Asia was removed. Politically, South Korea and Taiwan had been united by anti-Communist ideology during the Cold War era but this ended, leaving the island republic even more isolated, in accordance with Chinese interests. Overall, from China's perspective, normalising ties with Seoul would allow South Korea to move away from the influence of the US and Japan and make it less likely for the US and Japan to check China with inter-Korea issues.

The US–South Korean alliance

In order to exert more influence over South Korea, China will aim to pull South Korea away from the US orbit after normalising relations with South Korea. Accordingly, China will exploit any tensions arising between South Korea and the US, which came about partly due to changes in Korean domestic politics and society. In the past fifty years, the US–South Korean alliance has been sustained with ebbs and flows expected of an asymmetrical alliance between two states with markedly different capabilities. South Korea, however, did not remain simply a loyal client state, especially during the later stages of the Cold War. As the South Korean economy grew at an extraordinary pace, the Seoul government often sought to transform itself into a political actor, with increased discretion commensurating with its enhanced capabilities.[9] The legitimacy debts of the authoritarian regimes in Seoul during the 1970s and 1980s had rendered the cost of dependency acceptable as far as the ultimate security objectives were concerned. The question is whether the change in South Korean domestic politics will force some serious rethinking on this dependency on the US.

In general, the trend towards democratisation in domestic politics has indirectly translated into the call for a more independent South Korean foreign policy without overarching American influence. The political legitimacy of Seoul's new elites now seem to depend in part on greater independence in foreign policy and defence autonomy from the guarantors of the recent past. Although tensions still exist between a growing desire for political independence from the US and an ongoing concern of a possible attack from North Korea, it is possible to argue that decades of dependence on external protectors – China and the US – have inadvertently contributed to the rise of nationalism in South Korea. This tide of South Korean nationalism, more specifically anti-American feeling, has been growing in South Korea since the 1980s.[10] Moreover, democratic forces in South Korea would point out that America played a big role in propping up military dictatorships in their country in the past. For instance, it can even be argued that there was American complicity in 1980 Kwangju Incident that culminated in the deaths of hundreds of civilians in that city; the US had played leading role in South Korea army's operation because technically the head of this army was America.[11] This type of anti-US sentiment in South Korea can be exploited by China in order to counter perceived American hegemony in Northeast Asia.

Apart from anti-US sentiment, as South Korea advances to become one of Asia's most industrialised nations, its economic relations with the US will become more complex and competitive, bringing along a diverse array of trade disputes and problems. For instance, when the US accumulated an increasing trade deficit with South Korea in the 1980s, it brought up the issues of fair trade and market access to Seoul. In response, South Korea argued that its economy is still fragile with many infant industries and a high defence expenditure, it has to depend on the import of raw materials and crude oil, and it has problems of large foreign debts and a chronic trade deficit with Japan.[12] South Korea is now an economic power, having recovered from the recent Asian financial crisis, and the US is bound to bring up more trade issues and disputes with South Korea.

Another source of friction between the US and South Korea lies in the sharing of defence costs. The US has constantly pressed South Korea to increase its financial support for American forces stationed there, given that the Americans have a strong desire to make defence cuts in East Asia. Defence negotiators on both parties remained far apart on the amount of Seoul's contribution to the cost of keeping US troops on the peninsula, with South Korea asking for a 50 per cent reduction in its share due to the redeployment and the phased reduction of US forces while the US requested for a 10 per cent increase on the basis of modernising the joint command, control, communications and information technology systems.[13]

Moreover, the debate over the command of the South Korean armed forces tests the military co-ordination between South Korea and the US. Under an agreement reached with South Korea in the aftermath of the Korean War, the US would assume control of South Korean troops in the event of another war on the peninsula. Since 1994, Seoul has acquired the authority within the Combined US–South Korea Forces Command to control its military – but only during peace-time. Negotiators from both sides met in February 2006 to discuss whether South Korea should be allowed to exercise control over its own armed forces during wartime. A joint panel has been set up to work out detailed measures for the trans-fer of wartime command and this issue will be discussed at subsequent US–South Korea Security Consultative Meetings.

Perhaps the most sensitive issue question relates to the 'strategic flexibility' of US forces stationed on the Korean Peninsula. The US has sought acknowledge-ment from South Korea that these troops could be reshaped as 'rapid deployment forces' and deployed elsewhere in the event of a crisis, particularly a military contingency involving China in the Taiwan Straits.[14] There was an attempt to bal-ance the two governments' positions: South Korea acknowledged the rationale for the transformation of the US global military strategy and necessity for 'strategic flexibility' of the US forces in South Korea while the US recognised that South Korea does not really want to be involved in a regional conflict in Northeast Asia. Essentially, South Korea accepted the reality that the US could redeploy forces from the Korean Peninsula for a Taiwan contingency regardless of the views of Seoul; however, the US was put on notice that it could not expect South Korea's support for any operation that would disrupt South Korea's relations with China. In the long run, South Korea might eventually deny US troops on the Korean Peninsula leeway to expand their role and become involved in other Northeast Asian states without Seoul's consent.

On issues of blocking the transfer of weapons of mass destruction (WMD) by rogue states such as North Korea and Iran, it seems that South Korea gives only qualified support to the US. Its position is essentially one of co-operation on a case-by-case basis.[15] The Proliferation Security Initiative (PSI), to which about 70 countries are signatories, was launched in 2003, and it allows multilateral forces to intercept ships or aircraft suspected of carrying WMD from rogue states. South Korea has been reluctant to join the PSI out of concerns that it may provoke North Korea, given the direct military threat it faces from its northern neighbour.[16] In some ways, it follows from the example of South Korean refusal to join the US in the Theatre Missile Defence (TMD) project.

It is also worth noting that since February 2005, South Korea has expressed interest in a balancing role between China and the US as well as between Japan and China.[17] It is in some ways similar to the one that Australia wants to play as a balancer between China and the US. More importantly, South Korea has never been an aggressive state that sought to dominate others, and this makes it accept-able as a neutral party to China. This balancing role does not negate the existing South Korea–US alliance and may therefore be too ambitious a goal for the Roh administration to implement because China continues to harbour deep sus-picions over the alliance in general and over US hegemonic intentions in Asia in particular.

At the wider level, South Korea has ambitions to materialise a security and economic co-operation bloc in Northeast Asia.[18] Basically, this bloc would be formed on the basis of the six-party talks once the North Korean nuclear issue is resolved. South Korea does command some soft power and is well qualified to play a wider role in promoting regional development and co-operation, but one must also recognise the inherent limitations to its foreign policy options. The first limitation is South Korea's dependence on the US for national defence as it contends with a nuclear threat from North Korea. The second limitation relates to the size of the country; South Korea is at best a middle power and does not possess sufficient clout in international relations yet.[19]

In sum, one can discern that US–South Korean relations are now plagued with a host of disputes that in essence involve the difficult transition from the Cold War military collaboration to a new post-Cold War normal type of relationship. China has to manoeuvre between South Korea and the US, and enhance its security interests in the process. Basically, there is a growing equality in US–South Korea alliance. South Korea is now more confident as an independent actor. It is in Chinese interests to exploit those to its advantage. After all, China had been the security patron of South Korea before the arrival of Western powers in Northeast Asia; in the long run, China might even present itself as a guarantor of South Korea's security.

US and South Korea on North Korea

Obviously, a key divergence in US and South Korean strategic thinking can be found in their policies towards North Korea. As discussed in Chapter 6, the US has an interest in removing the North Korean threat. Accordingly, it has an important motivation for strengthening the US–Korea alliance, broadening its rationale beyond co-operation against a common enemy. The US has already imposed financial sanctions on North Korea for alleged US currency counterfeiting and sanctioned eight North Korean companies suspected of spreading WMD. As part of its campaign to eliminate terrorism, the US focuses on illicit financial activities facilitated by the North Korean government while calling for international efforts to combat money-laundering, terrorist financing and other financial crimes. In this light, the US has urged South Korea to join it in imposing financial sanctions on North Korea, but South Korea has its own methods to deal with North Korea.

Today, the government of Roh Moo-hyun in South Korea has continued the 'sunshine policy' towards North Korea and is generally critical of any US hardline stance towards North Korea. First proposed by former president Kim Dae-jung in 1998, the South Korean 'sunshine policy' entails a shift away from the rapid German style reunification towards a gradual negotiated transition on the divided Korean peninsula as well as offering unconditional economic and humanitarian aid to North Korea.[20] Despite its limitations, this proactive policy resulted in the landmark summit in Pyongyang between Kim Dae-jung and North Korean leader Kim Jong-il in June 2000.[21] Since then, South Korea has continued to push for economic engagement with its northern neighbour, with the Kaesong Industrial Zone under construction in North Korea some 40 miles north of the demilitarised zone being a prime example.[22]

Currently, Roh Moo-hyun has effectively ruled out using military options against North Korea in resolving the nuclear issue. The South Korean Unification Ministry has said that it was too early to call North Korea a nuclear state.[23] The 2004 South Korea Defence White Paper even dropped designation of North Korea as the 'main enemy' for the first time in a decade.[24] Basically, South Korea rejects regime change as a policy towards North Korea. Interestingly, the US may then feel it needs to enhance understanding with its ally on the North Korean issue. For instance, National Security Adviser Stephen Hadley has already stressed that America actually favoured the 'transformation' of North Korea by economic means, and not harsh measures that would bring about the collapse of the Kim Jong-il regime.[25] Such moves by key US officials might in the long run help to assuage the fears of North Korea and prod the reclusive state towards a more moderate foreign policy. From China's perspective, the differences in US and South Korea foreign policies towards North Korea are evident and a key task is how to exploit them to its advantage.

In general, South Korea's criticism of the neo-conservative proponents of regime change in the US might strengthen the hand of American officials who favour a more moderate, long-term transformation in North Korea, whereby economic incentives serve as a means to induce change in North Korea rather than a form of appeasement. This will allow moderates in the US to argue more vigorously that taking a harder line against North Korea, by threatening economic sanctions or military action, risks seriously alienating South Korea and weakening the US–South Korean alliance. Whether Bush administration will acquiesce totally to South Korea's position or is prepared to abandon the threat of military action or economic sanctions against North Korea remains to be seen but it is clear that any hardline stance adopted by the US can be tempered to some extent by its Korean ally.

On its part, the Bush administration realises the strategic importance of South Korea and has called for a more co-ordinated approach to North Korea. Essentially, this means asking South Korea to support the US position in relation to the North Korean threat. However, South Korean President Roh Moo-Hyun has responded by stressing the equality of the US–South Korean alliance; specifically, Roh and foreign minister Ban Ki-moon have explicitly referred to the need to balance the nuclear issue with inter-Korean reconciliation. From South Korea's perspective, the US appears unwilling to offer additional incentives for Pyongyang due to the fear of appeasing the North Korean regime. From the US perspective, it appears that South Korea might be prepared to undercut the common goal of countering the nuclear threat because of a fundamental desire to keep inter-Korean reconciliation on track. The fact that South Korea puts its relations with North Korea on an equal status with obligations to the alliance with the US must surely raise a degree of concern in Washington.

In the final analysis, it must be stressed that South Korea's role in the North Korean nuclear issue is fundamentally still a restrictive one. After all, South

Korea was largely shut out from the first North Korean nuclear crisis; its role was largely confined to providing financial support for the Korean Peninsula Energy Development Organization (KEDO) under the Agreed Framework. In the second North Korean nuclear crisis, South Korea's contribution must still be made through the US, primarily because North Korea still insists on bilateral dialogue with the US and on concluding a peace treaty directly with America. Furthermore, North Korea has criticised South Korea's nuclear testing, which it argues adds another obstacle for the smooth procession of six-party talks.[26] Within South Korea, it must also be noted that the sunshine policy of Roh Moo-hyun has come under attack, with the opposition Grand National Party criticising Roh as pro-Pyongyang while other observers viewed it as risky but necessary for asserting Seoul's role in the six-party dialogue. Technically still at war with its northern neighbour – a peace treaty has yet to be signed after the Korean War – South Korea's role on the nuclear issue continues to be most evident through checking any further hardening of the US line against North Korea.

At the same time, it must be noted that South Korea's frequent emphasis on policy differences with the US over North Korea runs the risk of making the US bypass South Korea and focus primarily on China as the partner for resolving the North Korean nuclear issue. It appears that ultimately, confronting US hardliners directly would not be a wise choice for South Korea. Better co-operation with the US – through extensive consultations in six-party talks and through a more overt expression of South Korea's own national interest in the context of those talks – may be more important in influencing the Bush administration's approach towards North Korea.

Influence on Korean affairs

Having influence on South Korea allows China to increase its presence on the Korean peninsula as a whole, with North Korea being the traditional client already. China can, for instance, have some inputs in the issue of Korean reunification. Overall, the lack of US and Japanese progress in establishing formal links with North Korea has helped to restrict the capacity of Washington and Tokyo to influence inter-Korean relations in a significant manner. This gives China the status of an important middleman between the two Koreas. A key principle is that Beijing prefers the Koreans resolve the process of reunification themselves, with outside pressure being kept to a minimum. China is wary that other foreign powers may get involved in the region. Its aim of reducing the probability of other powers getting caught up in Korean affairs has historical roots; regional powers such as Japan and Russia had competed for influence over Korea when China under the Qing dynasty was weak. Today, Beijing is anxious to avoid this scenario happening again, especially given that Japan may re-emerge as a great power. More critically, a key China aim is to avoid American intervention, such as those under the auspices of the UN in the Korean War. If the two Koreas can work out their problems by themselves, that would be more in line with Chinese strategic interests.

Apart from gaining more influence on the Korean peninsula, China's interest with regard to the task of Korean reunification stems from its goal of engendering a peaceful regional environment. Therefore, China constantly emphasises that only peaceful means must be used to achieve reunification on the peninsula in order to ensure that stability in the region will not be threatened. It is widely acknowledged that the cease-fire agreement signed in 1953 at Panmunjom by the Korean People's Army and the Chinese Volunteer Army on one side and by the UN troops on the other needs to be revised in order to reflect the post-Cold War situation. It should be replaced by a peace agreement, and China acknowledges this. In Chinese eyes, a key stumbling block for this to be achieved appears to be the ongoing tension between the US and North Korea.

Naturally, China is opposed to any aggressive behaviour on the part of either North Korea or South Korea – more likely from the former rather than the latter – because this will jeopardise regional stability and consequently impinge on Beijing's own security in the absence of a peace treaty. Any aggressive behaviour would also make it difficult for China to respond, given that Beijing still values its traditional friendship with North Korea while promoting closer economic ties with South Korea. Therefore, China welcomes historic pacts such as the 1991 Agreement on Reconciliation, Non-aggression and Exchange and Co-operation between the South and the North (the Basic Accord), which provides the basis for establishing a peace system on the Korean peninsula. The Basic Accord led to both Koreas agreeing on the Joint Declaration on De-nuclearisation of the Korean peninsula in 1992, with both sides agreeing to allow mutual inspections of suspected nuclear facilities. Here it must be noted that China desires a nuclear free Korean peninsula primarily because it wants to hold onto to its nuclear monopoly in East Asia. At the same time, the agreements of 1991 and 1992 have become largely irrelevant because of North Korea's nuclear brinkmanship.

To certain extent, one might also argue that China is keener on maintaining peace and stability on the Korean peninsula rather than specifically bringing about Korean reunification. After all, the central challenge for China is to make the external environment safe for its modernisation drive. Beijing's policies pertaining to Korean reunification are pragmatic, as its Korean policies in the current era have generally proved to be. From China's perspective, the ideal regional environment would be one in which it can pursue economic growth without regional powers – namely, the US and Japan – competing for influence on its doorstep. It is also evident that in Chinese eyes, maintaining a peaceful Korean peninsula includes some sort of Chinese influence over the region, and it is precisely this influence that gives Beijing a means to enhance its regional status. It is possible to argue that China's desire to acquire influence on the Korean peninsula is best seen as the starting point for a return to the Sino-centric world order.

Without doubt, the actual process of reunification of the two Koreas has important implications for China's security interests. For instance, China will be concerned if South Korea absorbs North Korea through peaceful evolution or if the regime in North Korea collapses. It knows that both scenarios are unattractive and even threatening to its security interests. South Korea absorbing North Korea, a communist state, can never be a desired outcome as this will have acute political legitimacy implications for the survival of the communist state system in China itself. From South Korea's perspective, a German-style absorption of North Korea may also not be affordable, partly because the South Korean economy is weaker than that of West Germany's and partly because the economic gap between the two Koreas is much larger in relative terms than that between East and West Germany. Hence, South Korea believes that the promotion of a regional bloc to resolve the tensions on the Korean peninsula can also lay the foundation for Korean reunification; the comparison with German reunification is instructive because West Germany laid the groundwork for German reunification by actively pursuing the European Union (EU).[27] If no regional bloc has been formed, South Korea will have to bear most of the economic burden in the event absorbing North Korea and regional powers such as China might be pressurised by the international community to offer some form of financial assistance. More importantly for China, economic dislocation of the North Korean masses could bring chaos on its borders. In short, Korean reunification will be beneficial to China only if Beijing is confident that its security interests are not being compromised.

At the same time, if the two Koreas were to achieve reunification, this could pose stiff challenges for China. For instance, a reunified Korea sympathetic to the West means that foreign powers such as the US will be able to ensconce themselves along the Yalu River. The experience of US intervention during the Korean War reminds the Chinese of this danger. Even if a unified Korea is not totally pro-US, it is more likely to pursue claims against China for territory along their common border, given that parts of southern Manchuria had been under Korean rule in the past. This relates to the order that China had imposed on large parts of Asia in the past, with Korea being a key vassal state. Today, it is disputed whether the ancient kingdom of Koguryo Kingdom (37 BC to AD 668) that controlled parts of Manchuria and North Korea was Chinese or Korean. For instance, one Chinese source declared that Koguryo was a regime established by ethnic groups in northern China some 2000 years ago and that it represented a key part of Chinese culture.[28] Such Chinese claims that Koguryo is China or was a Chinese vassal state strike at the heart of what it means to be Korean today; the very idea of China's Koguryo presents a threat to Korean identity.[29]

From the perspective of South Korea's leaders, the use of the past is also important to pursue national security goals. For instance, Park Chung Hee had sought to create a usable past to defeat communists and reunify the Korean peninsula. Like Sin Chae Ho before him, Park saw the Yi dynasty as the problem and Koguryo as the solution: the former had left an undesirable legacy of 'historical vassalism' that led to reliance upon others and 'blind obedience' to great powers such as China, contrasting with Koguryo, which was 'aggressive in war' and 'martial in temperament' and an Oriental power of the first rank with wide territories in what is now Manchuria.[30] The point is that pan-Korean nationalism might one day be whipped up in the event of Korean reunification against China, the traditional overlord.

At the same time, both Koreas share a common historical enemy in Japan and this is in line with Chinese interests. Despite their differences, both Koreas have issued a joint declaration that the 1905 treaty of annexation had been fundamentally invalid; under that treaty, Japan forced Korea to sign away its sovereign rights, paving the way for the eventual annexation in 1910 until the 1945.[31] Both Koreas also noted that Japan failed to return an 18th century stone monument of the Choson dynasty that was erected in Kilju County in North Korea in commemoration of a Korean general who defeated invading Japanese forces in the 16th century. Of significance is that this monument – seized by the Japanese during the Russo-Japanese War of 1904–1905 that was fought largely on Chinese soil and waters – still remains in the Yasukuni Shrine, a perceived symbol of Japanese expansionism. The impact of history on Korean–Japanese relations is highly relevant today, and it explains the difficulties that both Koreas have in coming to terms with a more powerful Japan. Certainly, both Koreas have agreed to co-operate on defending the history of Koguryo and share opposition to Japan's bid for a permanent seat in the UN, to Japan's claims to the disputed Liancourt Rocks (Tokdo/Takeshima) in the Sea of Japan and to the right-wing versions of Japanese history textbooks. The relevance here is that this historical pan-Korean enmity towards Japan is something that China can exploit to its advantage in its manoeuvres against Japan.

After all, China and the two Koreas had been victims of Japanese colonialism and aggression. Hence, China and the two Koreas continue to watch their neighbour to the east with a wary eye. Although Japan had already established relations with South Korea in 1965, the anti-Japanese sentiment is still pervasive among South Koreans and indeed throughout the Korean peninsula. Basically anti-Japanese sentiment represents one factor around which all Koreans can unite in the long term. In fact, Japanese colonialism is often perceived by both North and South Koreans as humiliating and oppressive. In contrast, Chinese dominance over Korea was more easily accepted with Chinese writing characters and Confucianism readily absorbed in Korean society for instance. Beijing will be eager to use such comparisons to its advantage in the pursuit of its Korean policy. It is possible that China and the two Koreas can even work together to constrain a rising Japan in the long term because neither will ever accept Japanese leadership of any kind in East Asian politics. In short, even though a unified Korea might pose some challenges to China, the fact remains that China can still use anti-Japanese sentiment in the two Koreas against Japan.

Conclusion

South Korea's importance in China's security interests will increase over time. Overall, China hopes to increase its influence on the entire Korean peninsula, protect its national security, secure a more advantageous political position and establish better economic opportunities for itself in the region. From China's perspective, South Korea can contribute to its economic development goals, and this is now viewed as almost important as any remaining ideological ties with

North Korea. By extending its official links to South Korea in 1992, China has attracted more investment from South Korea and thereby bolstered its economic security. This growing emphasis on economic interests in China's South Korea policy is likely to remain for the foreseeable future.

China also aims to enhance its political ties with South Korea as this provides leverage against major foreign powers such as the US. Today, one of the most important reasons why China wants to exert its influence on South Korea is to counter US unilateralism in international politics. While South Korea has retained some ambivalence towards the rise of China as a benign civilised power, the multi-faceted troubles in Seoul's relations with Washington gives China considerably expanded room to wedge into the Seoul–Washington alliance. There is no doubt that South Korea faces dilemmas and choices in the context of its alliance with the US but also choices posed by the fact that South Korean and Chinese thinking about North Korea has significant overlapping and complementary elements. As a key ally of the US, South Korea does have a limited capacity to moderate US foreign policy, especially that relating to the Korean peninsula. South Korea has its own engagement with North Korea, primarily in the form of providing economic assistance and reviving high level talks with the Stalinist state. To a certain extent, such efforts were not fully rewarded, due to structural constraints inherent in the asymmetric alliance with the US and the threat posed by North Korea.

Like North Korea, South Korea is important for China in its conduct of international relations. Traditional Chinese policy in the past towards the Korean peninsula was military oriented and North Korea centred. Today, it is clear that Beijing wants a more comprehensive approach to security that stresses the military, political and economic aspects, and China attaches equal importance to its relations with both North Korea and South Korea. Specifically, a divided Korean peninsula has given China an advantageous position as the single major power that maintains close relations with North Korea while simultaneously developing ties with South Korea.

Today, it is evident that in Beijing's eyes, maintaining stability on the Korean peninsula includes some sort of Chinese influence. This influence is important to China's quest for global power status in the 21st century. With regards to Korean reunification, China will give its support as long as this is achieved in a peaceful manner. China aims to sustain a stable regional environment so that it can carry out its own economic modernisation goals. Its fundamental objective is to avoid a situation on the Korean peninsula whereby war might break out and American intervention close on its doorstep is almost certain. In the meantime, a divided Korean peninsula enables China to assert its regional power role and enhance its overall security interests in the process.

8 The importance of Central Asia

This chapter explores China's growing interests in Central Asia, looking at various aspects of Beijing's security before examining its strategy vis-à-vis other great powers in the region. Today, Central Asia attracts the attention of all great powers, primarily due to its vast energy resources. China is no different as it seeks further supplies of oil to further its modernisation; a strong economic base provides the basis for China to achieve truly global power status in the 21st century. Hence, Central Asia is increasingly important for the economic security of China. At a wider level, Beijing generally adopts a Realist approach to international relations and therefore sees strategic competition with rivals in Central Asia as inevitable.

Military security

Currently, China does not face direct military threats on its northwestern flank. This can be contrasted with the past when Russia and then the Soviet Union frequently threatened China from Central Asia. Basically, China is no different from other states in that it needs to defend its territorial integrity and resist foreign involvement in the Xinjiang Uighur Autonomous Region, which is geographically part of Central Asia. Historically, this enormous region north and west of China's heartlands had represented a source of anxiety for Chinese emperors; these emperors expended considerable resources in pacifying Xinjiang and the surrounding border lands in order to bring under control the ancient oasis cities of the Silk Road. Writing in the 1930s, Owen Lattimore noted that the Chinese had effectively controlled Central Asia for only 425 out of 2000 years.[1] In the mid-18th century, China was strong and powerful and much of Central Asia was under its influence. However, as Qing dynasty weakened in the mid-19th century, China's control over Central Asia diminished, primarily due to growing Russian influence and local Muslim-motivated rebellions. One important rebellion took place in the 1860s, in the Ili area that borders present day Kazakhstan. The uprising was led by Yaqub Beg, who managed to set up an East Turkestan government until it was ended by the Chinese in 1878.

In 1884 Xinjiang was formally incorporated into the Qing empire but the Manchu dynasty was weakening and it subsequently collapsed in 1911. The successor

Republican government was not strong either; it had to contend with centrifugal tendencies in the form of warlordism and foreign encroachment in the form of Japan. Given this situation, the Soviet Union seized the opportunity to back the Uighurs of Xinjiang in establishing a Kazakh and Uighur East Turkestan Republic in 1933. This attempt was suppressed by the Chinese government, only to be re-established in 1944 and the Soviets managed to control the Ili region until 1946. Between 1937 and 1942, when China was preoccupied with the war against Japan, Xinjiang was ruled by a Chinese warlord Sheng Shicai, with Soviet support.[2] Xinjiang finally reverted to Chinese rule towards the end of the Chinese Civil War and was constituted as the Xinjiang Uighur Autonomous Region of the People's Republic of China (PRC) after the Communists took power in 1949.

During the late 1960s and early 1970s, when 'social imperialist' Soviet Union posed a military threat following the Sino-Soviet schism, China had to station large numbers of troops in Xinjiang to serve as a defensive line against attacks.[3] The Soviet Union had amassed large number of troops on the western and northern borders as well as in its satellite state of Mongolia, so Beijing actually faced a threat to its very existence.[4] Hence, the impact of foreign military threats – especially czarist or Soviet – in Central Asia still to a certain extent influences Chinese security thinking today, notwithstanding the fact that the threat from Moscow has diminished since the disintegration of the Soviet Union.

Additionally, it must be noted that security in Central Asia had been linked to the nuclear issue until 1995. Kazakhstan had inherited part of the Soviet Union's nuclear arsenals, hosting two strategic missiles launch sites at Derzhavinsk and Zhangiz-Tobe, a nuclear test zone at Semipalatinsk and one strategic bomber airbase. Astana eventually returned all those inherited weapons and their means of delivery to Russia through a deal backed by the US. This has made the military situation in Central Asia more stable. At a wider level, China has a fundamental interest in nuclear non-proliferation in Central Asia as it wants to maintain its nuclear monopoly in the entire Asia-Pacific. Interestingly, one of the largest Chinese nuclear testing site is located at Lop Nor in Xinjiang, which borders Central Asia.

Since the end of the Cold War, China has established confidence-building measures with Central Asian states on their land borders to enhance its military security. An important agreement on such measures was reached with Russia, Kazakhstan, Kyrgyzstan and Tajikistan in April 1996;[5] this far-reaching accord – arguably the most comprehensive arms control agreement in East Asia since the Second World War – restricts deployments and exercises along China's western border region and was uniquely lengthy and legalistic. The following year, in April 1997, China reached a troops-reductions accord with the aforementioned countries along their common borders.[6] Beijing stressed that, taken together with the 1996 document, this accord made China's northern 7,000 km common border 'a secure belt of mutual trust'.[7] In short, those moves were undertaken by China to bolster military security on its northwestern flank.

In addition, China's historical rivalry with Russia over Mongolia, a country which has strong historical links with Central Asia, has been largely resolved.

In June 1991, the last remaining Soviet combat troops were withdrawn from Mongolia. China sees this withdrawal as a military security gain since its northern border has now become less vulnerable. More importantly, China's military burden has been greatly relieved due to the disappearance of Mongolia as a springboard for Soviet invasion into China proper. It also means that the Chinese can now divert resources from military spending to promoting economic development. It is this linkage between military and economic security that holds the key to understanding China's security agenda.

Today, China does not want to see a volatile situation in Central Asia as a stable wider Asia-Pacific is vital for carrying out its economic modernisation goals. Beijing wants to see regional conflicts resolved peacefully. For instance, whilst recognising Russian special interests in Tajikistan, China had stressed that the Commonwealth of Independent States (CIS) should be the proper forum for settling issues such as the Tajik civil war of 1992–1997. Such security thinking also reflects the fear of further foreign military involvement, especially a Western one, in Central Asia, which has been magnified by the expansion of North Atlantic Treaty Organisation's (NATO) eastwards. Interestingly, common perceptions of NATO's policies with regard to Central Asia – driven to a large extent by the US – have helped cement some form of strategic solidarity between China and Russia. Today, both states remain apprehensive about a US-led attempt to dominate Central Asia, a tendency accentuated by American unilateralism in global politics in the light of the Iraqi War and the war on terror.

Political security

Central Asia also looms large when it comes to analysing China's political security. Essentially, the Western advocacy of human rights and liberal democracy is aimed at China as well as the newly independent Central Asian republics. The Soviet Union and the former eastern European states were to a certain extent viewed as having succumbed to the strategy of peaceful evolution; this is a lesson the Chinese have learned and still emphasise today. Most Central Asia states practise authoritarian rule, and this is congruent with China's illiberal system. Furthermore, the regimes in Central Asia were previously communist, and Communism still serves as the ideological basis for the current government in China. One might argue that overall, this comparison puts China in the position as a defender of authoritarian regimes in Central Asia, reducing its status as progressive country in the eyes of democratic states. Basically, China shares with Central Asian states the resentment against the promotion of ideas such as human rights by the West in general and the US in particular. This does constitute some form of unity between China and Central Asian states against the perceived Western strategy of peaceful evolution.

In discussing peaceful evolution, China has often highlighted the dangers of foreign powers fomenting internal dissent in a given state in order to modify that state's political system. The West's criticism of the Andijon event in Uzbekistan was a case in point. Hence, Uzbekistan might shift its policy and lean more towards China instead of continuing military co-operation with the US in the light of such criticisms; for instance, it might even invite Chinese forces for joint exercises on its soil, especially after the military withdrawal of the US in November 2005. With regard to another Central Asian republic, Kirghizstan, the Chinese have analysed the fall of the Askar Akayev government in March 2005 and expressed concern about any potential domino effect of more democratic forces in the region.[8] It is the shared commitment to resist the Western linked promotion of liberal democracy that binds China and most of the Central Asian states in ideological terms.

Moreover, China has paid a lot of attention to Uighur secessionist movements in Xinjiang and it argues that these are often abetted by the West. One Chinese assessment notes that the West in general and the US in particular support separatist forces in Xinjiang and other border areas with the aim of destabilising China in mind.[9] Certainly, a number of moderate and political organisations and media sources in the West are dedicated to publicising the Xinjiang issue: the Uighur American Association and the East Turkestan National Congress are two such organisations, while the Munich-based Eastern Turkestan Information Bulletin is a key media outlet. In general, the US government does take an interest in Xinjiang. For example, US Congress has pressed for the release of a prominent Uighur businesswoman from Xinjiang who was arrested in 2000 because of her US-based activist husband.[10] In reality, one might argue that such lobby groups in the West have a marginal impact, especially in an age of fighting terror; the US needs tacit Chinese co-operation and is therefore unlikely to pursue the Uighurs' cause in any vehement manner.

Essentially, it must be said that the separatist tendencies of the Uighurs in Xinjiang are mostly indigenous and motivated to a certain extent by Islam.[11] Descended from the Turkic people of Central Asia, the Uighurs share with the subjects in Central Asian states a common religion. Muslim communities with historical links to Central Asia have already played an important role in the history of the Ningxia Hui Autonomous Region and the Gansu, Qinghai and Shaanxi provinces of China. With Communism fading away as an ideology, Islam has often served as a cohesive and galvanising force for certain groups in Central Asian states as well as the Uighurs in China's Xinjiang. According to Jonathan Lipman, Muslims in Xinjiang are accorded with the 'stranger' status by Beijing.[12] Due in part to their affinity with the Turkic language and culture, they have maintained their aspiration to autonomy and have used religious factors to mobilise armed opposition to Chinese rule. One such attempt happened as early as 1990; it was unsuccessful but Chinese leaders took it seriously and warned of the danger of 'reactionary and splittist forces' carrying out their infiltration activities under 'banners of nationality and religion'.[13]

In the late 1980s and early 1990s, the Uighurs in Xinjiang watched not only the 1989 Tiananmen event and the Tibetan separatist movement unfold but also saw their ethnic cousins in former Soviet Central Asia gain independence. This lifted their long cherished hopes to achieve statehood. The disintegration of the Soviet Union has certainly raised political security problems in Central Asia for China as the newly independent Central Asian republics do have at least a modicum of sympathy for the Muslim people in China's westernmost regions. China is aware that the Uighurs could receive ideological support and military hardware from neighbouring Central Asian states today; a small number of arms have also flowed from Iran, Afghanistan and sympathetic brethren in Russia to insurgents in Xinjiang in the recent past. Today, China faces a host of Uighur insurgent groups – United Revolutionary Front of Eastern Turkestan, Xinjiang Liberation Organisation and Uighur Liberation Organisation (ULO), Wolves of Lop Nor, Free Turkistan Movement, Home of the East Turkistan Youth and Organisation for the Liberation of Uighuristan, although how big a political threat they actually pose to Beijing remains a moot point.[14]

Nevertheless, to counter any secessionist tendencies, China has often called upon the quasi-military/business conglomerate Xinjiang Production and Construction Corps (XPCC), known colloquially as the *bingtuan*, to crack down on any form of separatist activities. Originally comprising decommissioned People's Liberation Army (PLA) troops who remained as part of the 'Xinjiang Wilderness Reclamation Army' after 1949 to perform the role of 'economic vanguard', this force has grown in ranks and it accounts for a significant proportion of Xinjiang's economic output.[15] It is evident that Beijing wants to avoid a scenario reminiscent of Soviet empire's collapse, which ended in former Soviet autonomous republics declaring independence one after another. The basic Chinese strategy is to crack down on secessionist movements before they start to mushroom. At the same time, China emphasises that such attempts do not constitute an anti-Muslim campaign, lest they are perceived by neighbouring Central Asian republics as intolerance towards religious freedom. Essentially, China knows that there is a delicate balancing act to be performed as too forceful an approach against the Uighurs could invite a backlash by Islamic forces in Central Asia and even beyond.

Since the events of September 11, the Islamic movements in Central Asia have gained a global stage as the lone superpower pursues its war on terror. Four months after September 11, China issued an official document that marked its most direct attempt to justify and link its actions against the Uighurs in Xinjiang with the American campaign against Al-Qaeda.[16] Beijing shrewdly seized this opportunity to link Uighur nationalist movements to Islamic militants pursued by the US, without distinguishing between the violent or non-violent groups in Xinjiang. While the US refused to endorse China's intensified efforts to combat separatist forces directly, it did not highlight the issue specifically. It appears that Washington has recognised the value of having a strategic dialogue with China and a 'united front' against terrorists and therefore traded its previous patronage of the Uighur cause for Chinese co-operation on the war on terror, particularly because of the urgent need to oust the Talibans in Afghanistan. In reality, China knows that defeat of the Taliban regime and other Muslim extremists will bolster its political security in Central Asia and on the whole strengthen its grip on the region. Therefore, some form of tacit co-operation with the US to deal with Islamic extremists seems a good policy in the short term.

Since late 2002, China has enlisted the help of neighbouring Central Asian states to marginalise the Uighurs' few remaining supporters. It applied pressure on other countries to prevent or cancel political events organised by diaspora Uighurs and pushed the Shanghai Co-operation Organisation (SCO) to focus on Uighurs separatists networks.[17] Earlier, China had already sought the acknowledgement of leaders of Kyrgyzstan, Kazakhstan and Tajikistan that 'national separation is a harmful destructive force' and secured their full support on this issue; those leaders also promised to adopt resolute measures to oppose the separatists so that they would not gain a foothold in their countries.[18] Essentially, the presence of a restive Islamic minority on its western frontiers that affiliates to its neighbours has forced China to reach out to the SCO to diffuse any impending threats to its political security. It is clear that China has not become complacent after military security on its northwestern front was enhanced with the diminished Russian threat; it is aware that new political threats in the form of Islamic separatist movements may resurface to challenge its control in Xinjiang.

Closer to the Chinese capital, there is a potential for Mongolian nationalism to resurface to feel the void left by the retreat of Soviet-style communism. For instance, Ulan Bator could become a base for separatist activities in China's Inner Mongolia region. Specifically, increasing cross-border contact between Mongols in Mongolia and their kinsmen in China's Inner Mongolia region could engender some form of pan-Mongolian nationalism. This has implications for China's security interests. The Mongols do share a common history with the peoples of Central Asia, as their empire once covered the Eurasian landmass. More importantly, they had conquered China proper and managed to establish the short-lived Yuan dynasty in the 13th century. Apart from keeping a close eye on any signs of Mongolian separatism, China is also concerned that Mongolia could be subject to Western influence in the long run. Therefore, a sound strategy is to establish closer ties with Mongolia in order to prevent the West from making further inroads there.

In general, the erosion of central authority, exemplified by the collapse of the Soviet empire, has forced China to rethink its control over traditionally non-Han areas such as Xinjiang. Although the dominance of the Han people in China has been more complete than the ethnic Russians' in their vast empire, Beijing's control of its western frontiers is not as secure as it wishes. Threats of separatism by ethnic minorities to these frontiers still exist and China continues to see a long term threat to its security interests from Islamic fundamentalism and possibly even pan-Turkism.[19] Essentially, China knows that it must learn some critical lessons from the disintegration of the Soviet empire and avoid a similar outcome at all costs.

Economic security

Apart from military and political security, economic security is important to China's national interest in Central Asia. Here, the focus is primarily on the energy security. In relation to raw material reserves, Central Asia is critical to

China because it is widely regarded as second only to the Gulf in term of oil resources.[20] China knows that economic competition in Central Asia will intensify in the coming years and is worried that more powerful foes such as the US may become more assertive in the search for oil there. In addition, China needs access to world markets to achieve economic security, and the US holds the key to this because it is the most powerful trading nation and dominates most international economic organisations. In the light of this, the Chinese have often stressed that no country should be allowed to apply economic sanctions – including oil embargoes – to retaliate against the other states. This is especially of the US, which had imposed ban on oil exports to Japan during the Second World War. Furthermore, from China's perspective, the US has often tried to impede its economic progress with the aim of preventing its ascendancy.

For China's development programmes, access to global capital markets and international loans is important but so is the security of more energy resources; a strong economic base is key to the drive to truly global power status in the 21st century. China has become a net importer of crude oil since 1993, and it now relies heavily on the Middle East for its total imports. In terms of improving indigenous energy supplies, China expects the Tarim Basin in Xinjiang to replace the its northeastern region as the new energy base, possibly supplying over one-fifth of its total oil requirements by 2010, including an output of 35 million tons and an import of 10 million tons of crude oil from Kazakhstan.[21] Earlier, Beijing had managed to strike a deal with Western oil giants to construct a $20bn 4,000 km long pipeline from Xinjiang to the eastern city of Shanghai.[22]

At the same time, China will seek alternative sources of energy supplies in Central Asia. This means it has to compete with countries such as Russia and the US for the region's raw materials reserves. The competition is given further impetus by ongoing tensions in the Middle East, a traditional supply source, and will intensify if the countries in Central Asia increasingly become the major suppliers of energy resources to the world market. In fact, China has already taken steps to enhance its energy security interests in Central Asia. For instance, Chinese state-owned oil companies took advantage of neighbouring Kazakhstan's incentive to reduce its economic and political dependence on Russia and are already important entrants in Kazakh energy development, having outbid rivals for controlling interest of several major oilfields in western Kazakhstan. An example is the agreement with Kazakhstan to construct a 1,240-km long oil pipeline to Xinjiang.[23] China has also reached preliminary agreements on oil and gas development and other Chinese investments in Uzbekistan.[24] Furthermore, gas-rich Turkmenistan has considered the construction of a gas pipeline to Kazakhstan and further onto Xinjiang.[25]

In general, after gaining independence, these Central Asian states want to rely less on Russia's state-owned gas and oil monopolies in developing reserves and marketing their energy products to the wider world; in many cases, clashes over contract terms with Russia have pushed these states to try to integrate directly with the global energy markets and to solicit the assistance of international financial institutions. Hence, China as well as the Western countries can seize the chance to further their economic ties with Central Asian states and secure further sources of energy supplies, reducing the economic influence of the traditional regional power Russia in the process.

Overall, China also needs to develop its northwestern region more as this is in the overall national interest. Paralleling relatively successful economic experiments on the east coast, such as the Shenzhen special economic zone (SEZ), China is undertaking several attempts to modernise this region. The Great Western Development Programme is the most recent large scale incarnation of several initiatives designed to bring wealth to this poorer region.[26] Such development projects in the northwest bring some economic benefits for the Muslims in Xinjiang and may assuage some of the separatist tendencies, notwithstanding resentment towards such projects by the Muslim population because Han Chinese in the region could get jobs in the state industry more easily and often have a higher standard of living and status. The key question is whether China can dampen the demand for independence by the Uighurs in Xinjiang through offering better material well-being. Policies aimed at reducing demand for political change have so far been successfully applied in the country as a whole, barring a few setbacks such as the 1989 Tiananmen event; the Chinese Communist Party (CCP) has now substituted economic performance for ideology in its quest to continue monopolising political power. To fill the ideological vacuum created by the erosion of Communism, the CCP must above all justify its legitimacy on economic performance. It needs to find new substantive validating credentials in economic achievements in Xinjiang order to appease the local population that it rules over and still retains power over.

Here lies the link between economic security and political security, each reinforces the other to strengthen the CCP's position in China, including the northwestern region. Securing key resources, such as oil, will propel the economic modernisation drive further, resulting generally in a higher standard of living for the masses; the CCP hopes that this will assuage calls for political change or in the case of Xinjiang, demand for independence by certain ethnic groups. To achieve economic security or more specifically, to continue the modernisation drive, it is clear that China needs a stable and peaceful environment in Central Asia, which forms part of the wider Asia-Pacific. Any interstate conflicts or civil wars in Central Asia will impair the regional environment, which will in turn disrupt ongoing economic development programmes there as well as affect China's overall national development plans to some extent. More importantly, China knows that any instability in Central Asia is bound to invite the intervention of other great powers.

China and the great powers

From a wider perspective, Central Asia holds an important geopolitical position in the analysis of great power competition in the international system. In the present geopolitical reality, some strategic analysts have turned to Mackinder's Heartland Theory and China's Xinjiang can be included in Mackinder's framework.[27]

Although China's population, commercial activities and political centre are currently gravitated towards the eastern coast of the Eurasian land mass, population growth may shift the centre of gravity westwards in the future. The newly independent states in Central Asia are very weak and will not be able to resist the dominance of great powers such as China, Russia or the US should they chose to exert their influence over the area. As early as 1997, the Chinese noted that Central Asia has become of high strategic significance for the US in ensuring Washington's dominant position in leading the world; given that Central Asia links up Europe and Asia via the Caucasus, control over Central Asia could mean the 'containment of Europe' and have an impact on East Asia as well as containing Middle Eastern threats.[28] This is accentuated by the economic importance of Central Asia.

In general, the war on terror has changed the strategic landscape in Central Asia. There now exists a tripolar structure instead of bipolar one; in addition to Russia and China, the US is now a key player in Central Asia. Basically, China sees the purpose of US involvement in Central Asia as threefold: to weaken Russian influence in this part of its former empire, to contain the spread of Islamic fundamentalism and to curtail Chinese presence.[29] Although the West generally acknowledges that Central Asia is Russia's traditional sphere of influence, the NATO has stepped up its presence in Central Asia, to some extent motivated by the US. Under the auspices of NATO's Partnership for Peace (PfP) programme, the Central Asian Battalion (CentrasBat) – the joint peacekeeping force of Kazakhstan, Kyrgyzstan and Uzbekistan – was established. Apart from advocating the eastward expansion drive of NATO, the US has actually set up military bases in countries such as Uzbekistan and Kirghizstan to support waging of the war on terror.[30] Although the US withdrew from Uzbekistan in November 2005, it is possible that the lone superpower might return if there is more upheaval in the region. Basically, if the Central Asian states cannot co-opt the Islamic radical movements within, the US would have further opportunities to justify any military presence there in the name of fighting terrorists. After all, Central Asian states do to some extent value US presence as a bulwark against any Islamic separatist challenges from within.

Undoubtedly, America's arrival in Central Asia geopolitics was given an impetus by the events of September 11, which magnified the threat of Islamic terrorism. The US staged a successful military campaign against the Taliban regime in Afghanistan and is still on the hunt for Al-Qaeda in Central Asia. To a large extent, China acknowledges the US's underlying motives but also sees an imperialist logic to such recent American military actions, believing that the war on terror serves as an excuse for America to impose itself in the world in general and Central Asia in particular. Interestingly, such thinking is also evident in certain quarters in Russia.[31] Due to some commonality of strategic interests against the US, China could develop a partnership with Russia, possibly through platforms such as the SCO, to counter US advancement in Central Asia as well as American unilateralism in world politics.

Above all, China is aware of America's economic motives, and they regard US military presence in Central Asia as part of a wider plot to control energy resources in Central Asia and the Caspian Sea. The US does seek alternative oil sources to reduce its import dependence on Persian Gulf supplies; the plan to build a pipeline from Baku in Azerbaijan to Ceyhan in Turkey with the aim of avoiding hostile states such as Iran – as well as Russia – is a case in point.[32]

Besides the US, it must be stressed that China also competes with Russia for influence in Central Asia. This competition can be viewed as a continuation of the rivalry that has existed since czarist Russia expanded eastwards from the Urals. In many ways, Russia's current goal is to secure its southern flank, as was the case during the Soviet era. From Moscow's perspective, Central Asia complements Russian territory and is regarded as one of the gateways to oil-rich Middle East. Moreover, Central Asia is Russia's traditional sphere of influence. Therefore, Russia had intervened in the Tajik civil war of 1992–1997 in favour of the ruling regime, and its presence in Central Asia is still evident. Because Central Asia is Russia's traditional stronghold, China would therefore need to invest considerable time and resources to counter Russia's dominance there. China's active promotion of the SCO and more importantly, its attempt to lead the regional organisation can be regarded as indications of such efforts.

In addition to the US and Russia, China could face competition for influence in Central Asia from lesser powers such as Iran and Turkey over the longer term. Iran's influence is not extensive yet and is mainly restricted to Tajikistan, the only Persian-speaking country in Central Asia. Turkey was the first state to recognise the independence of the Soviet Central Asian Republics and the first state to open embassies in those states. The first Turkic summit was held in Ankara in October 1992 – attended by the leaders of Turkey, Azerbaijan, Kazakhstan, Kyrgyzstan, Turkmenistan and Uzbekistan. Since then, however, the call for some form of pan-Turkism has petered out. In general, Turkey and Iran have up till now not posed a serious threat to China's strategic interests in Central Asia. In contrast, stiff competition for influence has come from the US and Russia, therefore China has formulated its foreign policy in Central Asia primarily with those two great powers in mind.

China and the SCO

With regard to Central Asian security, China has taken an active role in promoting SCO as a credible regional organisation, largely out of self-interest. Beijing's aims in the region are threefold: to weed out separatist activities on its western front, to counter US and Russian influence in the region, and to demonstrate that it can act as a responsible regional power in Central Asia. Although events at Andijon in Uzbekistan and the change of power in Kirghizstan did not erode the stability in Central Asia totally, they have strengthened the need for China to use the SCO more; China still stresses the need to be vigilant so that extremist and terrorist forces will not take advantage of these situations.[33] Through the SCO, China was able to secure the inauguration of a regional anti-terrorist body, which intensifies its co-operation with Central Asian states in the war against the 'three forces of terrorism, extremism and separatism'.[34] What triggered this deviation from the traditional Chinese policy of non-intervention in a given state's domestic affairs was the fear of a global militant Islam network allying with separatist forces in Xinjiang. In this sense, what serves the US in its war on terror now coincides with China's predicament on its northwestern front. The manipulation of the SCO to serve the cause of eliminating separatism in Xinjiang is indicative of classic Chinese foreign policy manoeuvres, although this is not a difficult task as the other SCO members share similar concerns over separatist threats in Central Asia.

Involvement in the SCO also enables China to bypass Russia's traditional stake in Central Asia to a certain extent. For instance, promotion of the SCO means the Central Asian countries will be less reliant on Russia-sponsored plans for achieving state and regional security. These states will then have more alternatives instead of relying on Russian proposals such as developing rapid deployment forces for co-ordinated regional counter-terrorist actions under the Commonwealth of Independent States' Collective Security Treaty (CST) framework.[35] In fact, Uzbekistan has withdrawn from the CST, and this can be regarded as gain for China vis-à-vis Russia. In general, China aims to pull the former Soviet Central Asian republics further away from the grip of their ex-overlord. The SCO has in some ways served as a device for China to increase its influence over Central Asian states while checking a return of uncontested Russian hegemony in the region.

Furthermore, the SCO serves as a platform for China to boost its regional power status and to work more closely with international organisations. For instance, the setting up of the aforementioned regional anti-terrorist body entails the formulation of legal documents that include working together with the United Nations (UN) Security Council and its anti-terrorism committee. Such actions give China an opportunity to highlight its increasing importance in international affairs. This raises optimism for the country's further integration with international society. Such further integration can only be beneficial for the international community, which generally worries about the implications of China's ascendancy. It is clear that China can use the SCO to show the world its credentials as an upholder of peace in Central Asia as well as its commitment to regional security through a proactive regional policy. Recently, Chinese President Hu Jintao has called on SCO members to step up co-operation, acknowledging the importance of multilateralism and advocating the replacement of notions of 'absolute unilateral security' in favour of some form of co-operative security.[36]

At the same time, participation in the SCO does not fully vindicate any strong signs of China genuinely embracing multilateralism; it largely represents a means for China to achieve its security goals rather than indicates a radical departure from China's preference for bilateralism in international relations. Traditionally distrustful of multilateral security undertakings, China has often taken a zero-sum view of alliances, believing that mutual security pacts must have an explicitly identified enemy or they should have no reason to exist. The positive sum notion that an alliance can serve to preserve stability and deter aggression, without identifying specific enemies, is on the whole still rather alien to Chinese security thinking. In general, China still suspects that most alliances in international system, including NATO's PfP in Central Asia, are at least partly aimed at itself.

One can also view China's participation in the SCO as an indication of the constructive role of great power management in regional security, in this case involving at least Russia and the US.[37] Great powers such as China can to a large extent dictate security patterns in Central Asia and more importantly, help prevent conflicts between Central Asian countries or even intrastate political violence. The key is how effectively China, Russia and the US can manage their differences and how far they can reach a common ground on Central Asian security issues without sacrificing their own national interests. From the Chinese perspective, consolidating its position in Central Asia and being able to induce a cultural secular, inwardly authoritarian and outwardly moderate Central Asia would be ideal. The question here is how and to what degree does Russia or the US share these objectives. In the long run, in addition to great power management, the achievement of Central Asian security must also be underpinned by the indigenous states themselves. These newly independent states must learn to take on more responsibility and act collectively to stabilise the region. An expansion of the SCO to include countries such as Pakistan, Mongolia, India and Turkmenistan in future could have this in regard.

Conclusion

China has key security interests in Central Asia in the 21st century, and these will increase over time. In the military realm, the region is vital as it borders an old enemy, Russia, and the lone superpower, the US, is now establishing itself there. Politically, the growth of militant Islamic in Central Asia concerns Beijing as it can spur separatist movements in Xinjiang and undermine stability on the northwestern front. In terms of economic security, China knows that it has to compete with other great powers to secure future energy supplies in resource-rich Central Asia.

In geopolitical terms, Central Asia is generally analysed as one of the key areas for great power competition. Indigenous states in the region are rather weak and are unlikely to effectively resist the intervention of more powerful countries. Adopting a Realist approach to international relations, China therefore seeks to maximise its power and influence in the region, primarily vis-à-vis Russia and the US. In doing so, China will face stiff challenges from its rivals. One way of enhancing its role in Central Asia is through diplomacy; therefore having good relations with the newly independent Central Asian states is vital.

Another route is through the SCO whereby China exerts its authority in Central Asia as well as shows the international community that its presence there is indispensable for regional security. After all, the SCO does constitute a means for China to Asia. This is especially so given that Washington tends to put less emphasis on such regional platforms as it pursues its own unilateralist agenda and Russia's status as traditional Central Asian overlord might hamper its participation in the SCO. Therefore, China will seize the opportunities offered by the SCO to step up ties with its Central Asian neighbours and project its influence, thereby enhancing its security interests in the region.

9 The drive to global power status

To a large degree, achieving comprehensive security – maximising the military, political and economic aspects of security – today implies that China must attain truly global power status. In the recent past, China attained comprehensive security primarily by being at the top of the Asian hierarchy; no country was able to challenge China directly in military, political or economic terms before the 1830s. Attaining such a status in Asia – as well as in the international system – today means that China's security will be at a maximum once again. However, the drive to global power status raises questions on whether China will impinge on the security of other states. The two contrasting theories – China threat (*Zhongguo weixie*) and peaceful rise (*heping jueqi*) – will be examined here. China's role in regional security will also be examined. We first explore China's quest for comprehensive security over a longer time frame.

Sino-centrism

Before the coming of the Western powers, China's security was as at a maximum as no country came close to challenging this in military, political or economic terms. Due to its supremacy in Asia and its sheer size, China in general did not face serious security threats from its smaller neighbours. In fact, China was once at the centre of a regional security system, and other states had to conduct their relations with Beijing in a deferential manner. The Chinese empire regarded itself as the centre of the universe; all states had to revolve around it insofar as they paid tributes to the Chinese emperor.[1] This was especially the case with adjoining vassal states such as Korea and Vietnam. This type of Sino-centric thinking is still evident today and influences the Chinese security policies on the Korean peninsula to a certain degree.

One of the features of the Sino-centric world order is hierarchy, whereby 'political actors are formally differentiated according to degrees of their authority'.[2] In many ways, this hierarchical structure derives from the workings of domestic politics and social relations, whereby inequality exists in relationships such as those between the ruler and its subjects, the father and his son. Hence, the practice of such hierarchical relationships has been extended to the realm of foreign relations over the previous centuries. Essentially, China views itself as the most powerful state in Asia and it demands that smaller neighbouring countries acknowledge this in some form. It is useful to distinguish between four kinds of hierarchical structures in international relations: spheres of influence, protectorates, informal empires and empires.[3] China has always seen Northeast Asia as its sphere of influence. It had established protectorates in certain regions of Central Asia in the past. The tributary system might be regarded as some sort of informal empire. The most interesting point is whether China has the intention to establish a formal empire in the long run as this could represent one way to achieve comprehensive security.

Another feature of the Sino-centric world order is the notion of moral superiority, which is supported by the fact that China is a civilisation going back over some four thousand years. There is a connotation that the Chinese ruler had duties towards his counterparts in the periphery, who were regarded as his inferiors.[4] The surrounding states were regarded as equal to each other; the Chinese rulers did not discriminate against them but they were all deemed as beneath the Son of Heaven.[5] To a certain extent, this stands in sharp contrast to the European states system that emerged since 1648 following the Treaty of Westphalia, where each nation-state is regarded as equal in sovereignty and mutually independent. In certain areas of Chinese foreign policy, one can still detect a moral tone whereby insistence on principles reflects a political culture that long prized ethics over the law, moral consensus more than the judicial process and benevolent government more than checks and balances. For example, China had helped socialist regimes in Africa in the economic development in the 1960s and it gives aid to developing nations today. Another case in point would be the 1997–1998 Asian currency crisis. Deeply shaken by the suddenness and scope of the crisis, China argued that it acted responsibly by not devaluing its currency and by offering aid packages and low-interest loans to several Southeast Asian states. These actions were not only appreciated in Asia but also stood in stark contrast to the dictatorial posture taken by the International Monetary Fund (IMF) and international creditors in response to the crisis. To a large extent, China's stance altered the prevailing image of China in the region or hegemonic and portended the notion of China as a responsible power. The key question is how much this was driven by morality rather than strategic interests. In any case, comprehensive security was achieved under the Sino-centric world order.

However, the Sino-centric world order collapsed under the challenge of the Western power and Japan. It then took China about a century before reasserting itself in the international system. China's rise as a communist giant rivalled the Soviet Union at certain periods during the Cold War. Although significantly weaker than either of the two superpowers, China was adept at playing its role in the great power triangle and even managed to extend its influence considerably in global affairs. This unmistakably points towards China's global power ambitions, and the implication is that those ambitions must be fulfilled today. In short, China will drive to global power status in the 21st century, and this represents a way to achieve comprehensive security.

China threat?

One unintended consequence of China's search for comprehensive security and drive to global power status is the notion of a China threat. The term itself, *Zhongguo weixie lun*, is used here as a convenient device to look at the alleged threats that China's rise might pose to its neighbours and perhaps even to the wider world. Much of the basis of the China threat theory derives from China's high defence budget, although this is actually less than 10 per cent of the US's military budget. Official Chinese statistics indicate that defence spending to state financial expenditure fell by some 10 percentage points from 17.37 per cent in 1979 to 7.76 per cent in 2004.[6]

More importantly, the purpose of Chinese military spending has been questioned by US officials such as Defence Secretary Donald Rumsfeld, who argued that no nations currently threaten China; in addition, China's expenditure are much higher than published figures and its ability to project power is increasing.[7] In many ways, the Chinese have now been more transparent with its military modernisation, as evidenced by the publication of several defence white papers. Although one might argue that these fall short of Western standards in terms of accountability, it does indicate that the Chinese have addressed the issue and have accordingly offered more information about its capabilities. The latest publication, for instance, gave detailed accounts of the People's Liberation Army (PLA) doctrine and structure as well as the development of defence industries.[8] For the ultimate goal of achieving truly global power status, China needs to have a modern military to achieve its political objectives; it lags behind other states in military technology and sees keeping up with the revolution in military affairs (RMA) as essential.

It is also important to note that China's defence modernisation is affected by the increase in defence spending in East Asia as a whole. At present, there is an arms build-up in East Asia closely linked to regional concerns that an American military and perhaps even political retrenchment from the region might expose East Asian states to various tensions and confrontations. Anticipating such challenges, most countries in the region have embarked on arms spending, which is often veiled under the explanation of catching up or ongoing modernisation of their forces. In addition, there are also other factors driving the arms build-up, such as the need to police the extra-territorial economic zones and sea lines of communications as well as to defend offshore territorial claims. In some cases, the additional factor is prestige conferred by the possession of certain advanced weapon systems. To a large extent, this arms build-up is fanned by the growing wealth of many Asian countries. China is affected by this process and, in turn, is increasing its defence spending in reaction to the regional trend of acquiring further military capability. Keeping up with the regional arms build-up has inevitably influenced the thinking of China's military leaders. It is true to say that, currently, the end of the Cold War has provided a relatively peaceful environment for China to redefine its military strategy and modernise its weapons systems. Indeed, the early years of the 21st century can be seen as the take off phase in a military build-up that will enable China to challenge for undisputed leadership in Asia eventually.

Above all, it is important to note that the driving force for Beijing's current military expansion has less to do with any current military threats but stems largely from a 'century of humiliation' by the Western powers and the need to become a global power. China's military and political security had been violated in the past by foreign powers. This explains why during the Cold War, China acquired nuclear weapons. The basic aim then was to stand up to the super-powers.[9] Essentially, possession of nuclear capabilities is still regarded as a supreme symbol of self-reliance, a means for China to defend its sovereignty and pursue an independent foreign policy More importantly, China is able use its nuclear power status to elevate its standing in the world as nuclear capability is regarded as evidence of global power status. Therefore, an ambitious programme of weapons development continues, some indigenous in nature and some helped by purchases from abroad, mainly from Russia and Israel. The basic Chinese proposition is that strategic independence is still required today because the two nuclear powers US and Russia possess the largest nuclear arsenals with the most sophisticated weapons. Hence, China argues that it needs nuclear weapons primarily to maintain its military security while stressing that those weapons are developed solely for self-defence and not meant to pose a threat to any specific country.[10] China aims to catch up with the US with marginal weapons improve-ments, and this constituted, for instance, the rationale for its nuclear weapons testing in 1995, at a time when other powers had imposed a testing moratorium.[11] Overall, anti-imperialism and fears of the hegemonist potential of America drive China's military modernisation – including nuclear weapon development – to a large extent.

The China threat theory also implies that China will use force to achieve its objectives in international relations. However, the use of force, if ever applied, is more likely to be rational, calculated and limited in scope in the 21st century. Chinese military thinkers are after all, still influenced by a particular strand in ancient military thought; the famous Chinese military strategist Sun Tzu wrote around 400 BC. that the supreme art of war is to subdue the enemy without fight-ing. To most Chinese military analysts, winning a war, be it economic conflict or a total war, is best achieved by manoeuvres and deception, without bloodshed. In recent times, China has used its military power largely in Clausewitzian, political terms, and above all, in a defensive manner. For example, China had participated in the Korean War as well as supported the North Vietnamese in order to secure its frontiers. China fought a border war against the Soviet Union in 1969 along the Ussuri River to defend its northern borders. China attacked Vietnam in 1979 for its invasion of Cambodia, an action indirectly aimed at the Soviet threat build-ing up at Cam Ranh Bay at that time. All the above wars were conducted to demonstrate that China will no longer be weak, as it had been during the first half of the 20th century. They were also an indication of China's ability to stand up to the superpowers, be it the US or the Soviet Union. From a broader perspective, in a world of sovereign states with no central political authority, it is inevitable that states will defend their territories with the use of force if necessary. This is rein-forced by the fact that China had been the victim of foreign aggression in the recent past. In this respect, China is no different from any other states, as it goes through the process of maintaining its sovereignty and bolstering its security.

At the same time, one must note that although Chinese history includes several competing foreign policy traditions, the realpolitik strand runs deep. For example, during the Warring States period (409–221 BC), relations within the Chinese state system was characterised by constant manoeuvre and ruthless competition, with opportunistic alliances, treachery, accumulation of military power and the attendant use of force being important tools of statecraft. China will like to translate its economic success more fully into an offensive military capability at some stage.[12] Improved military power projection will undoubtedly give Beijing a wider choice in the pursuit of its national security interests. Whether this impinges on the security of neighbouring countries, as the China threat theory suggests, is more contentious.

The notion of a China threat can also take a more ideological form. For instance, Western analysts such as Samuel Huntingdon have predicted a neo-Confucianism ideological challenge – possibly led by China – to the West.[13] At present, no semblance of a unified Confucian challenge has appeared in real terms yet, apart from 'Asian values', which are better seen as a justification for the continuation of specific strands in Asian political culture rather than as a stern challenge to the West. Conversely, China rejects the universality of Western or US culture, which implies that the development of history will be accompanied by the Western culture wiping out other competing ones.[14] From the Chinese perspective, it will be dangerous if Huntingdon's theory finds its way into US foreign policy.

Interestingly, there are also analysts and scholars in the West who adhered to the China disintegration thesis in comparison to the China threat; these predictions of an imminent collapse of the Chinese state, based largely on the current social cohesion and legitimacy problems, represents a completely different scenario from the China threat theory. Hence, although China has been regarded by many as a great power, at least in regional terms, there are those that regard China as a weak state at the same time. Barry Buzan's distinction between the terms 'state' and 'power' is useful here.[15] The term 'power' is used to refer to the relations among states, which are largely seen in terms of their military strength although criteria such as political cohesion within a state and the level of economic development, are also important. The term 'state' specifically refers to issues such as the degree of social cohesion and here one views the state from inside.

The China disintegration thesis basically argues that economic problems will create domestic crises for Beijing and tests the unity of the Chinese state. Such problems arose primarily due to uneven economic development, with the eastern areas rising much faster than the inland and western areas for instance. It is true that issues such as income disparity, corruption, rural–urban migration, burden of a huge population, regional protests continue to undermine social cohesion, with spill-over effects being felt by the Chinese state. There is, of course, another way of interpreting the China disintegration thesis: a Chinese state on the point of collapse will try to use an aggressive nationalistic foreign policy as a form of internal cement. In short, a situation whereby China is facing a collapse can also magnify a China threat to the wider world.

Last, it is plausible to view the China threat theory purely as means for Western analysts and policymakers who advocate strategies aimed at keeping a rising China in check. In fact, China has often attributed its negative image as a potential regional hegemon to certain US hardline foreign policies. It can be argued that the ending of the Cold War deprived many countries of their most specific strategic aim, and many potential threats, such as the China threat, were soon brought to the fore to fill the vacuum of the strategic structure. Certainly, this type of thinking has been evident in some American academic and policy circles since the early 1990s. Here, the Chinese perception is that there is a foreign attempt to 'line up the different fractions of American society, or even the whole West, to fight an imaginary enemy'.[16] Basically the Chinese see such arguments as serving the agenda of US hardliners who need an adversary after the Soviet collapse. Taking a longer perspective, it is also important to note that the prime perceived threat to America was China in the 1990s, but this has since shifted more to militant Islam in the era of war on terror.

Today, Chinese analysts perceive that US officials such as Defence Secretary Donald Rumsfeld needs to find a pretext for prolonging their massive military expenditure and find a way for their armament sector, following the high tide of military action in Iraq.[17] In some ways, playing up the China threat can also justify US's continuing military presence in Asia and create the basis for intervention in the Taiwan Straits and for arm sales to Taiwan independence forces. Moreover, there is a Chinese argument that the US might use the China threat theory to create tensions in the Asia-Pacific in order to undermine any growing regional security co-operation mechanisms because this undermined the authority of the US; more specifically, America is afraid that it might lose to China the dominant position it currently possesses in regional security.[18]

In this vein, one can understand why China sees the China threat theory as a foreign attempt aimed to sow discord between China and its neighbouring countries so that benefits, such as those through arms sales, can be reaped, and China's development can be restricted and obstructed.

Overall, one utility of the China threat theory is the fact that it gives policymakers in the West a convenient framework for formulating their China policies. More specially, it provides some justification for those policymakers who wish to adopt a containment policy towards China.

Peaceful rise?

In order to counter the China threat theory, China has espoused the peaceful rise thesis, which basically argues that its ascendancy is more likely to be seen as peaceful rather than disrupting.[19] China frequently stresses that it needs to maintain a peaceful international environment so that its limited resources and energies can be concentrated on construction and development. Following this line of argument means that it is hard to imagine that China would harm the existence of a peaceful international environment at the risk of its own development programme. This is, of course, not only a refutation of the China threat theory but also an indication of China's desire to carry out its economic development. In reality, the Chinese are not calling for stable regional environment out of altruism. It is in their key interests to sustain the current high rates of growth for domestic reasons as well as external objectives.

Linked to the peaceful rise theory is that China's concept of advancement is based on cultural traditions and centres on non-aggressive development, which seems to contrast with the Western one. Chinese academics have contrasted Western colonialism with the Sino-centric world order, which was based on Confucian virtues and aimed at demonstrating the might of the Chinese empire rather than outright material gain or conquests.[20] It was pointed out that for instance, during the Ming dynasty, the naval exploits of Zheng He were aimed at enhancing trade and China's prestige rather than territorial gains.[21] Compared with nature of Western colonialism, one might argue that the Chinese path to ascendancy has less negative effects on the security of the other states.

Some evidence of China's peaceful rise can be found in the evolution of Chinese foreign policy since 1945. History shows that, as China progressed through the years, it had to abandon the Marxist inevitability-of-war thesis in its grand strategy in order to use the world capitalist system to achieve internal economic growth. On the whole, the concept of global interdependence appears to have replaced the Leninist-inspired theory of imperialism, and this constitutes the theoretical justification for China's growing reliance on the world capitalist system. There is a merit in the argument that a revolutionary state, as China had been in the 1960s, can be eventually 'socialised' into international society.[22] Nevertheless, at this point in time, it is true to say that China has been fully socialised into international society, although this process is steadily gaining momentum as China seeks to deepen its economic ties with the capitalist world in a bid to bolster its economic security. In the foreseeable future, it is unlikely that China will embark on all-out war to achieve its security objectives. China will not want to be seen as the first to initiate a large-scale conflict because this will risk hurting its economic ties with its trading partners and international financial institutions. These economic ties and a stable environment in East Asia are too important for China's economic modernisation and domestic stability. In addition, one can argue that continuing economic modernisation will increase China's general interdependence with the outside world, giving further support to the peaceful rise theory.

Economic interdependence with the outside world has to a certain extent restricted Chinese political and military behaviour in many ways. Complying with a set of international norms and standards in the realm of economics means that Chinese behaviour is being constrained. As Keohane and Nye put it, 'as a result of increased communications, movement of people across international borders, foreign investments and changes in export and import practices', significant changes in attitudes and conduct of states, such as those of China, can take place without the Chinese realising it.[23] For example, in order to obtain developmental loans from Europe, Japan, the US and international economic institutions, China will need to gain a degree of acceptance in the eyes of the developed nations. An expansionist foreign policy would hardly be ideal in this case.

To a large extent, China acknowledges that it cannot do without the world in its development, and the world in turn needs China for its prosperity; these mutually reinforcing trends will remain to validate the peaceful rise theory. An important corollary is that China's continuing modernisation can only help the world economy and contribute to stability. Hence, the peaceful rise thesis can be further extended to the notion that China's ascendancy is beneficial to the global economy; Chinese sources noted that in 2003, some 18 per cent of the growth in the world economy was generated by China, despite the fact China only accounted for 4 per cent of the world's gross national product (GNP).[24] As China's share of the global GNP increases, its contribution for the generator for global growth will magnify.

At the same time, there is no hard evidence to support the theory that economic interdependence automatically leads to peace. In fact, history shows that at least to date, increased economic co-operation and interdependence in their own right provide no guarantee against conflicts. Although increased economic co-operation and interdependence can increase the stakes and thus raise the consequences to the point where a potential aggressor such as China will have to think twice before choosing a military option in order to achieve its aspirations, they can also create a false sense of confidence that causes certain states to push too hard or too fast.

Even if one accepts that China's rise will be on the whole peaceful, there are ambiguities on the degree of its harmonisation with the international system. Interestingly, it has been suggested that a state's expectations of future trade are crucial determinants of whether interdependence causes war.[25] This is certainly on China's security agenda, given that its trade problems with the US still remain unresolved. A similar situation has in fact existed before China's ascendancy; Japan and the US clash over bilateral trade disputes frequently. Here, one witnesses the nexus between the economic and military aspects of a state's security. Enhancing one aspect could mean damaging the other, and it is therefore crucial for China to manage this nexus correctly.

Nonetheless, if China is enmeshed in a network of international ties, it will become more concerned about losing major trading partners. China might, therefore, become more constrained in its actions in the political realm, conducting itself in a manner more acceptable to the international community. In such circumstances, an aggressive Chinese foreign policy will be less likely. Therefore, it is in the interests of the outside world and in particular China's immediate neighbours to capitalise on China's reliance on the world economic capitalist and try bringing China into the international system; this is even more important because China remains unique among the great powers in having little experience of genuine multilateral interaction with the international community.

An analogy can be made to the case of other great powers. Japan has risen to be a major power again while accepting the constraints of the international system, primarily due to the restraint imposed by the longstanding US–Japanese alliance. As for the US, its rise to global power status in the 19th century also took place largely within the existing rules and was accompanied by a willingness to work within certain constraints with the objective of changing the international order from the inside. From China's perspective, the current challenges to enhance comprehensive security and achieve global power status mean making itself anti-imperialist, not so much through self-reliance and mobilisation for wars but instead through economic growth. In order to do that, China will need a stable environment. Therefore, it appears China might follow the examples of the US and Japan in scaling the global hierarchy within the constraints of an existing international system rather than modifying this system drastically to suit its ascendancy.

Role in regional security

Given China's desire for a stable environment, the next question will be whether China can contribute to regional and international security. In general, China still prefers to deal with most security issues on a case-by-case, bilateral basis before embarking on multilateral dialogues. Perhaps one reason for China's reservations in most multilateral security schemes relates to the fact that these schemes might simply serve to single out China for criticism, in particular for its military build-up. Beijing prefers a step-by-step incremental approach whereby it can ensure its security interests will not be compromised in any way. This partly reflects an adherence to a zero-sum view of alliances, in which mutual security pacts must have an explicitly identified enemy – or they should have no reason to exit. The positive sum notion that alliance can serve to preserve stability and deter aggression, without identifying specific enemies, remains alien to the Chinese security thinking. Moreover, the Chinese suspect that these alliance, in particular those in the Asia-Pacific region, are aimed at China. This is certainly true of Beijing's perceptions of the US–Japan alliance, the extension of North Atlantic Treaty Organisation's (NATO) Partnership for Peace proposal for Central Asia as well as US security ties with Australia, Thailand, Philippines and Singapore. Unfortunately, China's general unwillingness to subordinate its security interests to regional organisations, especially those initiated by the US, has contributed to fears of China being a threat to the region. In this sense, general Chinese suspicions of the Western goal of containment have carried over into regional security discussions.

However, as time goes by, it would not be China's interests to remain completely aloof from these regional security activities. Hence, it appears that China participates in selective dialogues in regional security discussions primarily to ensure that any solution to regional issues will be to its advantage. On its part, China has begun to reassess its attitude towards multilateralism. Until the mid-1990s, China had largely perceived such organisations as potential instruments of the lone superpower's strategy of containment and encirclement. It has now modified its assessment of multilateral organisations, with perception of such organisations evolving from suspicion to uncertainty and then to supportiveness.[26] The most important engagement with such organisations relates to the regions of Southeast Asia and Central Asia.

China currently participates in the ASEAN Regional Forum (ARF), which was founded in July 1994, and the non-governmental Council on Security Co-operation in the Asia-Pacific (CSCAP). It appears that China is beginning to see a virtue in regional multilateralism, perhaps as a way to exert counter-pressure against US presence in East Asia. Today, China has a role in the ARF, supports its CBMs and voluntarily submits annual security outlook report every year.[27] Such moves not only increases the transparency of China but is also aimed at allaying the fears of smaller states who feel threatened by a strong China. China is also a participant in the first ever East Asia Summit in 2005, where the long-term goal is to establish an East Asian Community which might actually be useful for countering US influence.[28] At a wider level, Chinese scholars have acknowledged that the ARF started some form of security co-operation in Asia and could in the long run resolve the security dilemma facing states, as the European Union (EU) has already set a good example on how to build up mutual trust among countries.[29]

Beyond Asia, China has stressed its willingness to play a constructive role in international affairs. It holds a permanent seat in the United Nations (UN) Security Council and has taken interests on issues such as the Middle East peace process and the nuclear impasse in Iran.[30] Chinese involvement in global affairs will become more apparent as it drives closer to truly global power status. In addition, China is important to the bigger goal of nuclear non-proliferation. China became a signatory to the Non-Proliferation Treaty (NPT) in March 1992. It has also reached a tacit agreement to abide by the Missiles Technology Control Regime (MTCR). On the Comprehensive Test Ban Treaty (CTBT), China was among the first signatories in September 1996. It is currently working on its domestic legal procedures for the ratification of the CTBT and has established a national agency to prepare for its implementation.[31] In the post-September 11 era, China supports efforts to ban biological and chemical weapons, acceding to the Biological Weapons Convention (BWC) and the Chemical Weapons Convention (CWC). However, in the eyes of many states, China, in general, still does not go far enough in its commitment to non-proliferation; from their perspective, although China no longer openly opposes these non-proliferation regimes, it has not taken effective steps to prevent the export of missile and nuclear technology to countries such as Pakistan.

Although China is gradually moving towards multilateralism, it must be stated that China's contribution to regional and international security arises primarily from its great power role. For instance, in order for any attempts at setting up confidence-building measures or forming security regimes in Asia to have any chance of success, great powers such as China must be involved. The case of the League of Nations is instructive: collective security institution had failed because not all the great powers were involved, given that the US had on the whole chosen to adopt an isolationist policy.[32] It is therefore plausible to argue that for the goal of security of the Asia-Pacific, China needs to be actively involved in some regional schemes. Here, it is important to realise that great powers can play constructive roles in a regional system. Generally, great powers are powers recognised by others as well as conceived by their own leaders and citizens to have special rights and duties in the international system.[33] These powers 'assert the right, and are accorded the right, to play a part in determining issues that affect the peace and security of the international system as a whole'; they do so 'by managing their affairs relations with one another, and by exploiting their preponderance in such as a way as to impart a degree of central direction to the affairs of international society as a whole.'[34]

Implicit here is the international society approach. In an international society, 'a group of states... not merely form a system, in the sense that the behaviour of each is a necessary factor in the calculations of the others, but also have established by dialogue and consent common rules and institutions for the conduct of their relations, and recognise their common interests in maintaining these arrangements'.[35] In a society of states, the consensus among great powers on certain issues often serves as a kind of norm, upon which international behaviour will be judged. This then places constraints on the foreign behaviour of all states involved in regional security arrangements, including on erratic ones such as North Korea. Such an international society may not yet exist in Northeast Asia due to reasons such as the lack of a long history of Westphalian-style international relations, the paucity of democratic states and the existence of territorial disputes in Northeast Asia.[36] If such an international society does not exist or count much in Northeast Asia, then it is even more important for the great powers to set some norms and then maintain them. At the initial stage, those norms could come from shared interests that have already been mentioned – maintaining the status quo, preventing nuclear proliferation and enhancing trade – in the Asia-Pacific. Here the emphasis is on China matching its interests with the US's, although the aspirations of Russia and Japan should not be totally ignored either.

Specifically, achieving regional security is linked to whether China and the US can act in a great power concert. For example, the US had envisioned a concert of powers involving the Soviet Union, Britain and China to maintain a liberal international order in the post-Second World War era although this eventually fell apart as the Cold War ensued.[37] In general, the historical record of great power concert is not particularly encouraging, even in cases where participants share similar worldviews and political systems. Given that China and the US have quite fundamentally different conceptions of world order, it might be difficult for them to work effectively on security issues such as the North Korean nuclear stalemate. From the US perspective, a sensible foreign policy might actually be one that seeks to identify more closely with fellow democracies in Europe and Japan.[38] This could mean continuing to engage China simultaneously or simply neglecting China. The former option is arguably better for Asia-Pacific security and international security, as the latter would be unwise given China's ascendancy.

Conclusion

China's search for ultimate security – the drive to global power status – is in many ways reinforced by the 'century of humiliation' that it previously suffered at the hands of various imperialist powers and by what Beijing perceives as the hegemonic ambitions of the US in the current era. To avenge for this 'century of humiliation', Chinese leaders believe that building up sufficient economic strength and military might to counter the perceived American threat is paramount today. From their perspective, the China threat theory is merely a reflection of US foreign policies that are replete with containment strategies. The classic Chinese proposition is that China will never seek hegemony or threaten its neighbours when it becomes powerful. At a wider level, it must be emphasised that in the anarchical international system, China faces the same problem of preserving its territorial integrity just like any other states and it also has to compete against other great powers in an uncertain era. Essentially, one might then argue that the much publicised China threat theory is better regarded as an unintended consequence of China's rapid economic growth and military modernisation.

Nonetheless, in its search for ultimate security, it must be said that China does raise some concerns for the security of other states. Even without expansionist ambitions, China's sheer size and potential for global power status will remain a key focus for its neighbours and the wider international community. Indeed, China's efforts to sustain growth in the economy in order to continue its drive to global power status is in many ways reminiscent of Japan's rise: the island nation had adopted reforms in the 19th century with the goal of a strong and militarily powerful country in mind. Asian neighbours are justified in worrying whether China's rise will resemble that of Japan in the early part of the 20th century. Overall, most scholars and practitioners of international relations will agree that the strategic orientation and military posture of China constitute to be key variables determining regional security in the 21st century, as Beijing builds up its comprehensive national strength and becomes more involved in international affairs.

At the same time, it seems unlikely that China will risk a major conflict in Asia and by extension, further afield because a stable regional environment is paramount for China's quest for economic growth. This is the crux of the peaceful rise thesis. Critically, economic growth provides the means for China to realise the aspiration of becoming a truly global power. Hence, it does not serve the interests of China to alter or damage the economic environment in Northeast Asia or the larger Asia-Pacific in any drastic manner. That will only hinder Beijing's modernisation and delay its drive to truly global power status in the 21st century, which is foremost on China's security agenda. In this vein, if one accepts the ideas embedded in the peaceful rise theory, China will inadvertently contribute to the enhancement of regional security and global security.

Conclusions

This final part of the book will restate the conclusions drawn from the study of China's security interests in the 21st century. First, the security situation that China faces today will be recapitulated. Then the chapter moves on to restate the salience of the economic and political aspects of China's security. Last, wider theoretical implications arising from the operationalisation of the concept of comprehensive security will be addressed.

China in the 21st century

Today, it is quite clear that Beijing cannot enhance its security interests on the basis of manoeuvring between opposing superpowers in a state of continued confrontation. China's leverage was lost as a consequence of Soviet–American rapprochement when the Cold War waned. Essentially, the collapse of Communism in the former Soviet Union and the end of the Cold War meant there was only one superpower left. This has spurred policymakers in China to re-examine its existing international relationships. Old enmities have evaporated and time-tested friendships have dissolved as Chinese leaders struggle to come to terms with the fluid and dynamic post-Cold War environment. Basically, China's leaders must now learn to adapt to new emerging security structures.

In one way, the end of the Cold War brought about a situation whereby Chinese leaders are able to address regional problems in Northeast Asia without subordinating them to the larger strategic context of meeting the potential threats of a superpower. Today, the relationship with Russia is less central to China than in the past, given the huge alterations in the regional and global security environment. For China, the decline of the Russian threat is definitely a major gain in the military realm: a northern border secure from any major military threat has long been a primary security objective of Beijing and this goal has been achieved within a rapidly changing and unanticipated international security environment as the Cold War faded away. China now faces a security environment in Northeast Asia that is less likely to be disrupted by a major international power than at any time in the past. Moreover, regional security trends since the late 1980s have generally been compatible with China's primary focus on internal economic modernisation and political stability. In this vein, one can argue that China currently enjoys the best security environment since the Communist Party took power in 1949.

Nonetheless, for China, the most important development in the post-Cold War era for its security is the relationship with the lone superpower. Today, the US is perhaps the only country in the world that possesses the combination of military capabilities and political will to constitute a threat to China. Japan has the economic and technological potential to do so but at present, Beijing is protected from that possibility by the Japanese Constitution and the continued strategic subordination of Japan to the US under the provisions of the 1952 US–Japan Security Treaty. In fact, China believes that restraining Japan's potential military is likely to require the continuation of Washington's security ties with Tokyo, at least until it becomes strong enough to meet the Japanese challenge. Similarly, American co-operation will be essential for a peaceful reunification of the two Koreas, which China might wish to support, not only to sustain stability in Northeast Asia but also to demonstrate its intentions of its reunification plans with Taiwan.[1] At the same time, China is deeply concerned that the end of East–West conflict might permit the US to be more supportive of Taiwan in an age where liberal values are more widespread.

At a wider level, if the objective situation in the external world – contradictions, configurations and balance – is in a perpetual motion, China does not see the need to keep any permanent alignments. From the Chinese perspective, it seems that adjustments in domestic and foreign policies are only natural as along as principles and goals such as striving for global power status remain unchanged. Due to external circumstances over which they have no control, Chinese leaders believe that those who can adroitly guide action according to circumstance are great leaders. In general, they still look for differences among the major powers that can be exploited to advance China's security interests. As the relations with the US continue to unravel, China might see Russia, western Europe or Japan as viable partners if it finds itself unable to make any reconciliation towards American policy in Asia – at least in the short term. In other words, there is a distinct possibility that some form of Sino-Russian tactical co-ordination and to a lesser extent Sino-Japanese convergence might emerge in the 21st century. In particular, leaders in Moscow and Beijing are already seeing eye-to-eye on a number of global issues, such as the Iranian nuclear issue, the eastward expansion of the North Atlantic Treaty Organisation (NATO) and hardline policies against separatists from within.

Studying China's security interests is important because China shapes the security environment in Northeast Asia. At the same time, the regional system also constrains Chinese foreign policy objectives. No state makes its foreign policy in a vacuum; foreign policies are at least as reactive as they are proactive. The questions of how China relates to the countries in Northeast Asia in the 21st century, and whether the nexus between China and Northeast Asia remains constant will have implications for China's security interests pertaining to the world at large. One consistency in Beijing's security agenda compared to earlier periods in its history is the quest to restore China to its rightful place in the world, which basically means achieving global power status today. After all, China's security agenda is shaped by its historical experience as a victim of Western and Japanese imperialism and its approach to international relations, derived from a mixture of

Marxist and Realist doctrines, identification with the Third World and historic Sino-centricism.

For those with an interest in thinking strategically about the international relations of the Asia-Pacific and international relations in general, one of the biggest challenge is to understand the nature and implications of China's search for comprehensive security. As this reality dawns on the public policy community, it must be said that the debate has often been simplistic. The exchange seems to be between those who assert that China will soon rise to be the world's largest economy and those who argue that China cannot sustain the current levels of growth. Some analysts suggest that China will muddle through difficulties in developing its economy, while others predict that it will face a major crisis of governance. On the policy towards China, some Western scholars argue that China can only be wrapped in the arm embrace of engagement whereas others stress the need to contain Chinese power.

While the issues raised by these questions are undoubtedly important, the debates on them have rarely been sufficiently sophisticated. Various participants have made references to a range of deep uncertainties about the basics of continued growth and stability; it is fair to say that no one has any great confidence in the reliability of the judgements made on a very fluid China. At the same time, it is argued here that in its search for comprehensive security, China is likely to bolster regional security because Beijing desires a peaceful environment in order to pursue its modernisation goals. If the environment in Northeast Asia becomes turbulent, Beijing's drive for economic development and in turn ambition to become global power in this century will be hindered. Analysing China's quest for comprehensive security leads to the conclusion that its security policies are characterised first by stability and second by practical realism. In this sense, using force to achieve short term objectives seems less likely.

In Asia and around the world, there is no doubt that China's growing economic, political and military strength has been the focus of much interest and some anxiety. From a negative viewpoint, it is contended that China's emergence from political and economic isolation since 1978 is likely to be marked by increasing and potentially dangerous friction with its near neighbours, with trading partners and others, and with international institutions. More hopefully, it is held that China's large and growing market and productive capacity offer enormous opportunities to add to the sum of world prosperity and that it is partly the task of the international system to find ways to accommodate China in accordance with the importance that Beijing thinks it deserves and will increasingly demand. In short, economic interdependence is not enough to make China moderate its behaviour, hence its neighbours and powers farther afield should combine engagement as well as the balance of power to constrain China from expansionism.

Economic security

Turning to the theoretical implications, it is evident that in addition to the military and political aspects, economic dimensions are important to China's security.

Chinese leaders now give prominence to the transition to economic power status and have taken economic construction as the central line, persisting in reform and opening up in the 21st century. The termination of the Cold War has brought about a situation long desired by the Chinese. Without having to subordinate its efforts to meet the threats of any superpower, China can now concentrate on economic development. Hence, one can detect that Beijing's security agenda has become increasingly economically driven, exemplified by its growing economic ties with countries such as Japan, South Korea and the US. For instance, China and Japan are now being pulled into each other's economic orbits: China wants to engage Japan's economic muscle for its development while Japan wants to see China develop as a responsible power in the region in the course of bilateral economic relations.

Essentially, China understands the urgent need to further its economic development and has put forward a plan of seizing trade opportunities in the capitalist world. It seeks a peaceful external environment in which it can pursue domestic reforms and expand trading and investment opportunities with as many states as possible. For the future security of the country, cultivation of close relations with Northeast Asian neighbours and indeed Asia as a whole is required. Asia is still widely regarded as the engine of growth for the world economy, notwithstanding the recent financial crisis. Moreover, China's growing economic strength within the region will enhance its global significance and help it achieve global power status in the 21st century. This does not mean that China's leaders have ceased to conceptualise their country in global terms but there is the recognition that Asia is important to China's economy and grand strategy.

Above all, China's philosophy on achieving comprehensive national security is based upon the notion of a powerful state underpinned by economic, technological and military strength. In many ways, economic power is regarded as the crucial element because it constitutes the necessary base to support a military establishment that is sufficiently robust to deter potential aggressors. This has been the guiding principle behind Chinese security policy in recent years and is likely to continue being so in the foreseeable future. Like their counterparts in the West, Chinese Realists focus on national capabilities including economic strength but they differ slightly with respect to the hierarchy of issues. While traditional Anglo-American Realists tend to consider military security as 'high politics' and social economic issues as 'low politics', contemporary Realists in China tend to place greater emphasis on economic and technological development. This is primarily because China is still a developing country, and it wants to catch up with the Western industrialised powers in economic terms. On the whole, with the end of the Cold War, bloc politics and ideological differences are now deemed as less important; instead, economic interests have risen to greater prominence in Chinese security planning.

Political security

Economic issues are also linked to the political security of the Chinese government. In fact, most of the internal political security threats faced by the Chinese Communist Party (CCP) are directly or indirectly related to the issue of development.

From the party's viewpoint, in the process of opening up its economy, China will be subjected to the infusion of Western ideas that might have negative influences on the current political system. On the whole, the 21st century is seen by China as a further consolidation of Western values such as democracy, human rights and the market economy. China has less qualms with liberalising economically but is adamant that its political values and system must be preserved at all costs. Today, key ideas underpinning the Chinese state are themselves subject to the alleged Western strategy of peaceful evolution. The reality is that the organising political ideology is so deeply ingrained in China that any drastic changes will have catastrophic consequences, as the collapse of the Soviet Union vindicates.

Specifically, political threats engendered by Western-style capitalism and democracy are perceived to be linked with the US. Hence, US actions, such as the response to the Tiananmen Incident in 1989, led to Beijing interpreting America's 'new world order' emphasising Western-style democracy and human rights as a fundamental security threat directed at the core values of the Chinese leadership. In Beijing's eyes, American efforts appear to be directed against the very legitimacy and stability of the CCP. Hence, when the US condemns China for abusing human rights, Beijing responds by accusing Washington of interfering in its internal affairs and attempting to subvert its socialist system. Whereas threats in the earlier era might have taken a more military dimension, challenges to China's security today tend to be more political in nature. Chinese leaders now have to cope with what they see as a continuous attack on their political system by the US-led Western democracies. This might trigger certain nationalist feelings in China. When equated with anti-imperialism, nationalism can be employed by the CCP to keep the Chinese state united against perceived foreign enemies. Being a fundamental factor in the Chinese worldview, nationalism has already guided Chinese analyses of international relations at various points in time.

China's perception of the American onslaught on its political security is also linked to domestic tendencies towards decentralisation, leadership issues and a possible split between the military and the CCP. This suggests that although China is a regional power, it is a weak state, given that the ruling party faces a rather high level of internal threats. The Chinese Communists are definitely facing a legitimacy crisis, especially after the ideological basis of their political power has been eroded by the collapse of Communism across the world. Political issues faced by the CCP have been explored in some detail in this book because it is felt that they should be given sufficient attention in writings on China's security.

As with the remaining Communist regimes, the prime goal of the CCP is to hold on to the reins of power. The current regime's central problem is how to run a closely controlled political system in concert with an open economy while ensuring that there are no spill-over effects from adopting the capitalist mode of production. The most dangerous spill-over effect is unquestionably the push in the direction of political pluralism, which will challenge the CCP's monopoly of political power in China. To a certain extent, therefore, it appears that the most serious threat to China's security is not an external military challenge (there are none at the time of writing) but rather the Western strategy to promote peaceful evolution. From China's perspective, this strategy aims to subvert Communist party leadership through political and cultural infiltration and is designed ultimately to make China a Western dependency.

At a wider level, one discerns that the economic imperatives upon which the Marxist–Leninist creed rests now threaten the political edifice that the Marxist–Leninists had constructed. China's leaders know that their country needs to absorb economic inputs from the outside world. At the same time, they are increasingly apprehensive of interdependence and submitting their national interests to those of an international economic system dominated by the Western powers. This is in many ways reminiscent of the dilemma facing the Self-Strengthening Movement reformers in the late 19th century. At a wider level, one might argue that the volatility of China's international relationships is in many ways a product of considerable ambivalence over a cost–benefit analysis of its interaction with foreigners.

It is clear that China needs a stable international environment in which it can expand its commerce and maintain access to technological and financial resources. These resources will come largely from the industrialised powers and international financial institutions as China tries to reap the benefits from the world economy without becoming overly dependent on it. As China seeks greater trading links with the outside world, it must come to terms with the concept of economic interdependence. Economic strategies are in general much more difficult to ascertain in an increasingly interdependent world and quite often not as clear-cut as geopolitical strategic initiatives.

Comprehensive security

The theoretical implications for the discipline of Security Studies/Strategic Studies that arise from this book need to be examined. Specifically, security cannot be conceived in narrow military terms any more. A more comprehensive definition must be adopted by analysts in order to enhance our understanding of national security interests in the post-Cold War era. In the Chinese case, military power and political clout combined with a vibrant economy is viewed as indispensable for China to drive towards global power status and to defend its sovereignty and territorial integrity.

In particular, the economics-security relationship constitutes one of the wider implications of this book. On one hand, it is sometimes argued that economic interactions exist only as a result of a nation-state's security interests; markets may ease the ways towards a state's relations with others but these cannot be sustained without governments agreeing to the bargain.[2] On the other hand, governments that attempt economic co-operation based solely on political motivations are bound to fail, if that co-operation is not grounded in economic rationality and cost–benefit analysis. Basically, this debate on the economic-security relationship has become increasingly sophisticated. As interdependence increases over time, domestic economic policy decisions will become more interconnected with the international financial and political systems. Accordingly, the need for states like

China to co-ordinate an array of fiscal and monetary policies alongside political considerations will become more critical. To the extent that economics are regarded as part of the domestic agenda in the 21st century, one can detect a closer link between internal stability and external threats in China's security thinking. The result is that China will employ both traditional military defence and non-military means, such as accumulating foreign currency reserves, in order to safeguard its territorial integrity and sovereignty.

At the same time, the linkage between the economic, political and military aspects of a state's security policy also leads to the problem of where to place the emphasis. To concentrate on one aspect at the expense of the others will be misleading and unrealistic. At a conceptual level, one can raise doubts regarding the extent to which economic and security issues were truly divorced in the past, and China's security can also be subjected to such questions. In general, it is practically impossible and even dangerously naïve to try and separate economic, political and military security issues. Almost all political or military security decisions have some economic implications. Conversely, economic considerations are now increasingly influencing the political and military security of states. Hence, one must recognise the inter-linkages and contradictions among the various aspects of national security. This often leads to policymakers needing to perform some sort of cost–benefit analysis because enhancing one aspect of state security could mean diminishing another. The task for Chinese leaders then is to balance and weigh the importance of security concerns on a case-by-case basis rather than adopt a straight-forward approach. In short, the aim is to enhance comprehensive national strength constantly by bolstering military, political and economic security simultaneously.

The preceding analysis also accords with the key notion in international politics that foreign policies are often intertwined with internal factors. Therefore, it comes as no surprise that China often states that foreign policy is an extension of its domestic policy. However, Chinese foreign policy is not being entirely internally generated either, it is also influenced and shaped by the evolving dynamics of the Asia-Pacific region and the wider world. The conventional wisdom in international relations is that foreign policy analysis does not take place in a vacuum. Hence, future developments in China's security policy will depend on the evolution of its economic priorities as well as its interactions with the international system.

In conclusion, this book has aimed to give more emphasis to the economic and political aspects in China's security, in addition to the traditional military one. We can now recapitulate, aggregate and reinforce some of the key conclusions drawn at the end of the various chapters. The first relates to the fact that China's security agenda is increasingly economically motivated as Beijing drives to global power status. The second relates to the fact that threats to China's security interests posed by other great powers, such as the US, are increasingly taking the form of the political rather than the military. These conclusions lead to the wider implication that in the 21st century, academics must better incorporate economic and political elements into their analyses of China's security interests, and those of other states as well.

Notes

Introduction

1 See, for example, Liu Xuecheng, 'Bush's re-election and Sino-US relations', *Guoji wenti yanjiu*, vol. 1, 2005, pp. 28–38.
2 Information Office of the State Council, *China's National Defense 2000* (Beijing, 2000), p. 8.
3 'Sino-Russian communiqué pledges to deepen economic ties', *Xinhua News Agency*, 3 July 2005.
4 'Chinese party paper commentary hails Central Asian border accord', *Xinhua News Agency*, 24 April 1997.
5 As usual, China stressed that the exercise is not aimed at any third party and will pose no threat to any country. 'Chinese, Russian commanders launch joint military exercise', *Xinhua News Agency*, 18 August 2005.
6 'Sino-Russian communiqué pledges to deepen economic ties', *Xinhua News Agency*, 3 July 2005.
7 The fifth centre of power is Europe.
8 For the concept of overlay, see Barry Buzan, *People, States and Fear: An Agenda for International Security Studies in the Post-Cold War Era* (Hemel Hempstead: Harvester Wheatsheaf, 1991, 2nd edn).
9 Michael Brown, Sean M. Lynn-Jones and Steven E. Miller (eds), *Debating the Democratic Peace* (London: MIT Press, 1996).
10 For a good discussion, see David Lampton, 'China's foreign and national security policy making process: is it changing and does it matter', in David Lampton (ed.), *The Making of Chinese Foreign and Security Policy in the Era of Reform* (Stanford, CA: Stanford University Press, 2001).
11 The 'bureaucratic politics' model is discussed in this classic text on foreign policy analysis: Graham Allison, *Essence of Decision: Explaining the Cuban Missile Crisis* (Boston, MA: Little, Brown, 1971).
12 At the Fourteenth Party Congress in October 1992, Yang Baibing was removed from the Military Affairs Commission, the key body controlling China's military; it appeared that Yang Baibing with his older brother, President Yang Shangkun, had built up a personal network of high-level supporters within the military before and after the 1989 Tiananmen Incident. Yang Shangkun was later removed as president of China when the National People's Congress convened in March 1993.
13 Samuel P. Huntingdon, *Political Order in Changing Societies* (New Haven, CT & London: Yale University Press, 1968), pp. 195–196.
14 Barry Buzan, Ole Wæver and Jaap de Wilde, *Security: A New Framework for Analysis* (London: Lynne Rienner, 1998).

1 The Chinese concept of security

1 W. B. Gallie, 'Essentially contested concepts', *Proceedings of the Aristotelian Society*, no. 56, 1956, pp. 167–198.

2 This type of approach has already been outlined in Barry Buzan's study on the theoretical aspects of security. See Barry Buzan, *People, States and Fear: An Agenda for International Security Studies in the Post-Cold War Era* (Hemel Hempstead: Harvester Wheatsheaf, 1991, 2nd edn).

3 David Singer, 'The level of analysis problem in international relations', in Klaus Knorr and Sidney Verba (eds), *The International System* (Princeton, NJ: Princeton University Press, 1961).

4 See Kenneth Waltz, *Man, the State and War* (New York: Columbia University Press, 1959).

5 However, Chinese scholars have increasingly noted the importance of 'human security'. See Wanming Yang, 'On the comprehensive security concept', *Guoji wenti yanjiu*, vol. 4, 2005, pp. 15–18.

6 See Ken Booth, 'Strategy and emancipation', *Review of International Studies*, vol. 19, no. 2 (April 1993), pp. 319–321.

7 Bill McSweeny, *Security, Identity and Interests: A Sociology of International Relations* (Cambridge: Cambridge University Press, 1999).

8 For instance, it has been argued that society should be the primary referent of security. See Martin Shaw, 'There is no such thing as society: beyond individualism and statism in international security studies', *Review of International Studies*, vol. 19, no. 2 (April 1993), pp. 159–175.

9 Michael Mann, 'The autonomous power of the state: its origins, mechanisms and results', in Michael Mann (ed.), *States, War and Capitalism: Studies in Political Sociology* (Oxford: Basil Blackwell, 1988).

10 At the same time, the CCP does have its own diplomatic initiatives outside the formal state apparatus. Examples include the party-level contacts with the Korean Workers' Party (KWP) and more recently, Taiwan's Kuomintang. See 'The Communist Party's diplomatic department', *Xinhua News Agency*, 22 June 2005.

11 See 'The non-military aspects of strategy', *Survival*, vol. 31, no. 6 (November/December 1989).

12 Joseph Nye and Sean Lynn-Jones, 'International security studies: a report of a conference on the state of the field', *International Security*, vol. 12, no. 4 (Winter 1988), pp. 5–27.

13 Joseph Nye, 'The contribution of strategic studies: future challenged', in Francois Heisbourg (ed.), *The Changing Strategic Landscape* (London: Macmillan, 1989), pp. 327–341.

14 Stephen Walt, 'The renaissance of security studies', *International Studies Quarterly*, vol. 35, no. 2 (1991), pp. 211–239.

15 See, for example, Qi Lin, 'An analysis of non-traditional security threats', *Journal of University of International Relations*, no. 1 (2005), pp. 27–32.

16 See, for example, Yu Xintian, 'China's strategic culture', *Xiandai guoji guanxi*, vol. 12 (2004), pp. 20–26.

17 See 'Roundup comparing security concepts', China Radio International, 29 December 1997 in *BBC Summary of World Broadcasts Part 3 Asia-Pacific*, 1 January 1998, p. G/2.

18 Information Office of the State Council, *China's National Defense 2000* (Beijing, Information Office of the State Council, 2000), p. 8.

19 See, for example, Liu Zhenmin, 'The current international order and China's road of peaceful development', *Guoji wenti yanjiu*, no. 1 (2005), p. 7.

20 Li Qinggong and Wei Wei, 'The world need a news security concept', *Jiefangjun Bao*, 24 (December 1997), p. 5.

21 'Chinese experts urge global co-operation to combat security threats', *Xinhua News Agency*, 22 June 2005.

22 'Chinese commentary says patience, consensus required on US reform', *Xinhua News Agency*, 11 June 2005.
23 'China hosts regional seminar on non-traditional security cooperation', *Xinhua News Agency*, 8 March 2005.
24 'Text of Sino-US joint statement on law-enforcement co-operation', *Xinhua News Agency*, 31 July 2006.
25 Li Qinggong and Wei Wei, 'The world need a news security concept', p. 5.
26 C. P. Fitzgerald, *The Chinese View of their Place in the World* (London: Oxford University Press, 1964), pp. 52–53.
27 The difference between Marxist and Realist theories centres on whether class interests or national interests drive state behaviour. See Robert Gilpin, *The Political Economy of International Relations* (Princeton, NJ: Prince University Press, 1987), pp. 25–64.
28 'China's oil consumption to rise by 5.4–7.0 per cent in 2006', *Xinhua News Agency*, 12 February 2006.
29 Zhang Wenmu, 'Economic globalisation and China's naval power', *Zhanlue yu guanli (Strategy and Management)*, no. 1 (2003), p. 90.
30 For a discussion of the pros and cons of the SPR, see Erica Downs, 'The Chinese energy security debate', *China Quarterly*, no. 177 (March 2004), pp. 32–34.
31 See Chong Zhongying, 'Major changes in international relations – East Asian financial crisis', *Shijie Zhishi*, no. 2 (1998), pp. 24–26.
32 'China's average tariff level drops to 9.9% in 2005', *Xinhua News Agency*, 28 January 2005.
33 For a useful analysis and review of the international relations literature on interdependence, see Dale C. Copeland, 'Interdependence and war: a theory of trade expectations', *International Security*, vol. 20, no. 4 (Spring 1996), pp. 5–41.
34 See Robert O. Keohane and Joseph S. Nye, *Power and Interdependence* (Glenview, IL: Scott Foresman and Company, 1989, 2nd edn).
35 Li Qinggong and Wei Wei, 'The world need a news security concept', p. 5.

2 The threat of peaceful evolution

 1 Qu Quansheng, 'Beware of the "peaceful evolution" scheme by hostile international forces', *Jiefangjun Bao*, 7 November 1989, p. 2.
 2 Tang Huihu, 'Western media interfering in China', *Dangdai Shijie Yu Shehui Zhuyi*, vol. 3 (1996), pp. 39–42.
 3 Cited in Tang Huihu, 'Western media interfering in China', pp. 39–42.
 4 Michael B. Yahuda, 'Chinese foreign policy and the collapse of communism', *SAIS Review*, vol. 12, no. 1 (Winter/Spring 1992), p. 134.
 5 'Problems posed by the Soviet Union – a talk given by Gao Di, editor of the Renmin Ribao, to Communist Party editors and cadres on 30 August 1991', in *China Quarterly*, no. 130 (June 1992), p. 484.
 6 'Problems posed by the Soviet Union', *China Quarterly*, p. 483.
 7 The Four Cardinal Principles are keeping to the socialist road, upholding the dictatorship of the proletariat, upholding the leadership of the CCP, and upholding Marxism–Leninism and Mao Zedong Thought.
 8 'Chinese paper denounces "peaceful evolution" approach of US monopoly capitalist class', *Guangming Ribao*, 4 September 1989 in *BBC Summary of World Broadcasts Part 3 Far East*, 19 September 1989, p. A1/2.
 9 See, for example, John Mearsheimer, *The Tragedy of Great Power Politics* (London: W.W. Norton, 2002).
10 *The National Security Strategy of the United States of America*, September 2002. This ties in with the 'democratic peace' theory. See Michael Brown, Sean M. Lynn-Jones and Steven E. Miller (eds), *Debating the Democratic Peace* (London: MIT Press, 1996).

11 *The National Security Strategy of the United States of America*, p. iv.
12 Condoleezza Rice, 'Promoting the national interest', *Foreign Affairs*, vol. 79, no. 1 (January–February 2000), p. 49.
13 Harry Harding, *A Fragile Relationship: The United States and China since 1972* (Washington, DC: The Brookings Institution, 1992), p. 18.
14 David Shambaugh, 'Peking's foreign policy conundrum since Tienanmen: peaceful coexistence vs peaceful evolution', *Issues & Studies*, vol. 28, no. 11 (November 1992), p. 68 and pp. 77–80.
15 Information Office of the State Council of the People's Republic of China, *Building of Political Democracy in China* (Beijing, October 2005).
16 For a further discussion on state-society relations in China, see Peter Hays Gries and Stanley Rosen, S*tate and Society in 21st Century China: Crisis, Contention and Legitimation* (London: Routledge, 2004).
17 'Confucianism and economic modernisation', *Renmin Ribao*, 19 September 1994, p. 1.
18 For a further discussion, see Daniel Bell, *East Meets West: Human Rights and Democracy in East Asia* (Princeton, NJ: Princeton University Press, 2000); Michael Freeman, 'Human rights, democracy and "Asian values"', *Pacific Review*, vol. 9, no. 3 (1996), pp. 367–388.
19 This is a reference to dissidents such as Fang Lizhi and Yan Jiaqi during the 'counter-revolutionary rebellion' in 1989. 'Chinese paper denounces "peaceful evolution" approach of US monopoly capitalist class', in *BBC Summary of World Broadcasts Part 3 Far East*, 19 September 1989, p. A1/2.
20 'Deng talks on quelling rebellion in Beijing', *Beijing Review*, vol. 32, no. 28 (July 10–16, 1989), pp. 14–17.
21 See Alexander Lukin, 'The initial Soviet reaction to the events in China in 1989 and the prospects for Sino-Soviet relations', *China Quarterly*, no. 125 (March 1991), pp. 119–136.
22 Information Office of the State Council of the People's Republic of China, *Human Rights in China* (Beijing, November 1991).
23 Information Office of the State Council of the People's Republic of China, 'On the part about China in the "1994 Human Rights Report" issued by the US State Department', *Xinhua News Agency*, 26 February 1995.
24 Communique of the Third Plenary Session of the 11th Central Committee of the Communist Party of China (Beijing, 29 December 1978).
25 See, for example, Larry Diamond, Juan J. Linz and Seymour Martin Lipset (eds), *Democracy in Developing Countries* (London: Adamantine, 1989).
26 For limitations of the Self-Strengthening Movement, see Frederic Wakeman, *The Fall of Imperial China* (New York: Free Press, 1975).
27 David Goodman, 'Reforming China: foreign contact, foreign values?' *The Pacific Review*, vol. 5, no. 1 (1992), p. 37.
28 See Samuel P. Huntington, *The Third Wave: Democratisation in the Late Twentieth Century* (Norman, OK: University of Oklahoma Press, 1991).
29 David Bachman, *Bureaucracy, Economy and Leadership in China: The Institutional Origins of the Great Leap Forward* (Cambridge: Cambridge University Press, 1991).
30 For instance, US Secretary of State Condoleezza Rice had earlier labelled North Korea as an 'outpost of tyranny' but later made a retraction. 'N Korea blames US "outpost of tyranny" comment for stalled talks', *Yonhap News Agency*, 14 May 2005; 'North Korea calls for US apology over "outpost of tyranny" remark', *Korean Central News Agency*, 1 April 2005.
31 The concept of a rogue state was initially popularised by the Clinton administration as part of a wider effort to identify threats to American security in the post-Cold War era. The definition of a rogue state varies but is generally understood to mean states that develop weapons of mass destruction (WMD), defy international norms and support terrorism. Robert S. Litwak, 'What's in a name? The changing foreign policy lexicon',

Journal of International Affairs, vol. 54, no. 2 (Spring 2001), pp. 375–392. See also Robert S. Liwak, *Rogue States and US Foreign Policy: Containment after the Cold War* (Baltimore, MD: John Hopkins University Press, 2000).

32 *Iraq Liberation Act of 1998*, 31 Oct 1998 (http://frwebgate.access.gpo.gov/cgi-bin/getdoc.cgi?dbname=105_cong_public_laws&docid=f:publ338.105.pdf).

33 See, for example, David Hendrickson and Robert Tucker, 'Revisions in need of revising: what went wrong in the Iraq war', *Survival*, vol. 47, no. 2 (2005), pp. 7–32.

34 See Michael Hunt, *Ideology and US Foreign Policy* (New Haven, CT: Yale University Press, 1987), p. xi.

35 Pioneering work on the impact of ideology on policymakers was done by Nathan Leites, in this case on Soviet elites in the 1950s. See also Alexander George, 'The "operational code": a neglected approach to the study of political leaders and decision making', *International Studies Quarterly*, vol. 13, no. 2 (June 1969), pp. 190–222.

36 Some American academics advocate a more multilateralist approach in world affairs. See Stewart Patrick and Shephard Forman (eds), *Multilateralism and US Foreign Policy: Ambivalent Engagement* (Boulder, CO: Lynne Rienner, 2002).

37 Ma Zhengang, 'A brief overview on the international situation and its prospects', *Guoji wenti yanjiu*, no. 1 (2005), pp. 1–3.

38 'China, Russia, India call for just world order with UN playing core role', *Xinhua News Agency*, 3 June 2005.

3 US global supremacy

1 From George Bush's speech to the Congress on 20 September 2001; see text in *New York Times*, 21 September, 2001, p. B4.

2 Anthony Lake, 'Confronting backlash states,' *Foreign Affairs*, vol. 73, no. 2 (March/April 1994), pp. 45–55. On the Iran–Libya Sanctions Act of 1996 aimed at isolating rogue states, see Michael Mastanduno, 'Extraterritorial sanctions: managing "hyper-unilateralism" in US foreign policy', in Stewart Patrick and Shephard Forman (eds), *Multilateralism and US Foreign Policy: Ambivalent Engagement* (Boulder, CO: Lynne Rienner, 2002), pp. 311–317.

3 Although Saddam Hussein has been defeated, the challenge of building democracy in Iraq remains. See, for example, David Hendrickson and Robert Tucker, 'Revisions in need of revising: what went wrong in the Iraq war', *Survival*, vol. 47, no. 2 (2005), pp. 7–32.

4 Liu Xuecheng, 'Bush's China policy in his second term,' *Guoji wenti yanjiu*, no. 1 (2005), pp. 28–32.

5 The 'axis of evil' comprises North Korea, Iraq and Iran, as George Bush stated at the State of Union speech in January 2002.

6 Su Ge, 'An assessment of US national security strategy adjustment', *Guoji wenti yanjiu*, vol. 2 (2003), pp. 15–16.

7 *The National Security Strategy of the United States of America*, September 2002, p. iv.

8 Today, the US faces four categories of challenges: traditional, irregular, catastrophic and disruptive. See *The National Defense Strategy of the United States*, March 2005, pp. 2–3.

9 David Hendrickson, 'Toward universal empire: the dangerous quest for absolute security', *World Policy Journal*, Fall 2002; Benjamin Barber, *Fear's Empire: War, Terrorism and Democracy* (New York: W.W. Norton, 2003).

10 *The National Defense Strategy of the United States*, March 2005, p. 10.

11 See Michael Walzer, *Just and Unjust Wars: A Moral Argument with Historical Illustrations* (London: Allen Lane, 1977), p. 81.

12 Su Ze, 'Kosovo War and the new military theory', *Jiefangjun Bao*, 1 June 1999, p. 6.

13 'China seeks to advance international nuclear disarmament process', *Xinhua News Agency*, 23 June 2005.

14 Dong Guozheng, 'Security globalisation is not tantamount to Americanisation', *Jiefangbao*, May 24, 1999.
15 See Wang Naicheng and Jun Xiu, 'Whither NATO', *International Strategic Studies*, no. 2 (1999), pp. 27–32 and Xie Wenqing, 'Observing US strategy of global hegemony from NATO's use of force against the FRY', *International Strategic Studies*, no. 3 (1999), pp. 1–9.
16 The strongest statements were made in Information Office of the State Council, *China's National Defence* (Beijing, July 1998).
17 See, for example, Liu Zhenmin, 'Current international order and China's road of peaceful development', *Guoji wenti yanjiu*, no. 1 (2005), p. 7.
18 Fears of encirclement are not new. China had seen the US deployed this strategy with a string of alliances in Northeast Asia, Southeast Asia and South Asia during the Cold War against the Soviet Union and itself. See, for example, John Lewis Gaddis, *We Now Know: Rethinking Cold War History* (Oxford: Oxford University Press, 1998).
19 *The National Security Strategy of the United States of America*, p. 1.
20 David Shambaugh, *Beautiful Imperialist: China Perceives America, 1972–1990* (Princeton, NJ: Princeton University Press, 1991), pp. 81–82.
21 For instance, the Qing dynasty employed the short-term tactic of using Russia to check Japanese encroachment in Manchuria in the 1890s. See, for example, Suisheng Zhao, *Power Competition in East Asia: From the Old Chinese World Order to Post-Cold War Regional Multipolarity* (New York: St. Martin's Press, 1997).
22 'Chinese president expressed sympathy to Bush, US government and people for disastrous attacks', *Renmin Ribao*, 12 September 2001.
23 Beijing's ties to the Taliban regime included providing assistance to build a national telecommunications systems in Afghanistan.
24 For example, this was called for by the Australian Defence Minister Robert Hill. See 'Regional security conference on terrorism', *Kyodo News Service*, 5 June 2005.
25 'China also under the threat of terrorism', *Xinhua News Agency*, 29 August 2005.
26 'UN adopts resolution to intensify global anti-terror campaign', *Renmin Ribao*, 9 October 2004.
27 'UN accord will curb financing of Chinese terrorists', *Xinhua News Agency*, 28 February 2006.
28 See, for example, Peter Gowan, *The Global Gamble: Washington's Faustian Bid for World Dominance* (London: Verso, 1999).
29 Liu Xuecheng, 'Bush's China policy in his second term', pp. 28–32.
30 'China becomes second biggest holder of US T-bonds', *Renmin Ribao*, 9 August 2002.
31 'China uses new programme on using foreign funds', *Xinhua News Agency*, 2 August 2006.
32 *The National Security Strategy of the United States of America*, p. 41.
33 *2005 Report to Congress of the US–China Economic and Security Review Commission*, November 2005 (http://www.uscc.gov/annual_report/2005/annual_report_full_05.pdf).
34 The US–China Business Council, *China's WTO Scorecard: Selected Year-Three Service Commitments* (30 August 2005).

4 The Taiwan issue

1 The Taiwan Affairs Office and the Information Office under the State Council, *The Taiwan Question and the Reunification of China* (Beijing, August 1993).
2 *The Sino-US Communiques* of 28 February 1972, 1 January 1979 and 17 August 1982 (http://usinfo.state.gov/eap/east_asia_pacific/china/china_communiques.htm).
3 'Defense minister says "PLA will not sit idle" over Taiwan independence', *Xinhua News Agency*, 31 July 1995.

4 'Chinese parliament adopts Taiwan anti-secession law', *Xinhua News Agency*, 14 March 2005.
5 They were Marshall Islands, Nauru, Palau, Solomon Islands, Tuvalu, Burkina Faso, Chad, Gambia, Malawi, Sao Tome and Principe, Senegal, Swaziland, St Kitts and Nevis, and St Vincent and Grenadines. See 'Taiwan thanks allies for UN letter protesting China's Anti-Secession Law', *Central News Agency*, 27 July 2005.
6 To defeat China blockade featuring a dozen advanced submarines, it is estimated that Taiwan will need to rely on the US Lyle Goldstein and William Murray, 'Undersea dragons: China's maturing submarine force', *International Security*, vol. 28, no. 4 (Spring 2004), pp. 161–196; Michael O'Hanlon, 'Strangulation from the sea: a PRC submarine blockade of Taiwan', *International Security*, vol. 28, no. 4 (Spring 2004), pp. 125–160.
7 'Military experts question motive behind Rumsfeld's China threat remarks', *Xinhua News Agency*, 10 June 2005.
8 'A severe step towards worsening Sino-US relations', *Renmin Ribao*, 5 September 1992, p. 1.
9 This includes acquiring diesel-electric submarines, P-3C anti-submarine aircraft and Patriot PAC-3 anti-missile systems. Opposition parties have blocked discussions of the bill over three dozen times, claiming that the cost is too high and that the weapons may not suit Taiwan's needs. See 'Debate over arms procurement package', *Central News Agency*, Taipei, 1 January 2006.
10 'US secretary says commitments to Taiwan not affected by arms deal', *Taipei Times*, 25 August 2005.
11 'Chinese expert warns of possible bad outcomes of US China threat theory', *Xinhua News Agency*, 20 June 2005.
12 This was also acknowledged by Taiwan. See Taiwan's Ministry of National Defense, *National Defense White Paper 2004* (17 November 2004), part I, chapter 4.
13 'Chen meets delegation of Japanese parliamentarians', *Central News Agency*, 13 January 2006.
14 'Taiwan to issue first national security report', *Central News Agency*, 10 November 2005.
15 'Puppet of America's double dealing policy', *Renmin Ribao*, 13 June 1995, p. 6.
16 'China's Taiwan Affairs Office issues statement on Taiwan vote', *Xinhua News Agency*, 23 March 1996.
17 Taiwan Affairs Office and the Information Office under the State Council, 'The One China principle and the Taiwan Issue', 21 February 2000.
18 Taiwan party urges US to support 'right to self determination', *Central News Agency*, 10 February 2006.
19 'The Taiwan Work Office of the CCP Central Committee and the Taiwan Affairs of the State Council issue a joint statement', *Xinhua News Agency*, 28 February 2006.
20 'US reiterates no support for Taiwan independence', *Xinhua News Agency*, 28 February 2006.
21 Chairman Su Chin-Chiang made this point. 'TSU head says China's rise threat to regional security', *Xinhua News Agency*, 18 July 2005.
22 'Pro-independence TSU celebrates fourth anniversary', *Central News Agency*, 6 August 2005.
23 'Text of KMT–Beijing agreement', *Xinhua News Agency*, 29 April 2005.
24 The Taiwan Affairs Office and the Information Office under the State Council, *The Taiwan Question and the Reunification of China* (Beijing, August 1993).
25 *The Taiwan Question and the Reunification of China*, August 1993.
26 'Xinhua commentary condemns Taiwanese foreign minister's offer of money to UN', *Xinhua News Agency*, 28 June 1995.
27 On the formation of the DPP, see Shelley Rigger, *From Opposition to Power: Taiwan's Democratic Progressive Party* (London: Lynne Rienner Publishers, 2001).

28 'President Li says "peaceful evolution" to continue in mainland China', *Central News Agency*, 26 December 1997.
29 'Taiwan president believes democracy will defeat China's authoritarian regime', *Central News Agency*, 1 April 2006.
30 'China strengthens legal work on the Taiwan issue', *Xinhua News Agency*, 6 February 2006.
31 'Hopes placed on the Taiwanese people', *Renmin Ribao (overseas edition)*, 28 February 1996, p. 1.
32 'Foreign Minister says Taiwan compatriots do not need to panic', *Xinhua News Agency*, 8 March 1996.
33 *The Taiwan Question and the Reunification of China*, August 1993.
34 'Opposition leader says "three direct links" with China best approach to ease tension', *Central News Agency*, 1 January 1998 in *BBC Summary of World Broadcasts Part 3 Far East*, 3 January 1998, p. F/2.
35 Figures from Beijing's Ministry of Commerce and Taiwan's Board of Foreign Trade (BOTC).
36 *The Taiwan Question and the Reunification of China*, August 1993.
37 Taiwan's National Security Council, *National Security Report 2006* (May 2006), pp. 53–60.
38 'Taiwan president says national security outweighs business interests in China', Central News Agency, 26 July 2005.

5 The challenge of Japan

1 This term is used by Takashi Inoguchi. See Takashi Inoguchi, *Japan's International Relations* (London: Pinter Publishers, 1991), especially pp. 142–143.
2 For an account, see Chalmers Johnson, *Japan: Who Governs? The Rise of the Developmental State* (New York: W.W. Norton, 1995).
3 Figures in January 2005 from the Japanese trade ministry.
4 'China becomes Japan's top trading partner in 2004', *Renmin Ribao*, 26 January 2005.
5 Meredith Woo-Cumings (ed.), *The Developmental State* (Ithaca, NY and London: Cornell University Press, 1999).
6 In August 1991, the Japanese leader at that time, Kaifu, visited Beijing; this was the first head of state among the industrialised nations to visit China since the Tiananmen Incident, marking the full restoration of Sino-Japanese ties.
7 These figures were published by ODA-Japan.com (http://www.euroact.co.jp/oda-japan/AboutODA/Recipient_Statistics/ODA_Loans/oda_loans.html).
8 'Economic relations with US, Japan reviewed', *Guoji Maoyi Wenti (International Trade Journal)*, no. 5 (19 May 1995), pp. 2–6.
9 Ministry of Economy, Trade and Industry, *White Paper on International Economy and Trade 2005*, pp. 4–8.
10 On the ODA, see Tsukasa Takamine, 'A new dynamism in Sino-Japanese security relations: Japan's strategic use of foreign aid', *The Pacific Review*, vol. 18, no. 4 (December 2005), pp. 439–461.
11 Reinhard Drifte, *Japan's Foreign Policy* (London: Routledge, 1990), p. 31 and p. 51. At that time, China even acknowledged Japan's right to provide for its own national security when the Japanese came up with the Report on Comprehensive National Security in 1980.
12 Christopher Hughes, *Japan's Security Agenda: Military, Economic and Environmental Dimensions* (Boulder, CO: Lynne Rienner Publishers, 2004).
13 Kenneth Waltz, 'The emerging structure of international politics', *International Security*, vol. 18, no. 2 (Autumn 1993), p. 66. Chalmers Johnson argues that Japan will have to re-acquire military power. See Chalmers Johnson, 'Japan in search of a "normal" role', *Daedalus*, vol. 121, no. 4 (1992), pp. 1–33.

14 Wang Guotai, ' "Resolution" that fails to distinguish tight from wrong', *Renmin Ribao*, 27 June 2005, p. 1.
15 See Task Force on Foreign Relations for the Prime Minister, *The Basic Strategies of Japan's Foreign Policy in the 21st* Century: New Era, New Vision, New Diplomacy (November 2002). This notion is similar to the concept of 'normal nation' (*futsu no kuni*). Ozawa Ichiro, *Blueprint for a New Japan: The Rethinking of a Nation* (Tokyo: Kodansha International, 1994).
16 'China "strongly demands" Japan end shrine visits', *Xinhua News Agency*, 15 August 2005.
17 Japan Defense Agency, *Defence of Japan 2005*.
18 Zhang Jinfang, 'Serious threat to China's security: experts comment on the strengthening of the Japanese–US military alliance', *Jiefangjun Bao*, June 4, 1999.
19 Japan Defense Agency, *National Defense Program Guideline for FY 2005 and After.*
20 Japan says China beginning to pose 'considerable threat', *Kyodo News Service*, 22 December 2005.
21 The proposal could win a majority in the General Assembly but probably not the two-thirds vote required to change the UN's charter.
22 Opening statement by Prime Minister Junichiro Koizumi at a press conference, 19 September 2001.
23 Zhou Yongsheng, 'Flexing its muscles: Japanese contingency bills pave the way for a more military approach', *Beijing Review*, vol. 47, no. 27 (8 July 2004), pp. 17–19.
24 'Article says plot to contain China lies behind islands dispute', Zhongguo Tongxun She, 9 September 96 in *BBC Summary of World Broadcasts Part 3 Asia-Pacific*, 11 September 1996, pp. G/1-G/2.
25 See, for example, Michael Armacost, *Friends or Rivals? The Insider's Account of US–Japan Relations* (New York: Columbia University Press, 1996), p. 251.
26 *The National Security Strategy of the United States of America*, September 2002, p. 26.
27 Institute for National Strategic Studies, *The United States and Japan: Advancing Toward a Mature Partnership* (Washington, DC: National Defense University, 11 October 2000). Although this report was unofficial, many of the group's members subsequently became key officials in the Bush Administration. Richard Armitage was the study group's co-chair, others included Michael Green, James Kelly, Robert Manning, Torkel Patterson and Paul Wolfowitz.
28 Ministry of Foreign Affairs Japan, *Joint Statement of the US–Japan Security Consultative Committee* (19 February 2005).
29 Similarly, China has expressed concern when Japanese Chief Cabinet Secretary Seiroku Kajiyama declared in August 1997 that the 'surrounding areas' covered by Japan–US collaboration 'should include the Taiwan Strait'; for this is regarded as the first time that a top Japanese official had openly 'interfered in Chinese affairs' since the normalisation of relations in 1972. 'Comment on Japan–US Defence Co-operation Guidelines', Zhongguo Xinwen She, 20 January 1998 in *BBC Summary of World Broadcasts*, 21 January 1998, p. G/2.

6 The alliance with North Korea

1 B. K. Gills, *Korea Versus Korea: A Case of Contested Legitimacy* (London: Routledge, 1996).
2 A good account of the Korean War can be founding in Bruce Cumings, *The Origins of the Korean War* (Princeton, NJ: Princeton University Press, 1990).
3 On the other hand, Russia abrogated its 1961 Treaty of Mutual Friendship with North Korea in the 1990s and came up with a new version that does not include military assistance to North Korea if it is attacked by another country.
4 In late November 2004, the International Atomic Energy Agency (IAEA) strongly criticised South Korea's failure to report scientific experiments, in 1982 and 2000, with

weapons-grade plutonium and uranium that could potentially be used in nuclear bombs. However, the Agency decided not to send the matter to the UN Security Council, sparing Seoul the possible imposition of sanctions.

5 Jonathan Monten, 'The roots of the Bush doctrine: Power, nationalism, and democracy promotion in US strategy', *International Security*, vol. 29, no. 4 (Spring 2005), pp. 112–156.

6 'North Korean paper supports China's position on US Security strategy report', Nodong Sinmun, 5 April 2006 in *BBC Worldwide Monitoring*, 7 April 2006.

7 'N Korea blames US "outpost of tyranny" comment for stalled talks', *Yonhap News Agency*, 14 May 2005; 'North Korea calls for US apology over "outpost of tyranny" remark', *Korean Central News Agency*, 1 April 2005.

8 *The National Security Strategy of the United States of America*, March 2006, p. 41.

9 'North Korea terms US rights act an "open challenge"', *Korean Central News Agency*, 18 October 2004.

10 The talks constitute a development from the four party-talks (US, China and the two Koreas) aimed at moving the 1953 Korean War armistice to a peace treaty.

11 'Agreement Adopted by Member Countries', http://www.tumenprogramme.org/tumen/news, 2 September 2005.

12 'North Korean leader "deeply impressed" by Chinese development', *Korean Central News Agency*, 18 January 2006.

13 Kim Dae-jung agreed with Kim Jong-il during their historic June 2000 summit meeting to build this complex, where it is envisioned to host 300 South Korean companies by 2006.

14 'South Korea outlines seven projects to help North once denuclearised', *Yonhap News Agency*, 28 June 2005.

15 North Korea made this public announcement on 10 February 2005. 'DPRK FM on its stand to suspend its participation in six-party talks for indefinite period', *Korean Central News Agency*, 10 February 2005.

16 'Text of six-party talks statement on North Korea nuclear issue', *Yonhap News Agency*, 19 September 2005.

17 In contrast to Chinese influence and control over Korea in the past, Japanese colonialism is often by North Koreans seen as humiliating and oppressive. See, for example, 'Rodong Sinmun on illegal "Korea–Japan Annexation Treaty"'. *Korean Central News Agency*, 19 March 2005 and 'KCNA Calls for Strict Precaution against Japan', *Korean Central News Agency*, 4 April 2005.

18 *South–North Joint Declaration on the Denuclearization of the Korean Peninsula* (February 1992).

19 Agreed Framework between the United States of America and the Democratic People's Republic of Korea (Geneva, 21 October 1994).

20 For an analysis of interdependence, see Robert Keohane and Joseph Nye, *Power and Interdependence: World Politics in Transition* (Boston, MA: Little, Brown, 1977).

21 'Conclusion of non-aggression treaty between DPRK and US called for', *Korean Central News Agency*, 25 October 2002.

22 North Korea has purchased several Soviet-supplied Scud-B missiles from Egypt in the late 1970s and developed them further. See Joseph Cirincione, Jon Wolfsthal and Miriam Rajkumar, *Deadly Arsenals: Tracking Weapons of Mass Destruction* (Washington, DC: Carnegie Endowment for World Peace, 2002), pp. 250–251.

23 Pyongyang's major exports include fishery products, textiles, minerals, metallurgical products and manufactured goods, including armaments.

24 See Joseph Cirincione's statement, 'Secretary of State Madeleine Albright's visit to North Korea', *Arms Control Today*, November 2000.

25 Iran's two other sources of nuclear assistance are Russia and China.

26 'US intention to launch nuclear war in Korea under fire', *Korean Central News Agency*, 3 April 2003; 'DPRK spokesman on US start of Iraqi War', *Korean Central News Agency*, 21 March 2003.

27 Those companies are Hesong Trading Corp, Korea Complex Equipment Import Corp, Korea International Chemical Joint Venture Co, Korea Kwansong Trading Corp, Korea Pugang Trading Corp, Korea Ryongwang Trading Corp, Korea Ryonha Machinery Joint Venture Corp and Tosong Technology Trading Corp.
28 A classic example is Britain and France surrendering to Nazi Germany's demands in Sudetenland under the 1938 Munich Pact.
29 Washington's foreign policy does contain elements of multilateralism whereby national security objectives might be achieved through international institutions. See for example, Steven Kull, Public 'Attitudes toward multilateralism', in Stewart Patrick and Shephard Forman (eds), *Multilateralism and US Foreign Policy: Ambivalent Engagement* (Boulder, CO: Lynne Rienner, 2002), pp. 99–120.
30 See Information Office of the State Council of the People's Republic of China, *China's Endeavours for Arms Control, Disarmament and Non-proliferation* (Beijing, September 2005).
31 China stresses the role in international institutions, rather than any unilateral action by the US. 'China calls on Iran to continue co-operation with IAEA', *BBC Worldwide Monitoring*, 25 November 2005.

7 The role of South Korea

1 To a large extent, the economic rise of South Korea was driven by growth in key sectors such as semi-conductors, shipbuilding, information technology, automobiles and petrochemicals. See, for example, Alice Amsden, *Asia's Next Giant: South Korea and Late Industrialization* (New York: Oxford University Press, 1989).
2 'Chinese president calls for further cooperation between China, South Korea', *Xinhua News Agency*, 17 November 2005.
3 Shandong takes half of nation's actual use of ROK capital, *Xinhua News Agency*, 15 January 2006.
4 'South Korean manufacturers suffer losses in China due to rising labour costs', *Choson Ilbo*, 25 May 2006.
5 South Korea does list the promotion of liberal democracy and human rights as its part of its national interest. See The Ministry of National Defense, The Republic of Korea, *2004 Defense White Paper*, pp. 59–61.
6 Samuel S. Kim (ed.), *Korea's Democratisation* (Cambridge: Cambridge University Press, 2003).
7 Figures from the Kyushu Economic Federation. *Interaction Transcending National Borders* (no. 24, August 2004). Obviously, Japan's Kyushu region is a key part of the Yellow Sea economic zone.
8 For instance, see Korea Institute for Economic Policy, *Regional Integration in Northeast Asia: Approaches To Integration Among China, Korea and Japan* (December 2004).
9 For ex-president Park Chung Hee's 'arms-for-allies' bargaining with the US, see Don Oberdorfer, *The Two Koreas: A Contemporary History* (Reading, MA: Addison-Wesley, 1997), pp. 85–94, 101–108.
10 David Steinberg (ed.), *Korean Attitudes Toward the United States: Changing Dynamics* (London: M.E. Sharpe, 2005).
11 Nicholas Eberstadt, *Korea Approaches Reunification* (Armonk, NY: M.E. Sharpe), p. 151.
12 See Roh Tae-woo, *Korea: A Nation Transformed* (Elmsford, NY: Pergamon Press, 1990), pp. 11–17.
13 In 2004, South Korea paid US$622 million to support those troops. See *2004 Defense White Paper*, Chapter 4.
14 *Joint statement on the Strategic Consultation for Allied Partnership (SCAP)*, 20 January 2006.
15 'South Korea consents "objective" of US proliferation initiative', *Yonhap News Agency*, 24 January 2006.

16 The US had requested that South Korea take part in eight PSI-related activities but South Korea decided to accept five of them. The five categories accepted are the inclusion of anti-proliferation drills in annual South Korea–US military exercise, dispatching observers to both theatre-level and non-theatre-level PSI drills and receiving briefings on both overall PSI activities and specific anti-proliferation drills. It is evident that the inclusion of anti-proliferation drills, in particular, is certain to anger North Korea, which sees the annual South Korea–US exercises a rehearsal for invading the communist state. The three categories that South Korea does not accept are the full-scale participation of PSI drills and material assistance to both theatre-level and non-theatre-level exercise.

17 South Korean leader reiterates 'balancing role' concept, *Yonhap News Agency*, 30 March 2005.

18 'South Korean president urges establishment of regional body', *Yonhap News Agency*, 28 September 2005. On the economic front, Roh Moo-hyun has urged countries in the Asia-Pacific to join forces to build a regional economic bloc modelled after the EU and North American Free Trade Agreement (NAFTA), arguing that the signing of bilateral free trade takes a considerable amount of time and effort and could reduce the effects of liberalisation originally intended.

19 However, South Korea's presence in international affairs will increase with the dispatch of troops to Iraq to assist in reconstruction being a case in point.

20 Chung-in Moon and David Steinberg (eds), *Kim Dae-jung Government and Sunshine Policy: Promise and Challenges* (Seoul: Yonsei University Press, 1999).

21 *North–South Joint Declaration* (15 June 2000).

22 Kim Dae-jung agreed with Kim Jong-il during their historic June 2000 summit meeting to build this complex, where it is envisioned to host 300 South Korean companies by 2006. For further details, see Republic of Korea's Ministry of Unification, *2005 White Paper on Korean Unification* (June 2005), pp. 74–84.

23 'South Korean minister says North announcement bid for upper hand in talks', *Yonhap News Agency*, 14 February 2005.

24 Republic of Korea's Ministry of National Defense, *2004 Defense White Paper*.

25 'Washington seeks "transformation" of North Korean regime: Hadley', *The Korea Times*, 8 December 2004 (http://times.hankooki.com/lpage/200412/kt2004120815151210220.htm).

26 In late November 2004, the International Atomic Energy Agency (IAEA) strongly criticised South Korea's failure to report scientific experiments, in 1982 and 2000, with weapons-grade plutonium and uranium that could potentially be used in nuclear bombs. However, the Agency decided not to send the matter to the UN Security Council, sparing Seoul the possible imposition of sanctions.

27 Roh gave the instruction while presiding over a meeting of the Presidential Committee for Northeast Asian Cooperation Initiative. 'South Korean president urges establishment of regional body', *Yonhap News Agency*, 28 September 2005.

28 Professor Wei Cuncheng from Jilin University was quoted. See 'China's ancient Koguryo Kingdom site added to World Heritage List', *Renmin Ribao*, 2 July 2004.

29 'Koguryo or Goguryeo?' *The Korea Herald*, 1 September 2004; 'Korean, Chinese academics debate claims to Koguryo kingdom', *Yonhap News Agency*, 16 September 2004.

30 Park Chung Hee, *Our Nation's Path: Ideology of Social Reconstruction* (Seoul: Hollym Corp, 1970), pp. 28–30.

31 'Koreas declare 1905 treaty with Japan invalid', *Yonhap News Agency*, 23 June 2005.

8 The importance of Central Asia

1 Owen Lattimore, *Inner Asian Frontiers of China* (Boston, MA: Beacon Press, 1940), p. 171.

2 Allen S. Whiting, *Sinkiang: Pivot or Pawn?* (East Lansing, MI: Michigan State University Press, 1958), p. 14.

3 The term 'social imperialist' was used by the Chinese to categorise the Soviet Union as a socialist country with imperialist ambitions, just like capitalist America. China had to face two hostile superpowers in the 1960s.

4 China fought a border war against the Soviet Union along the Ussuri River in 1969. See also John. Gittings, *Survey of the Sino-Soviet dispute: a commentary and extracts from the recent polemics 1963–1967* (London: Oxford University Press, 1968), Donald Zagoria, *The Sino-Soviet Conflict, 1956–1961* (Princeton, NJ: Princeton University Press, 1962).

5 'Five-nation border agreement signed in Shanghai', *Xinhua News Agency*, 26 April in *BBC Summary of World Broadcasts Part 3 Asia-Pacific*, 27 April 1996, p. G/1.

6 China said it would further cut its troops by 500,000 in 3 years on the basis of a reduction of one million troops in the 1980s. See 'Roundup comparing security concepts', China Radio International, 29 December 1997 in *BBC Summary of World Broadcasts Part 3 Asia-Pacific*, 1 January 1998, p. G/2. 'Chinese party paper commentary hails Central Asian border accord', *Xinhua News Agency*, 24 April 1997 in *BBC Summary of World Broadcasts Part 3 Asia-Pacific*, 26 April 1997, p. G/1.

7 'Defence minister says China's military diplomacy "unprecedentedly active" in 1997', *Xinhua News Agency* 26 December 1997, in *BBC Summary of World Broadcasts Part 3 Asia-Pacific*, 30 December 1997, p. G/112.

8 'Chinese agency notes Russia unusually cautious on Kirghizstan crisis', *Xinhua News Agency*, 26 March 2005.

9 'Chinese think-tank on Central Asia, NATO', *Zhongguo Xinwen She News Agency*, Beijing, in Chinese 20 January 1998, in *BBC Summary of World Broadcasts*, 21 January 1998, p. G/2.

10 'China cuts Uighur's sentence', *BBC World News*, 3 March 2004 (http://news.bbc.co.uk/1/hi/world/asia-pacific/3528535.stm).

11 'Li Peng addresses national conference on nationalities affairs', *Xinhua News Agency*, 20 February 1990 in *BBC Summary of World Broadcasts Part 3 Asia-Pacific*, 23 February 1990, p. B2/1.

12 Jonathan N Lipman, *Familiar Strangers: A history of Muslims in the Northwest China* (Seattle, WA: University of Washington Press, 1997). He contrasted the Uighurs with the traditional Huis, who have been less vocal and almost non-committal towards any form of nationalism, based on their primordial religious identity. The Huis are 'familiar strangers': they are familiar owing to their overall cultural affiliation with mainstream Chinese culture and their alienation is a product of their belief in Islam. For another account of Hui Muslims in China, see Michael Dillon, *China's Muslim Hui Community: Migration, Settlement and Sects* (Richmond: Curzon, 1999).

13 'Li Peng addresses national conference on nationalities affairs', in *BBC Summary of World Broadcasts Part 3 Asia-Pacific*, 23 February 1990, p. B2/1.

14 Dewardic McNeal, 'China's Relations with Central Asian States and Problems with Terrorism', in US Department of State, *Congressional Research Service Report for Congress*, 17 December 2001 (http://fpc.state.gov/documents/organization/7945.pdf).

15 Abigail Sines, 'Civilizing the Middle Kingdom's wild west', *Central Asian Survey*, vol. 21, no. 1 (March 2002), pp. 5–14.

16 Statement from the Information Office of the State Council, People's Republic of China, 'East Turkistan's terrorist forces cannot get away with impunity', 21 January 2002, Beijing.

17 The Shanghai Five originally comprised China, Russia, Kazakhstan, Tajikistan and Kyrgyzstan. Uzbekistan joined in 2001 and the organisation was renamed SCO.

18 'Central Asian countries promise Xinjiang military heads to suppress separatism', *Xinjiang Ribao*, 3 November 1997.

19 See, for example, William Safran, *Nationalism and Ethno-regional Identities in China* (London: Frank Cass, 1998) for discussion on China's ethnic minorities.

20 For a survey of the oil and gas resources in Central Asia, see John Roberts, 'Caspian oil and gas: How far have we come and where are we going?' in Sally Cummings (ed.), *Oil, Transition and Security in Central Asia* (New York: RoutledgeCurzon, 2003).

21 'China's to increase oil production in Tarim Basin', *Renmin Ribao*, 10 November 2004.

22 Chinese state-owned China Petroleum and Chemical Corp (Sinopec) and PetroChina have stakes in the joint venture with Shell, British Petroleum (BP), ExxonMobil and Russia's Gazprom. 'Trans-China pipeline deal signed 4 July 2002' (http://news.bbc.co.uk/1/hi/business/2092313.stm).

23 'Kazakhs agree to China pipeline', *BBC News*, 18 May 2004 (http://news.bbc.co.uk/1/hi/world/asia-pacific/3723249.stm).

24 China signs Uzbek accords', *BBC News*, 15 June 2004 (http://news.bbc.co.uk/1/hi/world/asia-pacific/3806217.stm).

25 G. Christoffersen, 'China's intentions for Russian and Central Asian oil and gas', National Bureau of Asian Research, *NBR analysis*, vol. 9, no. 2 (March 1998).

26 *China Quarterly*, volume 178 (June 2004), especially Nicolas Becquelin, 'Staged Development in Xinjiang', pp. 358–378.

27 Halford Mackinder, 'The geographical pivot of history', *Geographical Journal*, vol. 20, no. 4 (April 1904), p. 421. See also G. Robbins, 'The post-Soviet heartland: Reconsidering Mackinder', *Eurasian Studies*, vol. 11, no. 3 (Fall 1994), p. 35.

28 'Chinese think-tank on Central Asia, NATO', *Zhongguo Xinwen She News Agency*, in *BBC Summary of World Broadcasts*, 21 January 1998, p. G/2.

29 'Chinese think-tank on Central Asia, NATO', in Chinese 20 January 1998, in *BBC Summary of World Broadcasts*, 21 January 1998, p. G/2.

30 US ambassador Stephen Young said the Ganci air base is vital to the global war on terror. See US-led anti-terror coalition needs Kirghiz air base, Interfax, 16 June 2005 in BBC monitoring.

31 Interestingly, some Russians also share this view. Although Moscow officially supports the US in the 'war on terror', there are Russians who regard this war as outright US imperialism or want to support greater integration with the West while remaining still sceptical of Vladimir Putin's policies. See John O'Loughlin, Gearoid O Tuathail and Vladimir Kolossov, Russian geopolitical storylines and public opinion in the wake of 9–11: a critical geopolitical analysis and national survey', *Communist and post-Communist Studies*, vol. 37, no. 3 (September 2004), pp. 281–318.

32 See 'Caspian pipeline "unites nations"', *BBC News*, 16 October 2004 (http://news.bbc.co.uk/1/hi/world/europe/3749616.stm).

33 Shanghai body chief urges close watch on 'extremists' in Central Asia, *Iterates News Agency*, 18 June 2005 in BBC Monitoring.

34 This was achieved at the fourth SCO Summit Meeting in Tashkent. See *Xinhua News Agency*, 17 June 2004.

35 The Collective Security Treaty Organisation (CSTO) wants to build up its military capabilities to cope with new threats such as international terrorism, illegal circulation of narcotics, illegal migration and organised crime. See 'Head of CIS Collective Security Treaty outlines priorities', *ITAR-TASS News Agency*, 20 January 2005 in *BBC Monitoring*.

36 'Hu's speech at the fourth SCO Summit Meeting in Tashkent', *Xinhua News Agency*, 17 June 2004.

37 For the role of great power management in international relations, see Hedley Bull, *The Anarchical Society: A Study of Order in World Politics* (Basingstoke: Macmillan, 1977).

9 The drive to global power status

1 John Fairbank, The Chinese World Order; Suisheng Zhao, *Power Competition in East Asia: From the Old Chinese World Order to Post-Cold War Regional Multipolarity* (New York: St. Martin's Press, 1997), Chapter 2.

2 Barry Buzan and Richard Little, *International Systems in World History: Remaking the Study of International Relations* (Oxford: Oxford University Press, 2000), p. 440.

3 David Lake, 'Beyond anarchy: the importance of security institutions', *International Security*, vol. 26, no. 1 (Summer 2001), pp. 129–160.

4 Mark Mancall, *China at the Centre: 300 Years of Foreign Policy* (New York: Free Press, 1984).

5 Wang Gungwu, *To Act is to Know: Chinese Dilemmas* (Singapore: Eastern Universities Press, 2003), p. 306.

6 Information Office of the State Council, *China's Endeavours for Arms Control, Disarmament and Non-proliferation* (Beijing: September 2005).

7 'Military experts questions motive behind Rumsfeld's China Threat remarks', *Xinhua News Agency*, 10 June 2005.

8 Information Office of the State Council, *China's National Defence in 2004* (Beijing, December 2004).

9 For an account of the nuclear quest, see John Lewis and Xue Litai, *China Builds The Bomb* (Stanford, CA: Stanford University Press, 1988).

10 *China's Endeavours for Arms Control, Disarmament and Non-proliferation*, September 2005.

11 The testing was met with widespread global disapproval. Robert S. Norris, 'French and Chinese nuclear weapon testing', *Security Dialogue*, vol. 27, no. 1 (March 1996), p. 51.

12 This line of argument can be found in Paul Kennedy, *The Rise and Fall of Great Powers: Economic Change and Military Conflict from 1500 to 2000* (London: Unwin Hyman, 1988), pp. 447–458.

13 Samuel P. Huntington, 'The clash of civilisations?' *Foreign Affairs*, vol. 72, no. 3 (Summer 1993), pp. 22–49; Samuel P. Huntingdon, 'If not civilisations, what? Samuel P. Huntington responds to his critics', *Foreign Affairs*, vol. 72, no. 5 (November/ December 1993), pp. 186–194. See also Francis Fukuyama, 'Social capital and the global economy', *Foreign Affairs*, vol. 74, no. 5 (September/October 1995), p. 97.

14 'Chinese Communist daily rejects universality of western, US culture', *Xinhua News Agency*, 7 June 2005.

15 For the concept of the weak state, see Barry Buzan, *People, States and Fear: An Agenda for International Security Studies in the Post-Cold War Era* (Hemel Hempstead: Harvester Wheatsheaf, 1991, 2nd edn), Chapter 2, especially pp. 96–102.

16 Wang Jisi and Zou Sicheng, 'Civilisations: clash or fusion?' *Beijing Review*, vol. 39, no. 3 (January 15–21, 1996), pp. 11–12.

17 'Military experts questions motive behind Rumsfeld's China Threat remarks', *Xinhua News Agency*, 10 June 2005.

18 'Chinese expert warns of possible bad outcomes of US "China threat" theory', *Xinhua News Agency*, 20 June 2005.

19 Information Office of the State Council of the People's Republic of China, *China's Peaceful Development Road* (Beijing: 12 December 2005).

20 The expeditions of Chinese admiral Zheng Ho to the Southeast Asia were viewed as a case in point. Guo Zhenyuan, 'China's road of peaceful development and its prospects', *Guoji wenti yanjiu*, no. 1 (2005), pp. 12–13.

21 *China's Peaceful Development Road*, 12 December 2005.

22 On the 'socialisation' thesis, see David Armstrong, *Revolution and World Order: The Revolutionary State in International Society* (Oxford: Clarendon Press, 1993).

23 Robert O. Keohane and Joseph S. Nye, *Power and Interdependence* (Glenview, IL: Scott Foresman and Company, 1989, 2nd edn), pp. 3–37.

24 Xu Jian, 'Peaceful Rise: China's Strategic Option', *Guoji wenti yanjiu* (2004), no. 2, pp. 1–8.

25 Dale C. Copeland, 'Interdependence and war: a theory of trade expectations', *International Security*, vol. 20, no. 4 (Spring 1996), p. 23.

26 For further analyses of Chinese thinking about such organizations, see Alastair Iain Johnston and Paul Evans, 'China's Engagement with Multilateral Security Institutions', in Johnston and Ross (eds), *Engaging China: The Management of an Emerging Power* (London: Routledge, 1999), Chapter 10.

27 *China's Endeavours for Arms Control, Disarmament and Non-proliferation*, September 2005.

28 For a discussion of China's growing involvement in regional multilateral organisations, see Susan L. Shirk, 'China's Multilateral Diplomacy in the Asia-Pacific', statement before the US–China Economic and Security Review Commission, February 12–13, 2004 (http://www.uscc.gov/hearings/2004hearings/written_testimonies/04_02_12wrts/shirk.htm).

29 Wang Yong, 'Using Regional co-operation to resolve Sino-Japanese structural differences', *Zhanlue yu guanli (Strategy and Management)*, no. 1 (2004), pp. 41–47.

30 This was also echoed by Palestinian President Mahmud Abbas. See 'Palestinian leader urges greater role for China in peace process', *Xinhua News Agency*, 16 May 2005.

31 Domestically, China's nuclear export comes under the control of Commission of Science, Technology and Industry for National Defence (COSTIND) in co-ordination with other relevant government departments. *China's Endeavours for Arms Control, Disarmament and Non-proliferation*, September 2005.

32 For an account of the failure of the League of Nations as a collective security system, see E. H. Carr, *The Twenty Years Crisis, 1919–1939* (London: Macmillan, 1961).

33 This is the theme of Herbert Butterfield's essay on 'The Great Powers' in Herbert Butterfield and Martin Wight (eds), *Diplomatic Investigations* (London: Allen & Unwin, 1967).

34 Hedley Bull, *The Anarchical Society: A Study of Order in World Politics* (London: Macmillan, 1977), p. 207.

35 Hedley Bull and Adam Watson (eds), *The Expansion of International Society* (Oxford: Oxford University Press, 1984). See also Martin Wight, *International Theory: The Three Traditions*, Gabriele Wight and Brian Porter (eds) (London: Leicester University Press, 1991); Barry Buzan, 'From International system to International society: Structural realism and regime theory meet the English School', *International Organisation*, vol. 47, no. 3 (1993), pp. 327–352. Buzan argues that international society suggests a broader term the specific notion of regimes. It suggests 'a situation in which a whole set of regimes, multilateral organisations and rules exists which enables states to communicate on a regular basis, to establish modes and habits of consultation and co-operation, to co-ordinate and manage their relations, and to prevent their disputes escalating into conflict of war.'

36 There are plenty of discussions on prospects for some form of regional institutions in Asia. See, for example, John Ikenberry and Michael Mastanduno, *International Relations Theory and The Asia-Pacific* (New York: Columbia University Press, 2003); Barry Buzan, 'Security architecture in Asia: the interplay of regional and global levels'; *The Pacific Review*, vol. 16, no. 2 (June 2003), pp. 143–173; Ralph Cossa, 'US security strategy in Asia and the prospects for an Asian regional security regime', *Asia-Pacific Review*, vol. 12, no. 1 (May 2005).

37 Warren Kimball, *The Juggler: Franklin Roosevelt as Wartime Statesman* (Princeton, NJ: Princeton University Press, 1991), pp. 83–105.

38 This was advocated by Henry Nau, *At Home Abroad: Identity and Power in American Foreign Policy* (Ithaca, NY: Cornell University Press, 2003).

Conclusions

1 Interestingly, the unprecedented summit between North Korea and South Korea in June 2000 has led to Taipei calling for a similar meeting between China and Taiwan.

2 Some analysts argue that global financial flows ultimately do not undermine a state's decision-making authority, since 'if a crisis increases their willingness to bear the consequences, states can still defy the markets' Louis W. Paul, 'Capital mobility, state autonomy and political legitimacy', *Journal of International Affairs*, vol. 48, no. 2 (Winter 1995), p. 373.

Selected bibliography

Official documents

China

Communique of the Third Plenary Session of the 11th Central Committee of the Communist Party of China (Beijing: 29 December 1978).

Information Office of the State Council of the People's Republic of China, *Human Rights in China* (Beijing: November 1991).

Information Office of the State Council of the People's Republic of China, *Tibet – its Ownership and the Human Rights Situation* (Beijing: 22 September 1992).

Taiwan Affairs Office and the Information Office under the State Council of the People's Republic of China, *The Taiwan Question and the Reunification of China* (Beijing: 31 August 1993).

Information Office of the State Council of the People's Republic of China, *The Progress of Human Rights in China* (Beijing: December 1995).

Information Office of the State Council of the People's Republic of China, *The Situation of Children in China* (Beijing: April 1996).

Information Office of the State Council of the People's Republic of China, *New Progress in Human Rights in the Tibet Autonomous Region* (Beijing: February 1998).

Information Office of the State Council of the People's Republic of China, *China's National Defence* (Beijing: July 1998).

Information Office of the State Council of the People's Republic of China, *China's National Defense 2000* (Beijing: 2000).

Taiwan Affairs Office and the Information Office under the State Council, *The One China Principle and the Taiwan Issue* (Beijing: 21 February 2000).

Statement from the Information Office of the State Council, People's Republic of China, *East Turkistan's Terrorist Forces Cannot Get Away with Impunity* (Beijing: 21 January 2002).

Information Office of the State Council of the People's Republic of China, *China's National Defense in 2004* (Beijing: December 2004).

Information Office of the State Council of the People's Republic of China, *China's Endeavours for Arms Control, Disarmament and Non-proliferation* (Beijing: September 2005).

Information Office of the State Council of the People's Republic of China, *Building of Political Democracy in China* (Beijing: October 2005).

Information Office of the State Council of the People's Republic of China, *China's Peaceful Development Road* (Beijing: 12 December 2005).

Japan

Japan Defense Agency, *National Defense Programme Guideline for FY 2005 and After* (2004).
Kyushu Economic Federation. *Interaction Transcending National Borders* (no. 24, August 2004).
Japan Defense Agency, *Defence of Japan 2005* (2005).
Ministry of Foreign Affairs of Japan, *Joint Statement of the US–Japan Security Consultative Committee* (19 February 2005).
Ministry of Economy, Trade and Industry of Japan, *White Paper on International Economy and Trade 2005* (July 2005).

South Korea

Ministry of National Defense of the Republic of Korea, *2004 Defense White Paper* (2004).
Korea Institute for Economic Policy, *Regional Integration in Northeast Asia: Approaches to Integration among China, Korea and Japan* (December 2004).
Ministry of Unification of the Republic of Korea, *2005 White Paper on Korean Unification* (June 2005).

Taiwan

Ministry of National Defense of Taiwan, *National Defense White Paper 2004* (17 November 2004).
National Security Council of Taiwan, *National Security Report 2006* (May 2006).

US

Iraq Liberation Act of 1998 (31 October 1998).
George Bush's Speech to the Congress (20 September 2001).
US Department of State, *Congressional Research Service Report for Congress: China's Relations with Central Asian States and Problems with Terrorism* (17 December 2001).
George Bush's State of Union Speech (29 January 2002).
The National Security Strategy of the United States of America (September 2002).
US–China Economic and Security Review Commission, *China's Multilateral Diplomacy in the Asia-Pacific* (12–13 February 2004).
The National Defense Strategy of the United States 2005 (March 2005).
The US–China Business Council, *China's WTO Scorecard: Selected Year-Three Service Commitments* (30 August 2005).
2005 Report to Congress of the US–China Economic and Security Review Commission (November 2005).
The National Security Strategy of the United States of America (March 2006).

Others

Joint Communique of the United States of America and the People's Republic of China (28 February 1972).
Joint Communique of the United States of America and the People's Republic of China (1 January 1979).

Joint Communique of the United States of America and the People's Republic of China (17 August 1982).

Sino-Soviet Joint Communiqué (Moscow: 19 May 1991).

South–North Joint Declaration on the Denuclearisation of the Korean Peninsula (February 1992).

China–South Korea Joint Communiqué (Beijing: 30 September 1992).

Agreed Framework between the United States of America and the Democratic People's Republic of Korea (Geneva: 21 October 1994).

Joint Statement by the People's Republic of China and the Russian Federation (Beijing: 25 April 1996).

North–South Joint Declaration – North Korea and South Korea (June 2000).

Joint Press Statement on the Outcome of ROK–US Bilateral Meeting (20 October 2003).

Text of KMT–Beijing Agreement (29 April 2005).

Joint Statement on the Strategic Consultation for Allied Partnership (SCAP) – Japan and the US (20 January 2006).

News agencies

BBC Monitoring
BBC News
Korean Central News Agency
Kyodo News Service
Xinhua News Agency
Yonhap News Agency
Zhongguo Tongxun She

Newspapers

Choson Ilbo
Guangming Ribao
Jiefangjun Bao (People's Liberation Army Daily)
Korea Herald
Korea Times
Nodong Sinmun
Renmin Ribao (People's Daily)
Renmin Ribao (People's Daily) (overseas edition)
Xinjiang Ribao

Books

Allison, Graham. *Essence of Decision: Explaining the Cuban Missile Crisis* (Boston, MA: Little, Brown, 1971).

Amsden, Alice. *Asia's Next Giant: South Korea and Late Industrialization* (New York: Oxford University Press, 1989).

Armacost, Michael. *Friends or Rivals? The Insider's Account of US–Japan Relations* (New York: Columbia University Press, 1996).

Armstrong, David. *Revolution and World Order: The Revolutionary State in International Society* (Oxford: Clarendon Press, 1993).

Bachman, David. *Bureaucracy, Economy and Leadership in China: The Institutional Origins of the Great Leap Forward* (Cambridge: Cambridge University Press, 1991).

Barber, Benjamin. *Fear's Empire: War, Terrorism and Democracy* (New York: W. W. Norton, 2003).

Bell, Daniel. *East Meets West: Human Rights and Democracy in East Asia* (Princeton, NJ: Princeton University Press, 2000).

Brown, Michael, Lynn-Jones, Sean M. and Miller, Steven E. (eds). *Debating The Democratic Peace* (London: MIT Press, 1996).

Bull, Hedley. *The Anarchical Society: A Study of Order in World Politics* (London: Macmillan, 1995, 2nd edn).

Buzan, Barry. *People, States and Fear: An Agenda for International Security Studies in the Post-Cold War Era* (Hemel Hempstead: Harvester Wheatsheaf, 1991, 2nd edn).

Buzan, Barry and Little, Richard. *International Systems in World History: Remaking the Study of International Relations* (Oxford: Oxford University Press, 2000).

Buzan, Barry and Waever, Ole. *Security: A New Framework for Analysis* (London: Lynne Rienner, 1998).

Carr, E. H. *The Twenty Years Crisis, 1919–1939* (London: Macmillan, 1961).

Cirincione, Joseph, Wolfsthal, Jon and Rajkumar, Miriam. *Deadly Arsenals: Tracking Weapons of Mass Destruction* (Washington, DC: Carnegie Endowment for World Peace, 2002).

Cumings, Bruce. *The Origins of the Korean War* (Princeton, NJ: Princeton University Press, 1990).

Cummings, Sally (ed.). *Oil, Transition and Security in Central Asia* (New York: RoutledgeCurzon, 2003).

Dillon, Michael. *China's Muslim Hui Community: Migration, Settlement and Sects* (Richmond: Curzon, 1999).

Eberstadt, Nicholas. *Korea Approaches Reunification* (Armonk, NY: M. E. Sharpe, 1995).

Fairbank, John King (ed.). *The Chinese World Order: Traditional China's Foreign Relations* (Cambridge, MA: Harvard University Press, 1968).

Fitzgerald, Charles Patrick. *The Chinese View of their Place in the World* (London: Oxford University Press, 1964).

Gaddis, John Lewis. *We Now Know: Rethinking Cold War History* (Oxford: Oxford University Press, 1998).

Gills, Barry. *Korea Versus Korea: A Case of Contested Legitimacy* (London: Routledge, 1996).

Gilpin, Robert. *The Political Economy of International Relations* (Princeton, NJ: Princeton University Press, 1987).

Gittings, John. *Survey of the Sino-Soviet Dispute: A Commentary and Extracts from the Recent Polemics 1963–1967* (London: Oxford University Press, 1968).

Gowan, Peter. *The Global Gamble: Washington's Faustian Bid for World Dominance* (London: Verso, 1999).

Gries, Peter Hays and Rosen, Stanley. *State and Society in 21st Century China: Crisis, Contention and Legitimation* (London: Routledge, 2004).

Harding, Harry (ed.). *China's Foreign Relations in the 1980s* (London: Yale University Press, 1984).

Harding, Harry. *A Fragile Relationship: The United States and China since 1972* (Washington, DC: Brookings Institution, 1992).

Hsu, Immanuel. *The Rise of Modern China* (Oxford: Oxford University Press, 1990).

Hughes, Christopher. *Japan's Security Agenda: Military, Economic and Environmental Dimensions* (Boulder, CO: Lynne Rienner, 2004).

Hunt, Michael. *Ideology and US Foreign Policy* (New Haven, CT: Yale University Press, 1987).

Huntingdon, Samuel. *Political Order in Changing Societies* (New Haven, CT and London: Yale University Press, 1968).

Huntington, Samuel. *The Third Wave: Democratisation in the Late Twentieth Century* (Norman, Oklahoma: University of Oklahoma Press, 1991).

Inoguchi, Takashi. *Japan's International Relations* (London: Pinter publishers, 1991).

Inoguchi, Takashi. *Japan's Foreign Policy in an Era of Global Change* (London: Pinter Publishers, 1993).

Johnson, Chalmers. *Japan: Who Governs? The Rise of the Developmental State* (New York: W. W. Norton, 1995).

Johnston, Alistair Iain and Ross, Robert Ross (eds). *Engaging China: The Management of an Emerging Power* (London: Routledge, 1999).

Kennedy, Paul. *The Rise and Fall of Great Powers: Economic Change and Military Conflict from 1500 to 2000* (London: Unwin Hyman, 1988).

Keohane, Robert and Nye, Joseph. *Power and Interdependence* (Glenview, IL: Scott Foresman and Company, 1989, 2nd edn).

Kim, Samuel (ed.). *China and the World: Chinese Foreign Relations in the Post-Cold War Era* (Oxford: Westview Press, 1994, 3rd edn).

Kim, Samuel (ed.). *Korea's Democratisation* (Cambridge: Cambridge University Press, 2003).

Lampton, David (ed.). *The Making of Chinese Foreign and Security Policy in the Era of Reform* (Stanford, CA: Stanford University Press, 2001).

Lattimore, Owen. *Inner Asian Frontiers of China* (Boston, MA: Beacon Press, 1940).

Lewis, John and Xue, Litai. *China Builds the Bomb* (Stanford, CA: Stanford University Press, 1988).

Lipman, Jonathan. *Familiar Strangers: A History of Muslims in the Northwest China* (Seattle, WA: University of Washington Press, 1997).

Liwak, Robert. *Rogue States and US Foreign Policy: Containment after the Cold War* (Baltimore, MD: John Hopkins University Press, 2000).

McSweeny, Bill. *Security, Identity and Interests: A Sociology of International Relations* (Cambridge: Cambridge University Press, 1999).

Mancall, Mark. *China at the Centre: 300 Years of Foreign Policy* (New York: Free Press, 1984).

Mann, Michael (ed.). *States, War and Capitalism: Studies in Political Sociology* (Oxford: Basil Blackwell, 1988).

Mastanduno, Michael. *International Relations Theory and the Asia-Pacific* (New York: Columbia University Press, 2003).

Mearsheimer, John. *The Tragedy of Great Power Politics* (London: W. W. Norton, 2002).

Moon, Chung-in and Steinberg, David (eds). *Kim Dae-jung Government and Sunshine Policy: Promise and Challenges* (Seoul: Yonsei University Press, 1999).

Nau, Henry. *At Home Abroad: Identity and Power in American Foreign Policy* (Ithaca, NY: Cornell University Press, 2003).

Oberdorfer, Don. *The Two Koreas: A Contemporary History* (Reading, MA: Addison-Wesley, 1997).

Ong, Russell. *China's Security Interests in the Post-Cold War Era* (London: Curzon Press, 2001).

Park, Chung-Hee, *Our Nation's Path: Ideology of Social Reconstruction* (Seoul: Hollym Corp, 1970).

Rigger, Shelley. *From Opposition to Power: Taiwan's Democratic Progressive Party* (London: Lynne Rienner, 2001).

Roh, Tae-woo. *Korea: A Nation Transformed* (Elmsford, NY: Pergamon Press, 1990).

Safran, William. *Nationalism and Ethno-regional Identities in China* (London: Frank Cass, 1998).

Shambaugh, David. *Beautiful Imperialist: China Perceives America, 1972–1990* (Princeton, NJ: Princeton University Press, 1991).

Steinberg, David (ed.). *Korean Attitudes Toward the United States: Changing Dynamics* (London: M. E. Sharpe, 2005).

Stewart, Patrick and Forman, Shephard (eds). *Multilateralism and US Foreign Policy: Ambivalent Engagement* (Boulder, CO: Lynne Rienner, 2002).

Task Force on Foreign Relations for the Prime Minister. *The Basic Strategies of Japan's Foreign Policy in the 21st Century: New Era, New Vision, New Diplomacy* (November 2002).

Van Ness, Peter. *Revolution and Chinese Foreign Policy: Peking's Support for Wars of National Liberation* (London: University of California Press, 1970).

Wakeman, Frederic. *The Fall of Imperial China* (New York: Free Press, 1975).

Waltz, Kenneth. *Man, the State and War* (New York: Columbia University Press, 1959).

Walzer, Michael. *Just and Unjust Wars: A Moral Argument with Historical Illustrations* (London: Allen Lane, 1977).

Wang, Gungwu. *To Act is to Know: Chinese Dilemmas* (Singapore: Eastern Universities Press, 2003).

Whiting, Allen. *Sinkiang: Pivot or Pawn?* (East Lansing, MI: Michigan State University Press, 1958).

Woo-Cumings, Meredith (ed.). *The Developmental State* (Ithaca, NY and London: Cornell University Press, 1999).

Wu, Xuewen (ed.). *Shizilukou de Riben (Japan at the Crossroads)* (Beijing: Shishi Chubanshe, 1988).

Yan, Xuetong. *Zhongguo Guojia Liyi Fenxi (Analysis of China's National Interests)* (Tianjin: Tianjin Remin Chubanshe, 1996).

Zagoria, Donald. *The Sino-Soviet Conflict, 1956–1961* (Princeton, NJ: Princeton University Press, 1962).

Zhao, Quansheng. *Interpreting Chinese Foreign Policy: The Micro-Macro Linkage Approach* (Oxford: Oxford University Press, 1997).

Zhao, Suisheng. *Power Competition in East Asia: From the Old Chinese World Order to Post-Cold War Regional Multipolarity* (New York: St. Martin's Press, 1997).

Journal articles

Becquelin, Nicolas. 'Staged Development in Xinjiang', *China Quarterly*, vol. 178 (June 2004), pp. 358–378.

Booth, Ken. 'Strategy and Emancipation', *Review of International Studies*, vol. 19, no. 2 (April 1993), pp. 319–321.

Buzan, Barry. 'Security Architecture in Asia: The Interplay of Regional and Global Levels', *The Pacific Review*, vol. 16, no. 2 (June 2003), pp. 143–173.

Chan, Sarah and Kuo, Chun-Chien. 'Trilateral Trade Relations among China, Japan and South Korea: Challenges and Prospects of Regional Economic Integration', *East Asia: An International Quarterly*, vol. 22, no. 1 (Spring 2005), pp. 33–50.

Chan, Yul-Yoo. 'Anti-American, Pro-Chinese Sentiment in South Korea', *East Asia: An International Quarterly*, vol. 22, no. 1 (Spring 2005), pp. 18–32.

Chong, Zhongying. 'Major Changes in International Relations – East Asian Financial Crisis', *Shijie Zhishi*, no. 2 (1998), pp. 24–26.

Copeland, Dale. 'Interdependence and War: A Theory of Trade Expectations', *International Security*, vol. 20, no. 4 (Spring 1996), pp. 5–41.

Cossa, Ralph. 'US Security Strategy in Asia and the Prospects for an Asian Regional Security Regime', *Asia-Pacific Review*, vol. 12, no. 1 (May 2005), pp. 64–86.

Crawford, Neta. 'Future Security Studies', *Security Studies*, vol. 1, no. 2 (1991), pp. 283–316.

Downs, Erica. 'The Chinese Energy Security Debate', *China Quarterly*, no. 177 (March 2004), pp. 32–34.

Fukuyama, Francis. 'Social Capital and the Global Economy', *Foreign Affairs*, vol. 74, no. 5 (September/October 1995), pp. 85–103.

Gallie, W. B. 'Essentially Contested Concepts', *Proceedings of the Aristotelian Society*, no. 56 (1956), pp. 167–198.

George, Alexander. 'The "Operational Code": A Neglected Approach to the Study of Political Leaders and Decision Making', *International Studies Quarterly*, vol. 13, no. 2 (June 1969), pp. 190–222.

Goldstein, Lyle and Murray, William. 'Undersea Dragons: China's Maturing Submarine Force', *International Security*, vol. 28, no. 4 (Spring 2004), pp. 161–196.

Guo, Zhenyuan. 'China's Road of Peaceful Development and its Prospects', *Guoji wenti yanjiu*, no. 1 (2005), pp. 12–13.

Hendrickson, David. 'Toward Universal Empire: The Dangerous Quest for Absolute Security', *World Policy Journal,* vol. XIX (Fall 2002), pp. 11–20.

Huntington, Samuel. 'The Clash of Civilisations?' *Foreign Affairs*, vol. 72, no. 3 (Summer 1993), pp. 22–49.

Hwang, Balbina. 'Anti-Americanism in Korea: Implications for the Future of the U.S.–ROK Alliance', *East Asia: An International Quarterly*, vol. 20, no. 2 (Summer 2003), pp. 60–73.

Johnson, Chalmers. 'Japan in Search of a "Normal" Role', *Daedalus*, vol. 121, no. 4 (1992), pp. 1–33.

Lake, David 'Beyond Anarchy: The Importance of Security Institutions', *International Security*, vol. 26, no. 1 (Summer 2001), pp. 129–160.

Lin, Qi. 'An Analysis of Non-traditional Security Threats', *Journal of University of International Relations*, no. 1 (2005), pp. 27–32.

Litwak, Robert. 'What's in a Name? The Changing Foreign Policy Lexicon', *Journal of International Affairs*, vol. 54, no. 2 (Spring 2001), pp. 375–393.

Liu, Xuecheng. 'Bush's China Policy in His Second Term', *Guoji Wenti Yanjiu*, no. 1 (2005), pp. 28–32.

Liu, Zhenmin. 'Current International Order and China's Road of Peaceful Development', *Guoji Wenti Yanjiu*, no. 1 (2005), pp. 7–9.

Lukin, Alexander. 'The Initial Soviet Reaction to the Events in China in 1989 and the Prospects for Sino-Soviet Relations', *China Quarterly*, no. 125 (March 1991), pp. 119–136.

Ma, Zhengang. 'A Brief Overview on the International Situation and its Prospects', *Guoji Wenti Yanjiu*, no. 1 (2005), pp. 1–3.

Monten, Jonathan. 'The Roots of the Bush Doctrine: Power, Nationalism, and Democracy Promotion in US Strategy', *International Security*, vol. 29, no. 4 (Spring 2005), pp. 112–156.

Norris, Robert. 'French and Chinese Nuclear Weapon Testing', *Security Dialogue*, vol. 27, no. 1 (March 1996), pp. 51–66.

Nye, Joseph and Lynn-Jones, Sean. 'International Security Studies: A Report of a Conference on the State of the Field', *International Security*, vol. 12, no. 4 (Winter 1988), pp. 5–27.

O'Loughlin, John, Tuathail, Gearóid Ó and Kolossov, Vladimir. 'Russian Geopolitical Storylines and Public Opinion in the Wake of 9–11: A Critical Geopolitical Analysis and National Survey', *Communist and Post-Communist Studies*, vol. 37, no. 3 (September 2004), pp. 281–318.

Ong, Russell. 'Japan and China's Security Interests in the Post-Cold War Era', *East Asia: An International Quarterly*, vol. 16, no. 1 (Spring 1997), pp. 44–64.

Ong, Russell. 'North Korea's Enduring Importance in China's Security Interests in the Post-Cold War Era', *Asian Journal of Political Science*, vol. 8, no. 1 (June 2000), pp. 47–64.

Ong, Russell. 'China's Security Interests in Central Asia', *Central Asian Survey*, vol. 24, no. 4 (December 2005), pp. 425–439.

Ong, Russell. 'China, US and the North Korean Issue', *Asia-Pacific Review*, vol. 13, no. 1 (May 2006), pp. 118–135.

Ong, Russell. 'China and the US War on Terror', *Korean Journal of Defense Analysis*, vol. 18, no. 2 (Summer 2006), pp. 95–116.

Rice, Condoleezza. 'Promoting the National Interest', *Foreign Affairs*, vol. 79, no. 1 (January–February 2000), pp. 45–62.

Shaw, Martin. 'There is No Such Thing as Society: Beyond Individualism and Statism in International Security Studies', *Review of International Studies*, vol. 19, no. 2 (April 1993), pp. 159–175.

Sines, Abigail. 'Civilizing the Middle Kingdom's Wild West', *Central Asian Survey*, vol. 21, no. 1 (March 2002), pp. 5–14.

Su, Ge. 'An Assessment of US National Security Strategy Adjustment', *Guoji Wenti Yanjiu*, vol. 2 (2003), pp. 15–16.

Takamine, Tsukasa. 'A New Dynamism in Sino-Japanese Security Relations: Japan's Strategic Use of Foreign Aid', *The Pacific Review*, vol. 18, no. 4 (December 2005), pp. 439–461.

Tang, Huihu. 'Western Media Interfering in China', *Dangdai Shijie Yu Shehui Zhuyi*, vol. 3 (1996), pp. 39–42.

Walt, Stephen. 'The Renaissance of Security Studies', *International Studies Quarterly*, vol. 35, no. 2 (1991), pp. 211–239.

Wang, Jisi and Zou, Sighing. 'Civilisations: Clash or Fusion?' *Beijing Review*, vol. 39, no. 3 (January 15–21, 1996), pp. 11–12.

Wang, Yong. 'Using Regional Co-operation to Resolve Sino-Japanese Structural Differences', *Zhanlue yu guanli (Strategy and Management)*, no. 1 (2004), pp. 41–47.

Xu, Jian. 'Peaceful Rise: China's Strategic Option', *Guoji Wenti Yanjiu*, no. 2 (2004), pp. 1–8.

Yahuda, Michael. 'Chinese Foreign Policy and the Collapse of Communism', *SAIS Review*, vol. 12, no. 1 (Winter/Spring 1992), pp. 131–140.

Yang, Wanming. 'On the Comprehensive Security Concept', *Guoji Wenti Yanjiu*, vol. 4 (2005), pp. 15–18.

Yu, Xintian. 'China's Strategic Culture', *Xiandai Guoji Guanxi*, vol. 12 (2004), pp. 20–26.

Zhang, Wenmu. 'Economic Globalisation and China's Naval Power', *Zhanlue Yu Guanli (Strategy and Management)*, no. 1 (2003), pp. 90–92.

Zhao, Xiaochun. 'On New Changes in National Interests in the Post-Cold War Era', *Guoji Guanxi Xueyuan Xuebao (Journal of the Institute of International Relations)*, vol. 1 (1995), pp. 1–7.

Index

For Product Safety Concerns and Information please contact our EU
representative GPSR@taylorandfrancis.com
Taylor & Francis Verlag GmbH, Kaufingerstraße 24, 80331 München, Germany